ALSO BY PHYLLIS BURKE

*Atomic Candy*

# FAMILY VALUES

JRKE

LY

E S

*nd*

*Many poets have said that love asks nothing,*
*but I submit to you today that*
*love demands everything.*

—Superior Court Judge Donna Hitchens,
Valentine's Day 1991

*No one is going to give you power.*
*You have to take it.*

—Harvey Milk
1930–1978

# *Preface*

IN HONAUNAU, Hawaii, there is a walled city guarded by grimacing gods and surrounded by palm trees. It is called the City of Refuge, and it dates back to the twelfth century. If you were declared an outlaw for political or religious reasons, or if you had been defeated in battle, you were condemned to death, but you were given one chance to survive: If you made it to the City of Refuge alive, you were allowed to live within its walls. You were given a running head start, but you had to swim the last part of the journey.

In order to survive, you would have to be strong, but you would also have been traumatized. To survive, you would have to unite with the other outcasts, even though you might be coming from warring camps. You would have to use your wits and strength to outrun your pursuers, but you might lose your sense of humanity in the process of the chase. Once within the walls of the city, if you made it alive, you would have to become whole, perhaps for the first time. You would have to devise a way to love each other, which would be difficult because most of you would arrive broken. To lesbian, gay, and bisexual people, San Francisco is the City of Refuge.

When my lesbian partner had a child through assisted conception, I could no longer pass for straight. I was propelled into a world where every act, no matter how everyday, became political, whether I wanted it to be or not. Everything, from taking our child to the doctor for a checkup to enrolling him in nursery school, brought with it a kind of visibility I had always avoided, and an unnerving vulnerability to the attacks of the radical right. My life became a crash course in "the personal is political."

This book is not objective. It is partly my story, and it is the story of San Francisco's lesbian and gay civil rights movement. During the time when I was undergoing adoption proceedings that, if successful, would allow me to be recognized as Jesse's second legal mother, a controversial new force arose in the movement; it was embodied in a group called Queer Nation. Historians will probably call this the Third Wave. In the United States, the First Wave was the homophile movement of the 1950s and 1960s, which was an attempt to blend into society. This was not so much a political statement as a practical matter of survival. The Second Wave, gay liberation of the mid-1970s and the 1980s, was symbolized by the Stonewall Rebellion in New York City, where gays fought back against police brutality for the first time. The day after Stonewall, the poet Allen Ginsberg remarked that the "fags" had lost that wounded look. The post-Stonewall period was a time when the goal became inclusion in the power structure. The late 1980s produced the first thrust of the Third Wave with ACT UP ("Aids Coalition to Unleash Power"). ACT UP was founded to push for medical treatment and research to combat AIDS, which at the time of this writing has killed a hundred thousand Americans, almost ten thousand in San Francisco alone. The majority of the American dead are gay men. ACT UP tactics bypass the ballot box and the courts in favor of guerrilla street theater and dramatic actions tailored for the media. They believe there is no longer time to work through the system, which became impenetrable during the Reagan-Bush collaboration with the radical right.

In mid-1990, throughout the United States, dozens of chapters of Queer Nation were formed. Building on the street-theater model of ACT UP, Queer Nation based its tactics upon uncompromising visibility and the "in your face" premise that "We are not like you. We will never be like you. Trying to be like you is killing us." There is absolutely nothing accommodationist about Queer Nation, yet the group is anything but morbidly serious. The ethic of "queer wit," humor and satire, is their trademark. Lesbian and gay politicians who use the art of compromise, who patiently try to edge the general population toward recognizing lesbian and gay relationships and families, are anathema to the activists, whose power rests upon their status as outsiders to the system. The fact that it is still usually dangerous to hold hands in public is proof to the activists that working within the system has not worked, and that it will never work.

Those who have worked within the system, picking away for years at society's power structure and surviving death threats and onslaughts of organized hate, have taken their places as politicians and police officers, judges and teachers, union officials and church ministers. Their motto is "We're just like you. Let us be part of America." They believe that as they become part of the system, as they become insiders, their very presence will force the system to evolve. And it has evolved, but slowly.

While using very different tactics, both groups struggle against the common enemy of demonization. Demonization comes from the radical right and, ironically, the liberal, cloistered villas of Hollywood, that celluloid Oz of the world's psyche.

Twenty years ago, I never imagined that the adoption I was attempting could even be thinkable. I knew that my chance to be legally recognized as Jesse's mother existed only because of the painstaking years of work by the lesbian and gay civil rights attorneys, particularly Donna Hitchens and Roberta Achtenberg. Yet the emotional firestorm of the process, which at every turn pointed out to me that legally I was nothing and socially I was at best a freak, drew me to Queer Nation, whose specialty was transmuting rage into media-wise satire and wit. The strong presence of the activists and the targeting of the city by forces promoting our demonization are what make San Francisco emblematic of the lesbian and gay civil rights movement.

This is the story of the political descendants of Harvey Milk, the nation's first openly gay elected official, who was gunned down in his City Hall office by a homophobic fellow politician.

This is the story of the Third Wave of liberation asserting itself in the streets and malls with public art and theater when the radical right, and Hollywood, did not honor the walls of our city. This is also the story of the legal recognition of a new kind of family, and of a little boy named Jesse, who just happens to have two mommies, and to whom this book is dedicated.

# Acknowledgments

I WOULD LIKE to thank my agent, Bonnie Nadell, and my editor, Ann Godoff, for believing in this book at its earliest stages.

The following people graciously agreed to be interviewed for this book: Abby Abinanti, Roberta Achtenberg, Mayor Art Agnos, Tom Ammiano, Gilbert Baker, Kurt Barrie, Pam Bates, Gil Block, Harry Britt, Jo Daly, Judge John Dearman, Tamara Diaghilev, Michael Douglas, Joe Eszterhas, Jack Fertig, Annette Gaudino, Jean Harris, Judge Donna Hitchens, Cleve Jones, Jonathan Katz, Carol Leigh, Carole Migden, Lea Militello, Mark Pritchard, Tanya Tandoc, Ggreg Taylor, and John Woods.

The work, support, and advice of the following people were instrumental in the formation of this book: Rupert Adley, Glen Bates, Ed Bedard, Jolanta Benal, Michael (Wrong Way) Botkin, Derek Boyle, Maureen Brownsey, Ken Bukowski, Jeff Bullard, Allen Burry, Larry Bush, Joann Butters and the Bagdad Café, Bennett Carlson, Allen Carson, Michelle Carter, Cat Chang, Mark Chekal, Mary Corrigan, Gwen Craig, Michael V. W. Crain, Jigna Desai, Mark Duran, Michelle Feher, Julie Ginsburg, Nivedita Glace, Andi Gletty, David Green-Fyre, Ed Harrington, Lynn Hendee, Liz Hendrickson, Frank Herron, Elaine Hersher, Mike Housh, Anne Keating, Gerard Koskovich, Scott Mahoy,

Sue Martin, Judith Meskill, Jennifer Morris, Irene Newmark, Joyce Newstat, Daniel Paiz, Carol Peacock, Beth Pearson, Rink, Robert Rios, Cory Roberts, Carol Rossi, Suzanne Rotondo, Abigail Rudner, Ray Russ, Robbin Schiff, Tina Toriello and Toots, Jill Tregor, Ed Treuting, Terry Tricomi, Dean Tuckerman, Ellen Twiname, Erich Van Benschoten, and Doug Weinberg.

# Contents

# FAMILY VALUES

# CHAPTER I

# *Jesse Breaks Through*

AT THE TURN of the century, insemination was called "ethereal conception," as if a scientific.Peter Pan were breaking through into the world from Neverland. Above all stories, Jesse loved those of Peter Pan and his battles with Captain Hook. When Jesse turned three, in the summer of 1991, he liked to be Peter, and he wore the green felt hat with the turkey feather that Cheryl made for him. But by that winter, he was partial to Captain Hook. We have a dozen Halloween pictures of him in his red satin cape, black pirate's hat with the white skull and cross-bones, black boots with the red toes, a toy silver hook raised boldly above his head. He probably remembers the cape and boots, and even the green felt hat, but he might not remember that the reason Peter Pan came to the world was to hear stories, especially stories about himself. I'm writing this story, which is all true, for Jesse when he is a young man. I can almost see him: seventeen years old, involved in his own revolutions and adventures. That will be the year 2005. Some of this will probably sound very odd and dated by then, but it is a story about him, and about who I became because of him, and so he'll be interested, just like Peter.

As I write this, Jesse is still very small, just three years old, and it's almost Christmas. When he's a young man, he will want to know all about his ethereal conception, how he broke through into the world and came to have two mothers. By then, he certainly will have heard pieces of the story, but it's important to have the whole picture, which is about civil rights, political warfare, Hollywood, and scraping SpaghettiOs off the floor.

In the twenty-first century, this might not sound strange, but in 1987 it did. Cheryl decided that she was going to have a baby, and the fact that she was lesbian was not going to stop her. She had always been an independent frontier spirit. Having been raised as a Church of Christ fundamentalist, she had been taught that she was not of this world, but belonged to God. What other people thought of her was none of her business. I was apprehensive. I thought it was terrible to live in this society and be different. I spent a lot of time camouflaging myself. The things I heard when I was invisible made me even more certain that I should stay in the closet.

Although I could not commit myself to having a child with her, Cheryl surveyed the available sperm banks in the San Francisco area, and located the ones that did not discriminate against lesbians and single women. In certain states, only a doctor is allowed to perform insemination, and many of them refuse to inseminate lesbians. In other states, a husband's consent is required; it is a crime to inseminate single women, and certainly lesbians. Cheryl selected Pacific Reproductive Services, which describes itself as "Insemination Services for the Non-Traditional Family." After medical screening by your local doctor, Pacific Reproductive Services will even ship sperm on dry ice anywhere in the United States.

Cheryl brought home a little catalogue of sperm donors. She sat on the couch and opened it the way Jesse now opens his adventure books. Each donor had a number and a detailed description. We leafed through the pages, and came upon a journalist who was Irish, Dutch, English, and French. We picked him immediately, because his ethnicity and occupation were similar to mine. His hair was described as almost black, but Jesse's is blond, like Cheryl's.

I felt very strange looking through a catalogue and making a selection, almost as if I were in some kind of Orwellian social engineering experiment. I was uncomfortable at how calculated it all was. Cheryl, however, was not particularly romantic about the business of becoming pregnant. Nor was she thinking of herself as doing something "radical." This was just her life. When she was seven years old, she decided she would have two children, a boy and a girl, and that they would get a boat and take it down the Amazon River. She decided that I would be a good partner for the excursion, and that was that. As for the scientific aspect of choosing the donor, as time went on, I realized that Prince Charles's selection of Lady Diana Spencer was just as calculated a decision on his part, except that they would have to spend the rest of their lives as tourist attractions. I also learned that in pre-Christian times, temple priestesses would select the men with whom they wished to have babies, and these were often not the same men with whom they chose to live. The men were perfectly happy with the arrangement, and it did not affect the children's social standing, because inheritance was by matrilineal descent.

San Francisco at the end of the twentieth century is not exactly the milieu of pagan temple priestesses, but it did give me some sort of precedent and historical root.

The donor descriptions were very detailed, and when you selected a donor, precise and complete medical records were provided. The donors underwent extensive physical examinations, as did the birth mothers. The question always comes up as to why a man chooses to become a donor. There are many reasons: financial (the donor is paid for his semen); genealogical (the man may desire to father as many children as possible in order to keep his genes in the gene pool); political (the donor may wish to make his semen available to nontraditional families, such as lesbian families); and social (a gay man may wish to be a parent, but may not want to go through the charade of heterosexual marriage).

The donor we selected for Jesse's assisted conception, which is what donor insemination has come to be called, is a heterosexual man who is willing to be known to Jesse, if he wishes, when he turns eighteen years old. He is what's known as a "yes donor."

His name is with a lawyer, who acts as a go-between. If Jesse's donor should contract a fatal disease, he has the option of informing us so that Jesse will be able to meet him. I'm as curious as anyone about Jesse's donor, but it is only Jesse who has the right to contact him, though we can reach him, through the lawyer, on Jesse's behalf. We thought it would be important to Jesse to know his biological roots. But it might not be. Everyone is different. Before going to a sperm bank, we did look for a donor who would like to be an active father. The problem was, most of the men we knew were gay, and although many of them would have been lovely fathers, the AIDS epidemic rendered them unable to be donors.

Eight thousand gay men were prematurely dead in San Francisco by the time Jesse was two, and yet behind what was almost a shadowy membrane there was a lesbian baby boom. Lesbians were giving birth, adopting children, and building families with gay men, but none of this was widely publicized in the mainstream press. Fighting in the courts for the legal rights of lesbian and gay parents, the lesbian lawyers worked without fanfare because they did not want to draw unwanted attention to their activities, and so make the parents and children easy targets for the homophobes and the politicians who used them to build hate bases. It is time to tell the story now because there are simply so many of us, as a result of the work of these women in helping us to build our families, that we cannot mask it any longer.

Before Jesse's conception, I did believe that it was acceptable, perhaps even noble, to deny myself and my partner the full range of human experience because we were a detested minority. Yet I knew that I had a deep maternal urge that often expressed itself on my lovers. I also wondered if, perhaps, a child would help me to focus on and again become part of the exterior world. I had drawn into myself, away from the world, over a dozen years before, first with the death of the woman I loved, then with the witchhunt by John Briggs against gay teachers, and then finally with the assassinations of Harvey Milk and George Moscone.

But I did not want to look at myself. Instead, I grilled Cheryl on why she wanted to have a child. It had to be politically correct, theoretically correct, and socially acceptable. It had to be pure and egoless. The fact that she had always wanted a baby was not enough for me. When Cheryl was twenty-five years old, she told her girlfriend that she wanted a child. The girlfriend left. She told all subsequent girlfriends that she wanted a child, and they all left. Cheryl was now thirty-two years old and the biological clock was noisily interfering with our sleep. Finally, one night in exasperation, she looked at me and said, "I am going to have a child. I want the meaning in my life that only a child can give. You can stay, or you can go. I'm having a baby with you or without you." I didn't think she was lying. She confessed later that she had been bluffing, but I'm glad I believed her. She's had to drag me into many things that I have come to love. I realized that she had every right to have a child; that I, too, believed that because she was lesbian, she had to have special reasons; that the simple human desire to bring a child into the world could not be taken for granted. I had always known that wanting a child was not just a whim with her. When we had just met, we went up into the attic of her house. In one corner, carefully wrapped, were tiny baby shirts. She had been carrying them around with her for years. We dressed Jesse in them. They're probably still up there. Cheryl saves everything. She's got Jesse's first fortune-cookie message: "Love is a necessity to you." She's even got the vials that his donor's semen came in.

We had been together for two years, and she drove me crazy sometimes. She always said what she was thinking, and diplomacy was not one of her strong points, but I loved her. I thought everything through ahead of time, calculated reactions, strategized. I guess it was a relief to be with someone like Cheryl. She had a good heart, and that wasn't a strategy. She always had time for people who were a little crazy, or struggling, or just down on their luck. She didn't have a case of the "look-goods." I guess you could call her a Christian. I knew that the baby would certainly be loved and wanted, which I always thought the most important thing. I had been holding out because I didn't want to be the one to make the decision, or at least that's what I had been saying.

I was afraid. If I loved the baby as much as I thought I might, I wouldn't be able to stand the pain if the world treated him cruelly. I don't think you can walk through this world without a little cruelty grabbing at your ankles. I didn't want to be so vulnerable to the world. I knew how deep my rage could go if I ever tapped into it, and so I was afraid of that, too. I loved Cheryl and my friends and family, but I looked forward to leaving the world at the end of my life, and not leaving behind anything too sacred or dear to me. I wanted to be finished with the earth.

The solution was to distance myself from the baby. I decided, Yes, I will help Cheryl to raise the baby, but I would be his aunt. He would call me Aunt Phyllis, and everything would be just fine. In other words, no one would know he had two mothers, including me. I believed this would also make it easier for Jesse socially. Cheryl would spend the bulk of her time with him and the other birth mothers, and I would go about my business, writing political satire and taking on the role of a magical Auntie Mame type of character. This was my plan. I spent quite a bit of energy explaining to people that, obviously, one could only have one mother.

This settled, Cheryl began keeping ovulation charts. It seemed as if our entire life was dominated by her projected ovulation. There are lesbians all over the city doing this, tormenting their lovers by obsessing over their ovulation cycles. I realized that Cheryl had been secretly keeping these charts for months, even before I agreed to raise a child with her. Once she decides on something, she'll cut through a mountain to accomplish it. I think it's in her genes. Her father's family came to America from Germany in the early 1700s. They settled first in Pennsylvania, and were called Pennsylvania Dutch, and they fought in the American Revolution. But the piece of history I can see in Jesse is that on Cheryl's mother's side he is a descendant of Daniel Boone, the Kentucky explorer and frontiersman. At Jesse's nursery school, I have used this as an excuse for his trailblazing personality.

While Cheryl was charting her ovulation cycles, we were part of a "Lesbians Considering Parenthood" workshop. Every Sunday for six weeks, three couples met in our living room to discuss the realities of parenting and to draw up plans for when the baby came. The only thing missing from the plans was experience. We nicknamed ourselves the "Maybe Baby Group." Meetings were facilitated by a woman from the Lyon-Martin Health Clinic, a lesbian-staffed and lesbian-centered health provider named for two Old Crones of the lesbian and gay civil rights movement, Phyllis Lyon and Del Martin. That was where I first heard the phrase "nonbiological mother." I announced that I would be referred to as "Aunt." I remember Cheryl and the other women smiling at me, nodding their heads. They weren't smug, but it was close. The women in the group were not exactly the type that could be called radical or revolutionary. They fit the profile of most lesbians considering parenthood: working-class and professional women who play Monopoly or tennis, go camping, watch movies, dance, and cook. Rather than taking to the streets in a spontaneous political demonstration, sitting in a front-row seat at a k. d. lang concert would be a wild night for most of these women.

One couple in the Maybe Baby Group had not yet decided if they would have a child. Catherine and Caroline were nurses who worked primarily with dying gay men. The nonbiological mother was forty and thought she should be preparing for her retirement, not starting a family. Three years later, I would see them at the Freedom Day Parade, nine-month-old Sophie on Catherine's shoulders.

The other couple was also about to inseminate. An odd dynamic arose between Cheryl and the inseminating woman in the other couple: They seemed to be engaged in competitive conception. I thought this other woman might have been inadvertently sabotaging herself. She was obsessed with having a girl because she lived in a separatist environment and she wanted to stay in it. How to conceive a girl was a subject of endless conjecture. This has always been problematic. In Separatistland, which is like Neverland for girls only, boys are allowed to attend events and live with the women until they reach an age when they are determined to be particularly and unacceptably boylike, which is how I imagine it's handled in harems.

I was secretly hoping for a boy. If we could have had one of each, that would have been lovely, but it was a boy I really wanted. I even called Cheryl my princeling until Jesse came along. When Cheryl and I first met, she announced that she was a complete cross-dresser. I found this charming since she has always been quite feminine in her build and movement, and has a beautiful round cherubic face. Cross-dressing for Cheryl meant wearing comfortable work clothes and not having to engage in the sexual politics of the workplace. She is now quite varied in her dress, but when we met I was taken captive by her size 6 work boots.

When I announced to the Maybe Baby Group that I wanted a boy, I was studied rather curiously by the facilitator and group members. Now, considering that at this same time it was reported in the papers that in China people were allowed only one child, and that if the child was female the parents were routinely killing her, I must admit it was a refreshing change, this great desire for girls. The separatist woman in our group was going so far as to put the semen onto a vinegar-soaked sponge before inseminating, which supposedly would kill off the male sperm. She was also using fresh semen, which, according to lesbian lore, has more active female sperm. Fresh semen is more difficult to use. It only lives outside the human body for about two hours, and there's an awful lot of coordinating and the risk of sperm death if a go-between happens to get caught in a traffic jam on the Golden Gate Bridge. There was also some speculation that cryopreservation, or freezing the semen, was somehow affecting the odds of having a female child. Certain heterocentric speculators outside the lesbian community have a bizarre theory that lesbians have more male hormones, and so produce mostly boys, but I think the fact that the majority of lesbians were conceiving boys was a result of timing and finances. Sperm can become expensive, costing between $60 and $120 for each insemination. Although lesbians often have an initial preference for female children, they are usually far more interested in getting pregnant than in the baby's sex, and so usually wait until their trusty ovulation-kit sticks are bright blue and so signal the presence of The Egg. The boy sperm, which carry the Y chromosome, are lighter, and so travel much faster toward the egg. Therefore, they get there first. The female sperm, which carry the X chromosome, are heavier and so travel more slowly toward the egg. If by the time the female sperm reach the egg it is already fertilized by the male sperm, they're out of luck. So in order to get a girl, you have to inseminate just before you ovulate (which is difficult to determine), so that the male sperm race up, find no egg, and disappear into Neverland, while the meandering female sperm arrive just as the egg does. Because most lesbians inseminate when they are sure they are ovulating, the odds for boys rise astronomically.

There's a Walgreen's there now, but on the corner of Castro and Eighteenth streets, a gay crossroad in San Francisco, there used to be a drugstore called Star Pharmacy. The Star started stocking ovulation-prediction and pregnancy test kits. On almost any day, you could see lesbians, singly, in pairs, or in little groups, sometimes accompanied by a gay man, very seriously examining these kits.

Cheryl had been tested extensively; finally, all of the tests were back, and she was found to be in good health. Having finally gotten the go-ahead from Sherron Mills, the woman who founded Pacific Reproductive Services, she purchased her ovulation kit and began the process.

Each morning, Cheryl took the ovulation test, then placed the Ovustick upright in its slot in a little white cardboard holder on the kitchen windowsill. We had long and tedious discussions about how blue I thought the tip of the stick was. It started out a watery, pale blue, the blue deepening as ovulation neared. There was a sample gradation of blues on the outside of the box to which you could compare the blues on your sticks. We saw blue everywhere, we studied blues, we dreamed blues, and finally, it was a bright blue morning, a bright blue day, and I was awakened by my complete cross-dresser. She was holding before my eyes a little stick from the ovulation kit. To say that she was a woman on a mission is a gross understatement.

"How blue does this look to you?" she demanded.

"Bluer than yesterday. Definitely," I answered. I had to give this answer or she would stomp around in those size 6 work boots. You see, it was important not to miss the ovulation cycle by thinking that the next day would be bluer, only to find it paler than the day before, and so a signal that you had missed The Egg.

"Do you think it's as blue as it could get?" she demanded.

She had asked me this question for the last several days.

"I don't know, dear. There are so many shades of blue. There's cornflower and indigo, peacock and robin's egg. And then there are blue ribbons and blue moons."

She shook the little stick at me and with intense irritation demanded, "But is this blue enough? Could it get bluer?"

Cheryl was certainly determined to be part of the chain of nature, and although I was certainly involved, it did not seem quite real. I took the little blue-tipped stick in my hand, and sitting sleepily on the edge of our bed, I examined it. Cheryl was staring at the stick as if it had a life of its own. In a puppet voice I said, "I think I'm baby blue!" I have this terrible habit of teasing people, especially the ones I love, when they are being particularly determined and down to earth.

Cheryl grabbed the stick and I followed her to the kitchen, apologizing for my insensitivity as I trailed geisha-style behind her. She tromped on in there as if she were headed for battle. The Ovusticks were lined up in their slots like little blue-headed soldiers. She placed the one she was holding in its slot and, comparatively, it did look deep blue. Cheryl paced in front of the window, breaking the bands of sunlight as she moved. I took the sample card from the ovulation kit and compared the shades of blue to the ones on the windowsill. The prism hanging in the sunlight threw off colors. I looked at Cheryl and smiled. I noted that beautiful colors on an intense and irritated face do not a pretty picture make.

As much to end the tension as because I believed it, I said, "This is it! The Egg has arrived! Let the insemination begin!" I felt as if I were announcing the start of the croquet match in *Alice's Adventures in Wonderland*.

We called ahead to alert Sherron Mills's office that we were coming. I had never been there. It was a medical building, and a typical doctor's waiting room. I was disappointed because I expected something out of *Star Trek*. We were led to a brightly lit, generic-looking examination room, and on our way, I saw a nurse opening a cylindrical tube about four feet high. As the nurse lifted the lid off the tube, wisps of liquid nitrogen floated in the air. I stopped and saw that inside the tube, hanging on wire racks, were carefully numbered two-inch plastic vials of frozen sperm. I had never seen how cryopreservation worked. It was very sci-fi. Cheryl had the look of the queen bee calling the drones. We went into the examination room, where Sherron was thawing the little vial that had the number of Jesse's donor on it. As the sperm thawed, it returned to its prefrozen, active state. Sherron was a pleasant woman with dark curly hair. She was the type of woman who would be a perfect, unconditionally loving aunt. As she prepared the semen, I asked her, "How many children can one donor father?"

"After four pregnancies, we take the man out of the pool," she said. I thought how odd it will be for the "yes donors" when four eighteen-year-olds who don't know each other, but are indeed half-siblings, all knock on his door one fine day in the year 2006.

As she put the semen into the injection syringe, Sherron smiled and said, "My friends are calling me the Father of the Lesbian Nation."

I loved this, but Cheryl wasn't at all interested in pleasantries or postmodern sociological constructs. We were the drones, and that was it. Sherron deposited the semen near Cheryl's uterus. Then she paused and apologetically said to me, "Oh! I'm sorry! I should have asked if you would like to do it."

So there was an etiquette to this, I thought. Cheryl gave me a "Let's get this show on the road" look. She was not a person into ritual etiquette, having been brought up as a fundamentalist, but the Catholic in me was a lover of ritual. I squirted the remaining bit of sperm near Cheryl's uterus. I've always thought that was the squirt that did it. Sherron put a cervical cap in place, so that the semen would have the greatest chance of staying near the cervix. Three years later, I found the cap carefully stored in the attic. Cheryl really does save everything.

On the ride home, Cheryl remained prone. Once home, she didn't stand up for twelve hours. Determined woman. As she lay upon the bed, I brought her a meal. As far as my cooking goes, the best I can say is that it's edible. I think she was lucky that night and got a grilled-cheese sandwich that wasn't too burnt, and a bowl of Campbell's cream of mushroom soup without too many lumps. I then decided to entertain her by enacting a sex-stereotyped fallopian-tube race. I first enacted the female sperm by studying my cuticles and indecisively muttering to myself, "Oh, I don't know. Maybe I'll go and maybe I won't. I'd love to conceive but I just washed my hair." Then I'd be the boy sperm, charging forward and calling ahead to all those on earth and in heaven, "Here I come! I'm gonna win! It's me! Stella! It's me! Don't look at those other guys!"

The days that followed were tedious, and Cheryl was mercurial. As the conception watch proceeded, she would alternate between believing she was pregnant and believing that she was not. It seemed like a good time to travel east to visit my parents, who were just in the process of moving into my father's family home in Cambridge, Massachusetts.

My life in San Francisco bore little resemblance to the life I had left behind in 1976, but in many ways, the East Coast had not changed at all. Logan Airport was the same; the taxicab drivers were still maniacal. The air was crisp, and the leaves gold and red. There is no place so beautiful in October as New England. The taxi driver barreled down the North Cambridge side streets, and I saw that the front yards had political signs stabbed into the ground on long sticks. Politics in Massachusetts is sport, especially in my father's childhood neighborhood, which was Tip O'Neill's old district, and which sent John F. Kennedy to the United States Senate.

Over a cup of tea, I mentioned to my parents that Cheryl might be pregnant. Years ago, when I finally came out to my father, he had said, "Why didn't you just say something?" The fact that we were practicing Catholics did not seem to them to be a problem. I suppose I was the sensitive type, taking hell and torture literally. If the Catholic church in the United States ever did a truthful survey, they would probably discover that the majority of their parishioners are not only in favor of, but practice birth control; no longer believe their sisters, brothers, mothers, and fathers should be excommunicated for divorce; and more often than not have a live-and-let-live attitude about homosexuality—which, after all, has populated the rectories and convents and almost single-handedly kept Broadway musicals alive.

But even my parents were taken aback by my little announcement of Cheryl's possible pregnancy. They were not negative, but
they certainly were startled. I couldn't blame them. So was I.

I explained to them how it had come about, and they remarked
on how interesting it must be to live in San Francisco. They have
always been city people, and this was an advantage.

While I was in Boston, I made several trips to be sure I had
described accurately from memory several scenes for my first
novel, *Atomic Candy,* which my editor, Ann Godoff, had ac-
quired for the Atlantic Monthly Press. I went to Filene's basement and to the Swan Boats. As I watched the Swan Boats bob
in the water, I decided what to put on the book jacket about my
personal life: "Phyllis Burke lives in San Francisco with her family." I did not want to come out any more than that because I did
not want to be ghettoized as a writer. The author photograph for
the book, however, did feature me in a black leather jacket—just
one of those little visual cues for the sisters—and yet I looked
feminine enough to pass for straight.

When I returned from my excursion to the Swan Boats, my
mother was pacing in the kitchen. Cheryl had called, she said,
and I was to call immediately. It was very important.

I called Cheryl and found out that she had taken a pregnancy
test. This time the magic color was green. If the little ball turns
green, you're pregnant. She had taken the test twice, but the balls
seemed a pastel green. How green did I think they should be?

"Forest green," I said. I guess I panicked.

My father was sitting at the kitchen table, pretending to read
*The Boston Globe* but listening to every word I said. My mother,
who had emigrated from Ireland as a child, did not bother with
appearances. She stood a few feet from me, her eyes wide, a little
smile on her face, part intensity, part fascination, her adventur-
ous streak rising to the surface.

I hung up the telephone, sat at the table and dunked my tea
bag, and my mother took her chair opposite my father.

"Cheryl thinks she's pregnant," I said.

I smiled at my father and for the first time truly understood the
expression "You could have knocked him over with a feather."

"What will the baby call you?" my mother asked. Always the

practical one. She seemed to be particularly intense with her spoon as she stirred the sugar into her milky tea.

" 'Auntie!' " I said.

"I see."

Something seemed to be on my mother's mind.

"What is it?"

"What will we be?" she asked.

" 'Great-aunt,' 'Great-uncle.' "

"Fine," said my mother.

"Oh, boy," said my father.

And so my mother and I had tea, and my father had a cup of coffee. We decided not to tell the rest of the family until it was certain, and the next day, I left for San Francisco.

When I arrived home in San Francisco, there was a small glass dessert bowl on the center of the wooden kitchen table, and in it were two tiny pale green balls. The prisms hanging in the window threw rainbow lights on the walls and ceiling. Cheryl was not at home, so I sat alone at the table. I gave one of the little balls a push with my finger. My hands started to sweat. The little ball was hard and noisy as it spun around inside the dessert dish. It was a very pale green. Watercress. Not even close to forest green.

Cheryl arrived home with yet another pregnancy test kit. She had been so excited about the possibility of being pregnant that she had done the test too early. She had another kit, and the magic color for this one was blue.

I was asleep the next morning when she burst into the bedroom, jumped on the bed, and in a state as close to rapture as I had ever seen, announced that she was absolutely, definitely pregnant. I remember my mouth falling open as I sat between horror and amazement and thought of something gracious to say. Within a few days, Sherron Mills confirmed the pregnancy. Impregnation usually does not occur so easily. Cheryl had a very erratic ovulation cycle, so it was quite shocking that she got pregnant on the first try. The more mystical among us said things like "This child was determined to come here."

The reality of the situation was disorienting for me, but not for Cheryl. She began early nesting. She built a sturdy changing table and collected infant clothing that looked as if it belonged on a doll. She had a dream of a white crib, and so I bought one, with a thin blue stripe. I was still into the idea of a boy. Cheryl was ecstatic, and I found myself taken up into the drama. Cheryl had lists of things that would be needed: little white cotton shirts, little dressing gowns, baby bottles and pacifiers. The pregnancy took center stage; it was even more intense than the completion of my first novel. There were baby showers and outings to buy carriages, musical mobiles, and a playpen.

We joined a support group formed by Jenny Curley for ten lesbian couples who were pregnant. (As with our heterosexual counterparts, the couple, not just the birth mother, is said to be pregnant.) Among the members of our group was Debra Chasnoff, who a few years later would accept an Academy Award for best short documentary, and would acknowledge her partner, Kim, and their son, Noah, in her acceptance speech.

The birth mothers seemed to be puffing themselves up as much as possible, because they were still in early pregnancy. It was a source of great disappointment for Cheryl that she did not show much until she was five months pregnant.

Cheryl loved this group. "Once you're pregnant," she said, "you can talk to anybody else who's pregnant and you have so much in common that no one else wants to hear about. Weight gain. Belching. What it feels like to be hot. Just the practical nuts and bolts of being pregnant. It's like a tool project, like you were building something. Kind of shop talk. Shop talk for pregnant moms."

Our entire lives were about to be turned upside down, and Cheryl thought of it as a tool project. The talk at one of the get-togethers turned to donors. One of the women had inseminated with the sperm of a friend who would be an active partner. One woman's brother had been the donor for her partner, which made him legally the child's uncle. I was just wrapping my mind around that fascinating reality when up came the question of which sperm bank you had used. As the chitchat continued, I realized that it was possible that two of the children to be born to women in the room would be half-siblings. I brought this up rather gleefully and was met with silence. If the women had used the same sperm bank, they were keeping the number of the donor secret from each other.

Then there were the women who used go-betweens, which means that the birth mother and the donor did not know each other's identities. This is all well and good unless the donor and the mother travel in the same circles and one of the donor's lesbian friends suddenly turns up pregnant. One woman in the group tried to avoid her donor when her pregnancy began to show. They finally ran into each other in the kitchen at a house party and the mutual recognition was inescapable. Another woman worked at a sperm bank and had taken an unauthorized withdrawal. One of the women in the group had used the same donor, and the woman from the sperm bank knew it. When the children were born, she announced that they were half-siblings. This irritated the other birth mother, who did not know the identity of the donor. It was bad etiquette.

I asked who else had used Pacific Reproductive Services, but the Oakland Sperm Bank and anonymous donors with go-betweens were rather popular with this group. I found myself gravitating toward the other nonbiological mothers. We were a curious little group. Most of us were not quite clear as to what our role was. At one point, all of the nonbiological mothers wound up in the kitchen. Most of us had our hands in our pockets. We spoke in low tones to each other about the perils of living with a pregnant woman, while the biological mothers in the living room were busily exchanging morning nausea remedies. A hot topic among us nonbiologicals was the naming of the child, and whether, how, and where our last names would be written on the birth certificates. In some states, putting a woman's name where it calls for the man's name is a crime, and in any case, this provides absolutely no legal protection for the nonbiological mother.

The next-hottest topic was care of the baby after it was born. I confidently stated that, at three months, the baby would be put into child care during our work days. None of our plans ever took into account the emotions we would feel when we first held those babies.

There was a sudden commotion from the biologicals in the

living room, and we moved in to see what the debate topic was. We had already done cloth diapers versus Pampers. That had been very controversial. This time it was circumcision. (Eight of the ten couples were pregnant with boys.) We nonbiologicals hovered near the doorway, and as I listened to the women, I realized it was probably the first time in history that circumcision had ever been debated by a group like this.

I contributed the observation "Don't you think this is funny? A roomful of lesbians ardently debating whether or not to circumcise their infant sons?"

Not a laugh. Not a smile. Not even from my Cheryl, who was at least used to me. Cheryl was furious at one of the other biologicals, who was adamantly against circumcision as barbaric and, at the very least, patriarchal, a way for the patriarch to cause the first betrayal by the mother, who must turn the child over to the men for the circumcision and the pain. She was informing Cheryl that Cheryl should not even be considering it. Cheryl couldn't stand it when anyone told her what she could or could not do.

I had absolutely no information about or experience with foreskins, and was not terribly confident of this particular group's range and depth of knowledge on the topic. I suggested that we ask some men what they thought, but this served only to inflame tempers all around. Cheryl and I did, however, consult our fathers, brothers, male cousins, and friends. They all had their varied reasons why you should or should not be circumcised. The basic nonreligious reason was that the son should match the father, which did not apply to us, but the most compelling reason was that other boys would laugh at you in the locker room if you were uncut. This amazed me. How had we created a society where a normal piece of skin could be the cause of peer torment? I even received a long-distance phone call from my cousin Richard, encouraging me to consider doing circumcision for athletic reasons. We decided to delay our decision. Cheryl was, after all, just two months pregnant.

A few days later, Cheryl began to hemorrhage. We called the doctor, and the word was that nothing can be done before the first trimester is complete. Cheryl lay there, not moving, trying to will the embryo to stay in place, but the placenta was pulling away from the uterine wall. For hours she lay absolutely still and focused upon keeping the baby alive inside. She moved only to change the bloodied pads. This began one of the longest, most tedious periods of our lives. Each day, we were afraid we might lose the baby. Cheryl was put on complete bed rest. She lay perfectly still, hour after hour, day after day, month after month, forced to eat my pan-fried meat and overcooked vegetables.

At eight weeks, it was time for the first sonogram. We did not know if we would even see the fetus, because it might have been lost in the hemorrhage. But there it was. It looked to me like a little sea creature. Cheryl fought back tears when she saw the heartbeat as a burst of star-shaped lines on the sonogram radar. "I've got my reward," she whispered as she watched the pulsation on the screen. It was still there, still alive, still growing, but not yet viable. This word, "viable," haunted us.

We were told to consider what we would do if Cheryl reached the fifth month but entered premature labor, so that the baby was born dead. Would we have a funeral? Would we hold and name the child? If the baby did live, we had no idea what its physical condition would be. The early hemorrhage could have caused physical problems, but amniocentesis was not an option since it could well cause Cheryl to abort. We counted each day, each week. Twenty-seven weeks, and the baby would live, they said. Twenty-eight would be better.

But at twenty weeks, Cheryl again began to bleed, and a second sonogram had to be performed. The doctor was silent as he scanned for the fetus, and then he said, "There's the old stem on the apple!" That was one of the most splendid sentences Cheryl and I had ever heard, and I thought it a particularly charming way to refer to a penis. At this point, the question of whether we would have a boy or girl was of no importance. We only wanted a healthy child. That the baby was male presented an additional stress, however, because a boy's lungs develop more slowly than a girl's; although he would be viable at twenty-eight weeks, thirty-two weeks was preferable for a male. This required Cheryl to spend three weeks in the Trendelenburg position, which means that your hips must be above your shoulders, thereby enlisting gravity to forestall premature labor. Between being virtually upside down and having to eat my cooking, Cheryl's mood grew nasty. I would walk in the door, and she would shout, "Can't you make anything but pan-fried meat?"

Every day of Cheryl's pregnancy, I went to work and sat at my desk at the law firm where I had been the office manager for two years. This was before I began teaching at the university. I had not come out to the owners of the firm because one of the owners was the quintessential good old boy. On one of my first few days on the job, Mr. O. had ranted in his office, "We kept the broads out, and I'll be damned if we're gonna let in the fags." He was in the process of blackballing, with his buddies, an otherwise acceptable man for membership in the Olympic Club, a nationally known, exclusive, all-male bastion of privilege in San Francisco whose founding mission was the betterment of the White male, and which at the time included our present Supreme Court justice Anthony Kennedy, who had asked that his membership be immediately reinstated should he not be confirmed. The Olympic Club's principal asset was a world-class golf course. Unfortunately for the club, several of the golf holes were on public property and City Attorney Louise Renne would soon be filing suit against them for discrimination. I knew that in all probability Mr. O's delight with me was based as much upon my blue eyes, blond hair, and Irish mother as it was upon my skills. Finally, I do not "look like" a lesbian, at least not to those who cannot pick up on subtle cues like charm bracelets loaded with tiny labyrises.

When I agreed to manage the office, the outgoing manager sidled up to me by the coffee machine and whispered, "Don't ever hire any gays, because Mr. O. hates them."

"Right," I said.

After about a year, unbeknownst to Mr. O., I had surrounded him with lesbians who were extraordinarily well paid. I did bring one identifiably gay male secretary into the office for a short period of time. Mr. O. came up to me and said, "If you want to hire a gay, go ahead. But you tell him I'm gonna call him names like 'fruit' if he stays here." Mr. O., who was rather plump, would stomp through the office, past this man's desk. As Mr. O.

left the room, the gay man, who had a wonderful sense of humor, would look at me and gush, "I do love fatties!"

I drew the line with Mr. O. when he started making faggots-dying-of-AIDS jokes. In a fairly flat tone of voice, I told him that I had just lost a dear friend to AIDS and I would appreciate it if he saved his humor for the Olympic Club.

When I announced to Mr. O. that Cheryl was pregnant and that she and I would raise the baby together, there was nothing in his mind to accommodate that thought. I could certainly not be a lesbian, as I did not have a mustache and I was Irish. I imagine he wrapped his mind into some kind of convent scene. It never sank in until years later, when the friend to whom I had turned my job over was listening to his oration on "the gays." She herself was straight, and she asked Mr. O., "But what about Phyllis? You liked Phyllis, didn't you?" When I saw him after that, he never seemed to walk with his back toward me, or if he did, his head was always turned a bit in my direction, as if he weren't sure what I might do if he weren't on guard.

Every day of Cheryl's pregnancy, I would return home from the office, from the orations of Mr. O., to see if the baby was still growing, if there had been any bleeding. Fortunately for Cheryl, I learned to steam rather than boil vegetables. The food was tasteless, but nevertheless Cheryl ate green and yellow vegetables every day, milk for calcium, meats and fish for protein. We both got fat. When one member of a lesbian couple gets pregnant, often both women gain weight. "We" were indeed pregnant.

Our doctors were at the University of California, San Francisco Medical Center. Dr. Patty Robertson, herself a lesbian mom, was the high-risk-pregnancy specialist in charge of our case. When we passed the twenty-eight-week mark, Dr. Robertson decided that it would be all right for Cheryl to go to Lamaze class. I felt uncomfortable and self-conscious with all of the straight couples. I quickly realized, however, that they made the assumption that Cheryl was a single mother and that I was her friend. They had no idea that we were a postmodern lesbian family. Maybe I should have butched it up. I would have let the matter go, but Cheryl always clarified the situation during group introductions when she announced that I was her partner. This was startling to some of the couples in the group, but not so startling that anyone left. I, however, was suddenly defensive, on guard for disapproving sneers or judgments. This was the first time we had ventured out together to a nonlesbian environment as a pregnant couple. I was very protective of Cheryl, and did not want to have any bad vibes sent toward her. Cheryl, however, did not give a damn. She was confident in herself. But I began to take on a certain amount of "male" energy: I was going to take care of everything. My version of butching it up, however, bears more resemblance to Eva Perón than to Daniel Boone. Cheryl loved it. I could tell by the way she smiled and preened. At this point, my complete cross-dresser was no more. She was now wearing lots of flowery, pastel things, although she complained bitterly about the maternity clothes available and flatly refused to wear any-thing that said BABY with an arrow pointing to her pregnant belly. I was solicitous, and an absolute tiger to deal with if I felt Cheryl was being slighted in any way. Basically, I was a pain in the ass, I knew it, and I didn't care.

Each couple announced the gender of their expected child. Many of the men literally puffed up when announcing they were about to have a son. When they announced they were bearing girls, many of the straight women seemed either apologetic or defiant. This girl-boy thing was certainly not confined to the lesbian community.

I paid close attention during Lamaze class. Before Cheryl's pregnancy, I didn't even know what the fallopian tubes were, much less have an understanding of the birth process. It had never seemed relevant to my life. I had known I was lesbian for twenty years, and had long ago accepted that I would be child-less.

The instructor drew diagrams and launched into a long meta-phor, complete with little drawings, about climbing hills and reaching plateaus. You would have thought we were going hik-ing. My favorite part of class was when the partner breathes along with the mother. In the midst of this, I could only think of the Reverend Cecil Williams, the flamboyant African-American minister of Glide Memorial Church, and his sermon the previous Christmas. In referring to Mary giving birth to Jesus, Cecil Williams declared, "Childbirth is *painful*! Don't let them tell you it's not!" The word "painful" echoed and rattled against the rafters of his church in the Tenderloin section of San Francisco. What did Cecil know that was unknown to this Lamaze instructor?

Many of the lesbian women were having home births with midwives, but their pregnancies were not high risk. Because of Cheryl's high-risk status, there was no consideration of a home birth. I was so grateful that we were excused from the politically correct method. I wanted the hospital, with access to state-of-the-art equipment, blinking red and green lights, and, if needed, drugs.

Mid-May, we had to make the Decision. Dr. Robertson lent us a videotape of a hospital circumcision. Cheryl lay upon the open couch in the living room, and I sat at her feet, facing the television. I popped the tape into the VCR. There was a mellow male voice, very reassuring, very informative. He explained the technique of circumcision. He stressed that the infant boy would not feel any pain during the procedure, that babies do not feel pain like adults. This seemed to me profoundly illogical. A smiling nurse brought in the infant and strapped him into a white bucket-like plastic seat. Then the doctor took a pair of scissors and started to cut. Cheryl started to cry, tears streaming down her face, and I could only gasp in wonderment at the screaming infant, the steady stream of blood, and the calm medical voice-over explaining that the baby felt nothing as the blood and skin fell away from his penis. I started to scream along with the baby, and then clicked off the television: I didn't want Cheryl to go into labor. So that was it for Jesse's circumcision. We were trying so hard to get him into the world in one piece, the idea of snipping something off him when he got here seemed unconscionable. My bottom line was, I couldn't put it back on. I had also seen a very remarkable thing in a local newspaper a few weeks before. It was an announcement for a "Foreskin Restoration Support Group" that included working through the grieving process. That finished it for me.

On June twentieth, at about eight-thirty in the evening, four days after her expected due date, Cheryl's water broke. I ran around the house gathering things and trying to be under control, but I felt like a cartoon. I could see myself from above, sitcom style, Ricky Ricardo leaving with Ethel and Fred to take Lucy to the hospital to have Little Ricky. They are all, of course, out the door with everything except Lucy, the pregnant mother.

We drove to the hospital on the route I had plotted. Cheryl was relieved and happy. This should have been a clue that she was not far enough into labor, and so of course they sent us home. We played Crazy Eights, and then about midnight, I fell asleep on the couch. In the early-morning hours, I walked past the studio and saw that Cheryl was rocking in pain while writing at her desk. I quietly went in and read over her shoulder. She was writing a final note about the location of insurance policies. I realized that she was considering the possibility that she might die in childbirth. I hadn't thought of this. I had been worried only about the baby having all his fingers and toes and being able to live outside the womb. If Cheryl did die, there was no guarantee that a court would respect her last will and testament, which instructed that I should be the baby's guardian.

Just before dawn, we again got into the car. This time, she shouted at me at every movement, at each and every little bump in the road. She smacked me in the arm and accused me of deliberately hitting potholes. This looked a lot more like the Reverend Cecil Williams's version of childbirth than the Lamaze instructor's scenario.

At the hospital, a nurse demanded that Cheryl at least try to walk up and down the halls, but when she did, blood and water spilled all over the floor. The nurse quickly put Cheryl into a hospital bed.

The labor went on all day, all night, for thirty-two hours. When fully dilated, Cheryl began to push. She pushed with such intensity that her neck widened and flattened like that of a cobra about to strike. I began to think about a strange theory that some lesbian psychologists were coming up with. It seemed that a statistically high number of lesbians had difficulty giving birth; the psychologists thought that maybe lesbians didn't want to give their babies up to the world.

The labor continued. I am high-strung and terrible when I have sleep deprivation. Watching Cheryl in that much pain and being unable to stop it was humbling and disorienting. I had always been able to smooth things in the world for her a little. She looked at me and said, "Can't you do something about this pain?" And I couldn't.

Dr. Jeanette Brown, a lesbian mom and a member of Bay Area Physicians for Human Rights, was the doctor on duty. She inserted a little monitor into Jesse's skull, inside Cheryl's womb, to check his heart rate and oxygen level for distress. Cheryl pushed for two more hours. Dr. Brown came up to me and quietly said, "We can't let them go on any longer. We have to take her to the operating room to perform a mid-forceps delivery. I am the very best at this."

We prepared for the operating room, and it was difficult to keep my emotions under control. I had to put on a surgical gown, and it felt like a dress with no shoulders. As I tried to fasten it in place, I stood outside the operating room door and tried to make a deal with God. If you let this baby and Cheryl be all right, I'll give you . . . The spiritual barter system. But then I stopped. I looked at the clock. It was the middle of the night, about three-fifteen. I could do the footwork, but I knew I was powerless, that I would have to accept whatever came, and so I said the only little prayer I could think of: Thy will, not mine, be done.

The operating room was sterile and bright, crowded with pediatricians, obstetricians, nurses, and an anesthesiologist, all in white. A little cart to put the baby on was in a corner. I heard someone call it a crash cart, and for a moment, my knees trembled. Cheryl lay on the table under the mushroom-shaped lights. All movement in the room paused like the seconds before the curtain on a play.

Then Jeanette Brown began the mid-forceps delivery. Dr. Brown was a small, yet very strong woman. She and another woman, a young intern, both worked the forceps under her guidance. They used their full bodies. I had never seen women use that much strength. They widened the birth canal with careful precision, the muscles on their arms bulging as they leaned the weights of their bodies away from each other, each gripping one handle of the tonglike forceps.

Jesse's head crowned and with a swift movement, Jeanette had him in her hands. He was covered with blood and mucus and his eyes were wide open.

"Oh my God. He's beautiful," I said.

The anesthesiologist looked at me and quietly said, "Your son was born at three fifty-one A.M."

That was the strangest phrase anyone had ever said to me. "Your son." Jesse looked at the world with such intensity, so fully awake, and then they cut the cord. He was rushed to the pediatric crash cart, and I followed. I watched as Jesse appeared to go limp. The pediatrician and nurses at the crash cart did not conceal from me their sense of emergency, although it was concealed from Cheryl. It was clear that the baby was in distress. Hands moved quickly all around him as they snorkeled fluid out of his lungs. Finally, he was breathing on his own, but he was what is called a floppy baby. I watched and breathed and breathed. I was trying to breathe into him. On the Apgar scale, which is a test for newborn responsiveness, he was only a 4 out of a possible 10. He began to breathe, but his little chest labored furiously as he struggled to pump air into his lungs. They determined that he would be all right for a few moments, wrapped him, and brought him to Cheryl. She was concerned about the brightness of the lights on his eyes, and she managed to lift one hand to shield him from the glare. Then the doctors lifted him from her to take him to the infant-care unit. I identified myself, and they were startled. I had always wanted to be invisible because I found out so much about what people really thought, but this was no longer useful. I put out my hands for the baby, and they handed me the little bundle, his chest still pumping.

In the hallway outside of the operating room, the doctor asked if I was authorized to consent to medical treatment, and I told him I was. I showed him the legal document I kept on my person at all times that gave Cheryl's consent to my right to authorize medical treatment for Jesse. The doctor told me they had to do a spinal tap on him. Cheryl's water had broken so early in labor, and the baby was so low on the Apgar scale, that they feared infection. They asked me to sign a piece of paper. Sleep deprivation made it seem all the more surreal as the doctor explained to me that the test had to be done, but that I had to understand that the baby could be crippled if anything went wrong. I had to sign a paper that said I understood this. I looked through the small window into the operating room and saw that it was impossible for me to consult Cheryl. A nurse was literally pounding the afterbirth out of her.

I signed the paper, and handed the baby to the doctors. I thought I would faint, but fear keeps the adrenaline running. The nurses called me to a nursing station. Cheryl's mother was on the phone from Ohio and wanted to know how the baby was. I told her to say a prayer, then hung up. I was not allowed to be present for the procedure on Jesse. For half an hour, I walked the hospital corridor and tried to imagine how I could ever tell Cheryl that the baby was disabled. As I passed the nursery, I saw that he had been returned to the incubator. He was still breathing in that exaggerated manner. The nurses and doctor had failed to inform me that the test had been successful and was negative.

The baby was crying; I went into the nursery. It took a while to convince the on-duty nurses that I was entitled to enter. I scrubbed my hands, put on the gown, and through the portal of the incubator slipped my hand, which I lightly rested upon his chest. He stopped crying, and the pumping, labored breathing slowly regulated.

And then the phone calls began, announcing Jesse's arrival, setting off what I call the lesbian tom-toms. Dozens of women, lesbian and straight, brought gifts for him. When there is a birth, or a new child comes to our community, that child is welcomed as an honored guest.

Three days after the birth, on the day Cheryl and Jesse were to return home, I filled the house with vases of white carnations. It was as if the Prince of the Peacocks were coming to visit. His cradle was ready in the living room, to be near our bedroom until he was old enough to sleep in his crib in the nursery. I took the clothes out of the cradle. Cheryl had laid out the coming-home outfit a month before: The peaked white hat, the lavender-trimmed snap-suit with tiny purple lilacs and green leaves, the cloth infant diaper. One friend commented that Cheryl had laid out Jesse's first clothes as if she were going to give birth directly into them.

Cheryl was ecstatic as she held her child, and as she handed him to me, she watched my face carefully for every expression. She saw what I did not and could not see.

I dressed Jesse in his first outfit, then propped him up in the hospital bed to take photos. One of the pictures is a "miracle photograph." He looks like a little Buddha: the peaked hat, his arms to his chest, his knees high with legs crossed at the ankles. Three bright pink orbs surround him, one above his head, one to each side. Real photographers see the picture and say, "Overexposed." Cheryl saw it and said, "Look at the angels!" This photograph was prominently displayed in many houses in the city. It was tacked to bedroom doors, taped to mirrors, pasted in albums, framed upon mantelpieces. Some of my gay men friends, who were losing their friends and lovers in the AIDS epidemic, handled Jesse's picture with special tenderness. One particularly gentle man, who had suffered so many losses that he could barely speak of them anymore, placed the photograph upon his little altar to Buddha and those he loved.

When the doctors told us we could bring Jesse home, I felt complete anxiety. He was so small. Where would the doctors and nurses be if he again had trouble breathing? I drove the car at about twenty miles per hour, my knee trembling as I tried to regulate my foot on the accelerator. I parked the car in front of our house, and when I opened the front door the scent of carnations drifted to the sidewalk. Cheryl had never been more radiant—and I had never been more directorial, especially for someone who identified herself as an aunt. We brought Jesse inside our house, and sat beside each other on the couch, the infant tucked between us, our arms around each other.

My mother called to ask if we were going to have the baby christened. I told her that I did not think it necessary to renounce Satan because I did not believe children came into the world with sin. She laughed and said that no one believed that anymore, and she was asking only so she could know when to send birth presents. I told her I would christen him myself. Immediately.

At twilight on his fourth day I lit a candle. Cheryl held Jesse between us, close in the crook of her right arm, and I stood beside her, a long-stemmed white carnation in my hand.

In a quiet voice, I told him, "With great respect and love, I welcome you to this world. You are an honored guest in this house, and you honor us with your presence. Your name is Jesse, which means Gift of God. Thank you for coming."

Cheryl kissed his head, and I took the flower and touched its petals to the crown of his cap of blond hair, then to his forehead and cheeks. He was so tiny, his backbone still curled, a sensory being, pre-thought, in touch with that which becomes hidden from us as we become part of this world. I put the white petals near his hand. He grasped the flower with the remarkable strength of the newborn, the way he held onto Cheryl's breast when he was feeding, and then he looked directly at me. This was no easy feat. He could not move his head. His eyes had to travel up with profound determination. He looked squarely into my eyes, and I experienced his presence as a being completely separate from Cheryl, from me, with his own destiny. At that moment, I believe he recognized me, but I did not know who he was. He sank quickly back into the Neverland of the newborn, but he had come out from it just long enough to make me his.

# CHAPTER II

# The Birds Sing at Night
# in San Francisco

ALL OF THE PLANS we had devised in the Maybe Baby Group fell apart. As Jesse was about to turn three months old, I came home and found Cheryl in tears, holding the baby close. She had called one of the child-care providers we had on our carefully prepared list, and had heard several infants crying in the background.

Cheryl stood and handed me the baby. I walked through the rooms of our small house, and I could feel her watching me. I knew what she was thinking, and what she was asking. There was no way that Cheryl could stay home. She had to return to her work as a technical engineer at Rolm, an IBM subsidiary, not just for the income, but for the health insurance. I could not tell Cheryl to stay home with Jesse, which she wanted to do, because my insurance could not cover him.

Legally, I was nothing to him, a biological stranger. It was not yet possible for me to attempt to become Jesse's second legal parent, in which capacity I would be able to insure him. Unusual adoption proceedings of this type had succeeded several times under the care of civil rights attorney Donna Hitchens. If successful, the adoption would allow Cheryl to retain her natural birthmother rights, while granting me legal adoptive-parent status. Jesse would, in effect, have two legal mothers, and I would be able to extend to him all the benefits that would naturally be his were Cheryl and I a married heterosexual couple. (Ironically, Cheryl and I would still have no legal relationship, while we each, separately, would have a legal relationship with Jesse.) Just before Jesse's birth, Donna Hitchens, who was our lawyer, had advised against attempting to do the adoption too early, before we could prove that I was his co-parent and had financially and psychologically supported him. Three years was considered a good time, because at that age he would be able to talk to the judge. Family-law judges preside over an almost feudal territory, their opinion on "the best interests of the child" being greatly subjective. The lawyers worked, therefore, case by case, tediously and quietly. They did nothing that could jeopardize the families, and they recognized that they had to work judge by judge, not through the court of public opinion. What they did do was have independent studies undertaken to determine if lesbian parents adversely affect such developmental stages as gender development. The clear answer was no.

But Jesse was only three months old, and we could not prove in a court of law that I was his co-parent. In truth, I myself did not believe it. The decision was made. I would take my chances and go without insurance, Cheryl would return to work, and Jesse would be fully covered. I was still carrying on my person at all times the legal document stating that Cheryl gave me her consent to authorize medical treatment for Jesse. I felt empowered and humiliated by this piece of paper in my wallet.

When I realized the full impact of being Jesse's full-time caregiver, there was only mild shock. I had known it would happen. I knew the lovely pie charts on time allotment from the Maybe Baby Group would break apart with the reality of the child. But there was something more, and that was that I wanted to do it. I wanted to be with him, to find out who he was, because I loved him.

Everything was fine as long as I stayed in the house. The moment I went outside, to the supermarket or playground, I became self-conscious. I could not for a single moment forget that I was assumed to be straight, and Jesse's birth mother. In some ways, I felt as if I were passing for his parent, since I had no legal connection to him; I was an impostor in my own heart.

People tend to speak to women with small babies. I didn't like speaking to strangers. I was not at all a public person. While I was standing in line at the supermarket, trying to quickly read a *TV Guide* article about *Roseanne,* a woman asked me what kind of labor I had had.

"Teamsters," I said.

I was trying to exchange a stuffed animal for some Pampers, and the lady behind the return counter asked me if I was breast-feeding.

"I'm his aunt."

"Does your sister breast-feed?"

"She's not my sister."

"Sister-in-law?"

"He just came to my house, okay? Can I do this exchange?"

And then there was the playground.

"Does he look like his father?"

"How should I know?"

As Jesse grew, we worked out a system for self-entertainment. I would put him in his high chair with little crackers and a bottle of warm milk. I would sit beside him with a good book and a cup of tea, and he would listen to Pavarotti while I read Susan Sontag essays.

We had just finished our ritual. Pavarotti and Jesse belted out the finale.

Jesse looked at me and smiled.

"Mama," he said.

I looked at him, and my book went down. He smiled with satisfaction. He had never said this word. It sounded so sweet and alien to me.

"No, dear," I corrected him. "Auntie. Auntie."

He smiled but said nothing.

"Auntie," I said.

He tossed his head back and laughed. "Mama, Mama."

I tried to distract him by giving him his toy telephone. He

imitated me, laughing uproariously then jabbering away into the phone.

"Mama," he said as he held the phone out to me. I put the phone in its cradle and lifted him into my arms.

Cheryl was soon christened "Mudner." As Jesse's speech evolved, Cheryl became "Mama Cher," and I was "Mama Phyllis."

Cheryl said nothing during this process. She had known it would only be a matter of time before I realized who I was.

I called my mother and father.

"I'm Mama Phyllis."

"We knew that, dear," said my mother, who said to my father in the background, "We're grandparents!"

Jesse knew who I was, Cheryl knew who I was, even my parents knew. Yet the best I could do was to refer to myself as his "other" mother, sort of like a spare.

In late May of 1989, a reporter from the *San Francisco Examiner* called. She had been given my name by friends. The *Examiner* was doing a groundbreaking sixteen-part series entitled "Gay in America," and they were looking for lesbian mothers who might like to be photographed and interviewed. Also, did we happen to know anyone who was going to have a baby born in June, during Lesbian and Gay Pride Week? Jesse had been born on June twenty-second, and his first birthday would indeed be during Pride Week, but no, we did not wish to be interviewed.

I read the "Gay in America" series with fascination, but the article that worried me concerned the St. Petersburg, Florida, battle of a nonbiological mother for the child she had raised with her partner, who had died suddenly of lupus. The deceased partner's parents had for a time won custody of the child, in spite of the deceased birth mother's wishes, but after two trials in a four-year period, the child had been returned to the nonbiological mother. What I noticed was that the reporter had hastened to describe the bedroom of the little girl as being decorated in "white and blue frills." I thought the reporter was trying to be helpful, to assure the readers that although the nonbiological mother appeared somewhat butch, the little girl was having proper gender training. I went into Jesse's room and saw that there were small gold birds and tiny flowers on his bedroom wallpaper. I decided they were butch flowers.

On Jesse's first birthday, we did not feature him in the *San Francisco Examiner*. We took him to the beach. He insisted on racing along the water's edge on all fours in his usual style: head down, eyes straight ahead, like a baby ram. He was very strong, and he made a crablike trail in the sand. When he tired of this, he gave each of us one of his hands, and we walked along the shoreline. He looked up into the sky at the gulls, lifted his legs into the air, and swinging between us, cried out, "Bird!" in a long-drawn-out call. We took him home, diapered him, and put him to bed, and as he fell to sleep, we sang "Happy Birthday."

As Jesse was about to turn two years old, in June of 1990, Donna Hitchens challenged an incumbent judge who had been appointed by the governor to a vacated seat. Although these judges must run for office in the next general election, they usually run unopposed. Such is the power of incumbency that a sitting San Francisco Superior Court judge had not been defeated in sixteen years. Donna founded the Lesbian Rights Project, which evolved into the National Center for Lesbian Rights. She had been a civil rights attorney for many years, and also had broad support among ethnic minorities, liberals, and progressives. She had put into place the legal team that would win the first civil rights case against the San Francisco Fire Department for discrimination against women and people of color. The lesbian and gay community united behind her challenge for the judge's seat; her campaign was not so much against the incumbent as in favor of diversity on the bench. Lesbians had never before united with such intensity behind a lesbian candidate for political office. (Let there be no mistake about it: The judiciary is political.) But when the election results were first announced, the incumbent was listed as the winner. I was now teaching creative writing at San Francisco State University, and I went to my classroom that day with a heavy, resigned feeling, but when I left school at the end of the day, the headlines had changed. The final tally had been made, and for the first time in history, without the benefit of incumbency by way of appointment, an openly lesbian woman had been elected to the judiciary by a general popular vote. Hitchens, a master of coalition politics, had toppled a sitting judge. She would take the bench in January of 1991. Yet, as I would come to understand, the more visible we became, the more power we took, the easier the targets we made for the radical right, some of whom were advocating the death penalty for lesbians and gay men.

On the traditional last Sunday of June, the Lesbian and Gay Freedom Day Parade was held. I usually walked with one group or another, but I always liked to watch the beginning of the parade and then join in. The traditional phalanx of hundreds of riders in the Women's Motorcycle Contingent, known informally as Dykes on Bikes, led the parade, followed by the parade committee, carrying the banner. The parade committee was not getting the attention it usually did. Behind it, there was a crush of photographers facing the other way. When I first saw the object of their attention, I was horrified: a man who looked exactly like a dime-store Jesus, except that his body was painted pink. He wore a loincloth fashioned from an American flag, and a crown of pink thorns. He was carrying a pink cross, with a green scroll across the top that said, MARTYR FOR ART. Behind him was a multicolored banner that stretched the width of the street. In bold letters it read, NOT SPONSORED BY JESSE HELMS. Every few yards "Jesus" would stop and pose. I was shocked by him. He was so blasphemous. He stopped near me, and all I could see was this terrible joke. My eyes went down, and I saw that he was wearing pink high heels. It was the most bizarre thing I had ever seen. Pink Jesus had large, soft brown eyes, the eyes of a maniac or a theater master. It was impossible to tell if he was brilliant or insane. Whatever he was, he was certainly an artist, meticulous in his preparations. As I looked closely at him, I realized that Pink Jesus was Gilbert Baker, the creator of the rainbow flag, which is flown internationally as a symbol of lesbian and gay pride. The rainbow flag had been a stroke of genius, but I did not think Pink Jesus was a good idea. How were we to make inroads into society at large with such a bizarre presence as this man? We were becoming empowered. Donna Hitchens was going to be sworn in as a judge. I felt that this type of behavior threatened everything we had worked so hard to attain. I just wanted my life. I was not part of a circus. I did not want who I was to be represented to the world by this media junkie, however powerful the image.

In September, we received a letter from Donna Hitchens's office, with a list of lawyers from whom to select her replacement. We chose Abby Abinanti, whom Cheryl had known socially. Early in October, Abby called to tell us it was strongly suggested that we immediately begin proceedings for my second-parent adoption. The lesbian lawyers were now concerned about the upcoming state elections. The Department of Social Services, which had been flexible in these second-parent adoption cases, was under the control of the attorney general, and it was not known if a new administration would have that same flexibility. The governor could always override any decision by his attorney general, but there was some suspicion—which would prove to be all too accurate—that Pete Wilson could not be trusted. I did not like the idea that Jesse's legal protection was so vulnerable to an election.

There had been many signs that things were loosening up: Barbara Bush had even come out in support of P-FLAG, Parents and Friends of Lesbians and Gays. In a letter she addressed to them, she stated, "I firmly believe we cannot tolerate discrimination against any individual or groups in our country. Such treatment always brings with it pain and perpetuates hate and intolerance. I appreciate so much your sharing the information about your organization and attitudes. Your words speak eloquently of your love and compassion for all gay Americans and their families." For writing this letter, and for lighting candles in the White House windows as part of an AIDS memorial vigil, the first lady was condemned by conservative activists.

Some of those who had attacked the first lady were dinner guests at a Pete Wilson GOP fund-raiser. Especially entertaining to them was the rainbow flag incident. On October 11, 1990, National Coming Out Day, the rainbow flag flew for four hours

over the state capitol; after that, then-Governor Deukmejian had
the flag removed, despite prior approval of its presence by the
Joint Rules Committee of the California legislature. One Sacramento attorney was shocked that the flag was removed, since
"they've flown everything up there except the Jolly Roger." At
Wilson's dinner, the guests were asked by the master of ceremonies to "rise and face the fag—I mean the flag." Some laughed
so hard they had trouble standing for the Pledge of Allegiance. As
they concluded with the traditional "With liberty and justice for
all," they shouted, "regardless of sexual orientation!"

This felt confusing. How could we be making such gains, and
then have such ridicule? These people were in Sacramento, outside of my city. They would stay there, and I would live in San
Francisco with my family forever.

On October 12, 1990, Abby Abinanti filed my petition for
adoption in San Francisco Superior Court. It stated, in part, that
I was a single woman. This was not a line of which I particularly
approved, but I was encouraged by my friends to look at "the big
picture," at what I really wanted, which was to give Jesse the
protection of a second legal parent, and to be sure that if anything ever happened to Cheryl, he could not be taken from me.
I had worked that fantasy to death in my mind. I had hidden him
with me in Paris and London so many times that I was beginning
to teach him a few words of French, just in case.

This fantasy of having to go underground was triggered by the
political fight over the lesbian and gay civil rights bill, AB-101.
AB-101 had finally made its way out of committee and onto the
floor of the California State Assembly. Lou Sheldon and his
group, the Traditional Values Coalition, were viciously fighting
it, condemning lesbian and gay civil rights as anti-family. They
testified to the Assembly that letting this bill become law would
be the same as granting special privileges to people who practice
bestiality, to pederasts, and to child molesters. Sheldon's tactic
was to find the sickest among us and hold that person up to the
public as an example of the homosexual threat. This is equivalent
to declaring heterosexuals unfit for parenthood because of Bonnie and Clyde. The fact that all criminal records, federal, statewide, and local, clearly show that ninety to ninety-five percent of

child molestation is performed by heterosexual men did not affect a mind like Lou Sheldon's. Demonizing lesbians and gays was his ticket to wealth and fame. I worried at the effect this type of campaign would have on Jesse when he grew up and understood what these people were saying.

I knew that I had to go through with this legal procedure, however invasive it might be. If anything happened to Cheryl, I could not bear to lose Jesse, and in any event, my French wasn't that strong. I also knew that it is almost impossible to overturn a decree of adoption. Even Lou Sheldon would have trouble with that.

The petition for adoption read, in part:

> The child has no legal father.
> The decision to conceive and bear Jesse was actually a joint decision by Petitioner and her partner.
> They have acted in all respects as equal parents to the minor child since the moment of the child's birth.
> They have jointly parented the child. They share child care responsibility as well as economic support for the minor child.
> Petitioner acts in all respects as a parent to the minor child and the child considers Petitioner to be his parent.
> Wherefore, Petitioner prays . . .

As I read the petition, I felt an intensity of gratitude. It was the first time that my relationship with Jesse had been officially asserted; in some ways, the same went for my relationship with Cheryl. That night I was alone at the house with Jesse. He wanted to dance. I held him in my arms, and we waltzed around the living room. It was a warm night, which is odd for San Francisco, and the windows were ajar. The air was still, and Jesse suddenly lifted his head and took a quick deep breath.

"Mama Phyllis!" he said.

I stopped dancing, to see what was wrong.

"Mama Phyllis. The birds are singing!"

And although it was dark, they certainly were. The birds tend to sing at night in San Francisco. I don't know why.

One week later, I received in the mail the "Independent Adoption Questionnaire." Someone had forgotten to take a yellow Post-It off the questionnaire. The note said, "Priscilla. Another insemination case." For the sake of discretion, I will refer to the adoption caseworker as Priscilla Judkins. I felt uncomfortable, realizing that the department might have a list of us and obviously were separating our case from the other cases for some reason. We were not just part of the normal adoption process, but were categorized in a special way. Why would this be? If they wanted to find us, it would be easy if there was a special list.

Every single line on the "Independent Adoption Questionnaire" posed a problem. There were two possible places for me to write my name: Under "Man," with surname called for, or beneath that, under "Woman," with maiden name called for. It took fifteen minutes to decide where to write my name, because the man's spaces implied that he was the principal adopting party, which I was, but I did not want the caseworker to think I suffered from "gender confusion." Besides this difficulty, the adoption form was designed for adopting a stranger's child. I was not qualified for the simple stepparent adoption procedure, because Cheryl and I were not allowed to be married. (There was, however, nothing in the California Civil Code that said that the parents of a child had to be of opposite sexes.) Some of the questions even implied that Cheryl was giving Jesse up for adoption, which naturally terrified Cheryl, who had to be reassured that this was not at all the case.

I crossed out the man's area on the form, and the word "Maiden" from beside the word "Woman." This was just the first question, and it was clear that legally married heterosexual couples were assumed to be the only acceptable adopting parents.

Ever had any traumatic experiences? the questionnaire asked.

No, I wrote.

The Lou Sheldons of the world were screaming, "Pederast! Child molester! Sodomist!"

Any particular adjustment problems?

No. None at all.

That night, Cheryl awoke from a nightmare. She rushed from our bed and went to Jesse's room. I followed her, and asked what was the matter. She woke up. She had been walking in her sleep.

"I had a dream," she said. "A straight couple knocked on the door. They came to take Jesse. They said the court had given him to them because I signed the paper."

I assured her that I would never proceed with the attempt to adopt Jesse if there was even the slightest hint that he could be taken away from her.

The next morning I took the questionnaire to be photocopied. I was a block away from Abby's office. The woman at the copy shop was sleepy when she put the questionnaire into the automatic feed. I waited patiently, sitting in a chair by the plate-glass window. I was already quite emotional when I heard the sound of paper ripping. I walked to the counter, and saw that the questionnaire had jammed in the feed. The woman was slowly tearing into pieces the first of seven pages in order to extract it from the machine.

"What are you doing?"

"It was meant to be," she said. She was Hindu, and was wearing her traditional sari.

"Stop!" Tears ran down my face, and I was furious. I went behind the counter and to the machine, which startled her. She backed away as I pulled the remaining pieces out as carefully as possible, but it was useless. She had ripped it into several pieces.

"This is an important paper. It's an adoption form. It's for my child!"

"It was meant to be! Nothing happens that is not!"

"Please do not share your religious beliefs with me right now, thank you."

I held the extracted pieces, and I could not stop the tears. The woman brought me some tape, and I taped the paper together as carefully as possible. I was embarrassed at my behavior, and put on my sunglasses to try to mask my eyes.

"It is difficult when we are fighting for a child," the woman said. "I am sorry about your paper."

"You didn't do it on purpose."

I left her shop, and walked the block to Abby Abinanti's office above Café Commons. It was embarrassing to feel so out of control. I had never cried in public as an adult, and I was unprepared for these feelings. I did not like to ask the legal establishment for anything. I was illegal in many states, in many countries could be put to death. Visibility did not seem wise, but Jesse was not going to be able to hide the fact that he had two mothers.

I did not take my sunglasses off in Abby's office, but she could certainly see my condition. I told her what had happened; she took the taped-together form and said, 'We'll just Xerox this, and send the copy.'

"It will be all right?"

"Yes."

There are times when we just have to decide to believe in someone's skill. While Abby photocopied the ripped and taped questionnaire, I noticed a framed picture of her on a bookcase. She was participating in a Native American ritual with her tribe, the Yurok, who are from Northern California. Abby Abinanti is a beautiful woman, tall and graceful, centered the way a person is only when they have survived the darker side of the world. In Northern California, a cross had been burned on her mother's lawn by the Ku Klux Klan, and as a child, Abby was subjected to constant racist verbal abuse, and as an adolescent, she was no longer invited by her peers to house parties. When she was graduating from college, she was pushed by the women on the Advisory Committee for Indian Programs to take advantage of an Indian law-school-scholarship program. She had no desire to go to law school. But there are now fewer than a dozen Indian lawyers in California, and at that time there were none, so she felt it was her duty to become an attorney. While in law school in New Mexico, she did trial practice work in the district attorney's office. The D.A. was working on the case of an Indian woman who had been raped, but the woman was not comfortable speaking with him. The D.A. reasoned that, as an Indian woman, Abby might better be able to communicate with the victim. He asked the judge if Abby could do the direct examination, and the judge responded that Abby could not possibly be an Indian because she was going to be a lawyer. The D.A. explained to Abby that the judge could not see her as an Indian because she was not drunk and wrapped in a blanket.

She did not identify herself as lesbian until after law school. Being a lesbian did not thrill her. She was a woman. She was an Indian. She didn't feel she needed the third category. But her philosophy was, What's done is done. She would accept the hand she had been dealt, believing that somehow there was a reason for it. No use getting excited, she said.

"No use getting excited" is a philosophical stance I wish I could claim. It is in my nature to get excited.

It was the day before Halloween. I had received a further packet from the Department of Social Services. This packet featured instructions for taking fingerprints, which were to be forwarded to the California Department of Justice. Early that morning, I went to a real estate office where there was a fingerprinting service. As the agent rolled my thumbs and fingers on the card, he inquired as to the purpose of the prints.

"Adoption," I said.

"That's really nice of you. I really respect people who adopt," he said. He was a pleasant man, in his mid-forties, slightly balding. I did not for a moment believe that if he knew the real situation he would be so admiring. This might not have been true, but everything was becoming "us and them" as I prepared for my day in court.

Late that morning, I was sitting at the kitchen table, sipping my coffee and reading the front page of *The Wall Street Journal.* I thought the paper was rubbing off on my hands, but I realized it was traces of black ink on the tips of my fingers from the morning's fingerprinting session. There was something primitive about having to have a part of my body identified in order to legalize an emotional bond.

*The Wall Street Journal* had a front-page article about San Francisco. An uninvited guest was coming to the city's party Halloween night: Larry Lea, a Texas-based televangelist, and Richard Bernal, pastor of the Jubilee Christian Center in San Jose, were going to lead their Prayer Warriors into battle against the high-ranking evil spirits that had infested San Francisco. These were not just street-level demons, Lea warned, but those of the greatest power and danger. Larry Lea vowed to exorcise the city of its demons, and the primary target was the lesbian and gay community. I thought the article was amusing until I read the next paragraph and learned that they planned to bus in ten thousand warriors. Ten thousand seemed to be a large number! I was accustomed to the odd one here and there, carrying signs on Lesbian and Gay Freedom Day, hanging around at the cable-car turntable at Powell and Market streets, calling on me to repent or face eternal damnation. The same old thing. Cheryl didn't pay much attention to these people, but I always saw them. I was streetwise and knew to watch my back, but Cheryl, who came from a very small Ohio town, was not. She had grown up around fundamentalists. She knew them and dismissed them, but I thought it best not to ignore people who believe you are inhabited by demons, people who are waiting to hear God's voice informing them as to an appropriate action to take against such demons. I had been ignoring the fundamentalists for years, but I was now concerned that they might target Jesse as not being quite human and inhabited by evil. Apparently, there had been much discussion in their circles as to whether or not a child such as Jesse had a soul.

According to *The Wall Street Journal,* Larry Lea's call to arms was "I think it's terrible to live in a city where it's easier to get a condom than it is to get a Bible." This seemed funny until I read on to his promise to "bind the strongman," an act that apparently had something to do with exorcism. "Then we will name them," he said, "come against them, execute written judgment against them and command them to obey us." People like Lea and Bernal had actually been invited guests at the White House. The only consolation was that Barbara Bush probably did not look forward to having dinner with them.

I sipped my coffee and waited for Cheryl and Jesse to reveal their Halloween costumes for that afternoon's party at Jesse's nursery school. I was sold on the school when the nursery teachers, Mary and Theresa Haas, assured me there were several other alternative families at the school. In an attempt to be sensitive to different realities, the school taught its own lyrics to "The Farmer in the Dell." The children sang: "And the farmer takes a partner."

Jesse was going to be a clown. I had spent four hours shopping for his costume, which included a comprehensive experience of Toys "Я" Us. I had never been to Toys "Я" Us before he was born, and it amazed me to have been so wholly unaware of the intense merchandising directed at the American child. Hundreds of parents and children had been tearing through the costume boxes, but apparently the boys all wanted to be Ninja Turtles, the girls, fairy princesses.

Cheryl and Jesse were thrilled by Halloween and the opportunity to dress up and make believe, and so I went along with them. There was a certain amount of suspense in waiting to see Cheryl's costume, because she could materialize as almost anything. There is a myth that only gay men understand female drag, but Cheryl was just as great a master of the art. When we were first dating, I had once looked out into the garden of the Haight-Ashbury cottage I was living in, only to see what appeared to be Marilyn Monroe waving to me from behind the hanging fuchsias.

For years, Cheryl had tried to interest me in Halloween, but I drew the line when she presented me that morning with a dinosaur costume fashioned from a black body stocking, with large bright yellow spikes, cut from sponges, sewn along the backbone. Parents were being encouraged to come in costume, but I flatly refused to appear in public wearing yellow sponge spikes.

Cheryl had considered wearing black leather to Jesse's Halloween party. She thought the children would love it, and she was right, but I absolutely forbade it. I was very concerned with appearances, and I wanted Jesse to be accepted in the straight world. Cheryl in leather with slicked-back hair doing her Billy Idol imitation was definitely not part of my public agenda. I would know that Cheryl was playing, but the other parents might not. I did not believe that the straight world was superior, but I had a great belief in camouflaging because of my extensive experience in the closet. Wearing leather would certainly not allow one to blend in at nursery school.

As I waited for Cheryl and Jesse, the thought of ten thousand Prayer Warriors being bused into San Francisco jarred something inside of me. It felt as if I were asleep beside a window left open at night in a strange neighborhood.

*The Wall Street Journal* reported that the Prayer Warriors were trying to get a permit to march through what they considered San Francisco's more demonized locales, such as the gay neighborhoods, in order to effect a more efficient mass exorcism of "sexual perverts." Kickoff time for the exorcism was 7:14 in the evening; Larry Lea claimed the timing was inspired by II Chronicles 7:14, an Old Testament verse wherein God promises Solomon that he will forgive his people's sin and heal their land if they pray and turn from their wicked ways. That invading a peaceful community might qualify as a "wicked way" never occurred to the Prayer Warriors. The deadline atmosphere of 7:14 P.M., October 31, 1990, heightened the excitement. That Lea chose San Francisco on its high holiday of Halloween was very astute of him. San Francisco had long been a city that everyone, from the Midwestern tourist to the Hollywood producer, used as a backdrop for their fantasies.

I was now extremely irritable. This happens when you are referred to as a "sexual pervert" by ten thousand organized fanatics. The *Journal* further reported that the mayor of San Francisco, Art Agnos, had spent the first two days of his vacation praying and fasting at a Greek monastery. His two days complete, one hundred and fifty monks had told him they would pray for San Francisco. Scott Shaefer, the mayor's press secretary, said that he would put their one hundred and fifty monks up against ten thousand Prayer Warriors any day.

Jesse made his entrance into the kitchen, and I gave him my undivided attention. He was delighted with his red and gold jester's costume and its royal blue pompoms down the front. A little jester's cap sat snug and cocked upon his white-blond hair. He ran toward me and stopped a few inches away, his little chest pumped with pleasure, his green-blue eyes round and expectant, his beautiful face decorated with two large red dots at the tips of his cheekbones. It was very difficult to be so much a part of society, but he made it worth it.

"I a clown," he said, and he slowly nodded his head, an all-knowing expression sweeping his face. Cheryl then appeared in the doorway to the kitchen. She stood demurely, framing herself in the manner of a Southern belle. She wore a long white dress with ruffles, short white gloves, and a string of pearls. Her blond hair was curled and fluffed. Jesse and Cheryl's facial resemblance to each other was so remarkable that it sometimes seemed to me that no man had been involved in Jesse's conception, an idea that had been greeted with some glee by our more radical lesbian friends, who were still holding out for parthenogenesis.

Cheryl sashayed down the front steps to the sidewalk where, of course, she waited for me to open the car door. I was impressed with her costume. It wasn't really the June Cleaver look. It was more Tennessee Williams's Laura, from *The Glass Menagerie,* before she got her limp. Jesse climbed into his car seat, I snapped the safety belt securely, and we were off to the party.

As we got out of the car and walked along the sidewalk to Jesse's school, I realized I would be meeting many of the other parents for the first time, and I became apprehensive. Inside the schoolyard, Cheryl floated off to deposit cupcakes on the dessert table, and probably to compare them with the other women's if she was, as I suspected, staying in character. I stood near Jesse in the play area, where he was digging in the sand, and a heterosexual couple dressed as tap-dancing raisins came up to me. Evidently, their child was a particular friend of Jesse's, and they wanted to meet Jesse's parents. I introduced myself, and at that moment Cheryl, in her best Tennessee Williams fantasy, drifted to my side. I could see that she was moving into Blanche DuBois territory. She smiled and cocked her head artfully as she tucked her arm into mine, where she hung like a leaf on a humid summer afternoon. She loved to tease me, especially in public. The most remarkable thing about Cheryl's performance was her absolute vacancy of expression; she looked like a Stepford lesbian. The mother and father became nervous, and then very solicitous. I think that Cheryl and I were their first lesbian couple, and they certainly were not prepared for this particular incarnation of Cheryl. Perhaps Billy Idol in leather would have been easier to relate to, or at least more expected.

In an attempt to be friendly, the woman asked me, "Which one of you is the real mother?"

Jesse was just within earshot. He stopped digging in the sand-box and looked up at me.

"Real in what sense?" I asked, the slightest edge to my voice, although I did smile. I was, after all, talking to tap-dancing raisins, and I myself was wearing a gold satin shirt and a felt tricorn pirate hat with three large peacock feathers jutting from the brim. Cheryl gave a little giggle and squeezed my arm in the most charming way.

"We're both pretty real," Cheryl said politely. Edging toward Scarlett O'Hara before Tara burned, she then drifted to Jesse in the sandbox, where she descended onto the sand, skirt floating down like a mushroom cloud, Jesse shrieking with laughter.

"I'm his nonbiological mother," I said to the other parents, "and Cheryl is his birth mother. We co-parent Jesse. Jesse calls me Mama Phyllis, and Cheryl Mama Cher."

The couple seemed grateful that I had not been offended, and in truth they had not meant to be offensive. A completely new vocabulary has come up around alternative families, and it is not yet common knowledge. In truth, I could not quite grasp who I was, so how could I expect them to? We chatted for awhile about costumes and the length of the lines at Toys "Я" Us. I was actually quite good at this sort of thing, when I felt like it, but as we talked, it was as if I were watching myself from the outside. The question of whether I was Jesse's real mother disturbed me. It came up all the time.

Over the heads of these two parents, I could see Cheryl playing with Jesse in the sandbox. I also noticed that the parents who had never before met Cheryl seemed to have no idea that she was in costume and in character. So perfect was her performance that most of the parents thought she was "real." This in spite of the fact that she was very demurely helping Jesse to dig in the sand while wearing white gloves and pearls. I did want to explain to the parents watching Cheryl that she was indeed in costume, in a role, but I gave it up. Cheryl did not come out of character all afternoon, and this is one of my many reasons for loving her: She knows how to play.

Jesse joined the other children for the finale, the costume parade. I was uncomfortable with the number of Ninja Turtles and fairy princesses. The children were not getting these images from their churches or schools. They were getting them from television and the movies. At least they were not dressed up like Larry Lea's Prayer Warriors. I was certain that the Prayer Warriors could not be ignored. If they could get away with this, they would escalate. I remembered all too well how Anita Bryant in 1977 had spearheaded a fundraising campaign to build "rehabilitation camps" and "ranches" for lesbians and gay men. Larry Lea might be another, more effective Bryant.

I was afraid to go near the Civic Center Auditorium that evening, but followed closely the media coverage, which had the intensity of a Super Bowl: The radical left and the radical right go at it in Flake City. That evening, GHOST (Grand Homosexual Outrage at Sickening Televangelists) spokesperson Mark Pritchard was featured on the five o'clock evening news. He was identified as a member of Queer Nation. Queer Nation was definitely not a moderate or even progressive lesbian and gay civil rights group. Pritchard told the reporter, "If any fundamentalists or gay-bashers get the idea that they're going to come down to the Castro to beat on us, then we're going to defend ourselves."

I was stunned that anyone would actually refer to himself as queer, would actually go so far as to use the word for the name of an organization. Would one put "Member, Queer Nation" on one's résumé?

The ten o'clock news had extensive coverage of the confrontation at its height. Most of the warriors had been bused in from the suburbs. They held their hands in the air, waved Bibles and spoke in tongues as the colorful demonstrators shouted, "We the perverted/Will never be converted!" Yellow buses bearing the inscription ASSEMBLIES OF GOD in bold black lettering, and carrying hundreds of Prayer Warriors, pulled in front of the auditorium. This was the peak of the confrontation, at the doorway of the Civic Center Auditorium, where over two thousand demonstrators confronted Larry Lea's security forces.

A strong tenor voice demanded, "Who's in charge of this room? I want to see the producer. *Right now.*"

There was an intense crush of press around the door, and the bright lights of the television cameras shot up and illuminated the face of Pink Jesus.

There he was again, being turned away at the door of the prayer meeting, shouting about violations of the state's Unruh Act, which protects against discrimination in public places like the Civic Center Auditorium by making it illegal to arbitrarily deny anyone access to a public place.

"No costumes!" shouted security.

"No costumes?" Pink Jesus shouted back into their faces. "What about their costumes?" he said, pointing at the sea of polyester suits and shirtwaist dresses just visible in the auditorium lobby. He turned to answer a reporter's question, which was not quite audible.

"We're trying to shock with humor," said Pink Jesus. "We are living political cartoons."

This had occurred earlier in the evening. A lone newscaster reported that all was now quiet at the Civic Center. He stood in front of a huge banner anchored in the grass across from the auditorium. The banner declared, BORN-AGAIN BIGOTS BE GONE. It moved gently in the breeze while distant drumbeats and shouts rattled and fell in shards of sound around the big foam tombstones implanted on the grass. Among the names on the tombstones were Larry Lea, Jimmy Swaggart, the KKK, and Lou Sheldon.

And there again was Gilbert Baker as Pink Jesus. I was still uncomfortable about him, but I was no longer categorically opposed to his tactics. If ten thousand fanatics could come to San Francisco with impunity, with the intent of exorcising world-class evil spirits from my soul and threatening the emotional well-being of my child, was this liberation? Was this the safe space I wanted to raise Jesse in? Was this a City of Refuge? Yet Gilbert Baker's tactics seemed radical and on the verge of being out of control, of playing into their hands. Video and photographic images of Pink Jesus, both in the Lesbian and Gay Freedom Day parade and at the GHOST demonstration, would become the biggest fund-raising tool and political-mobilizing image of the radical right for several years.

I wondered if Gilbert had a death wish. Surely he must know

that someone could easily take a shot at him, and wearing pink high heels and a loincloth would not make for an easy getaway.

There was little violence that night. The Prayer Warriors had apparently stayed at the Civic Center. There had been only one incident in the Castro. Four young men in khaki camouflage uniforms had beaten some lesbians and gay men, but they had been caught, taken into custody, and turned over to their commanding officer from the Army Reserve.

I spent the rest of the evening helping Jesse sort his hard candies, lollipops, and Gummi Bears. The Castro and Pink Jesus were only over the hill, but they might as well have been on Venus.

That night, the Prayer Warriors had been challenged at the Civic Center by a new kind of force, a force of which the country was just hearing, which had existed in San Francisco only since mid-July. Its motto was "In your face." It played with gender and power, and it called itself Queer Nation.

A few days after Halloween, I received my first phone call from the caseworker, Priscilla Judkins, at the Department of Social Services. She identified herself and asked if I had ever been married. I said I had not. She was very perky. She asked if it was true that Jesse did not have a legal father, and I confirmed that it was.

She then said, "Well, that's it."

Confused, I gripped the phone as if it were a fish that might slip away.

She paused, and insisted, "It's not personal."

"Of course," I said.

"It's just department policy. You understand?"

"Yes," I said. "It's just department policy."

"You'll get the notice."

"Oh, of course. Thank you. Yes, thank you so much for calling, and of course I understand that it's just department policy, nothing personal."

I hung up the phone, and contacted Abby. Apparently, on the basis of this phone call, the right to a home visit would be decided.

Yes, this is the procedure. Don't worry, everyone said. This is just the procedure. You have to understand. Don't be dramatic. It will be fine. There will probably be a denial. As soon as the official first denial arrives, a hearing will be requested, and at that time, the judge will be asked to sign an Order Compelling a Home Visit. In other words, the judge would force the Department of Social Services to at least come to my house.

I assured everyone that I had been very nice to Priscilla, who had even apologized for department policy. Wasn't that nice of her? I asked my friends. I could get quite excited, so there was tremendous encouragement for me to be . . . nice, calm—perhaps, if possible, someone else. I felt as if the room were on fire and the only door out was locked. I hated the idea of someone from the state in my home, peeking through the details of my life, invading my privacy. Yet I was willing to go to court to force that invasion to take place.

Later that afternoon, I went to get Jesse from his nursery school. I drove, but I felt as if someone else were driving. I was unusually careful. Perfect. I lifted Jesse into the air, as usual, and kissed him, as usual, but I felt like an unwanted guest in someone else's house.

I brought Jesse home and turned on *Mr. Rogers' Neighborhood*. Jesse was now almost two and a half years old, and he had some understanding of what people were saying. Today, Mr. Rogers's show was about feeling angry. Jesse and I ate rice cakes and apple slices while King Friday proclaimed himself the only one in the kingdom to have feelings.

# CHAPTER III

# Bright Lights,
# Queer City

ONE WEEK AFTER the GHOST demonstration against the Prayer Warriors, an extraordinary phenomenon occurred at the San Francisco polling booths. It became known nationally as the Lavender Sweep. Three openly lesbian and gay politicians were elected, and domestic partnership was passed. The term "domestic partners" was defined as two adults who have chosen to share one another's lives in an intimate and committed relationship of mutual caring, who live together, and who have agreed to be jointly responsible for basic living expenses incurred during the domestic partnership. Ironically, the way the legislation had been written, domestic partners could theoretically be responsible for medical and other bills incurred by a partner who died, yet were granted no tangible benefits.

Tom Ammiano was elected to the school board. He was a teacher and a gay man who had valiantly fought for reform of the San Francisco school system since the early 1970s. His campaign posters had featured his name, the position he sought, and a bright red apple. His campaign did not have much money, but it did have enthusiastic grass-roots support. Not only did he win a seat on the board, but he received more votes than any other candidate. He would become the first openly gay person in the country to sit on a school board, a fact that did not escape the attention of the radical right. Tom was probably also the first stand-up comic to sit on a school board, which made for some lively interchanges during debate on condom distribution as part of an AIDS-prevention plan for sexually active high school students.

Carole Migden, a lesbian woman who had been active in the California Democratic party for years, was elected to the Board of Supervisors. Winning in virtually every neighborhood of the city, she would eventually sit on the platform committee of the Democratic party. A seat on the Board of Supervisors also went to Roberta Achtenberg. In 1989, she was the chair of the Mayor's Task Force on Family Policy. Mayor Agnos's appointment of Achtenberg to that position had generated much heat from conservative elements. In July 1990, Achtenberg had also published "Preserving and Protecting the Families of Lesbians and Gay Men." Achtenberg took the position that to be pro-gay was to be pro-family. She would be chosen for the elite 12-member Democratic Party Drafting Committee, which would formulate the party's platform for the 1992 presidential race. Harvey Milk's dream was coming true. Lesbian women and gay men were taking their places at the table.

There were setbacks, but there were victories—and apologies. That week, General Motors chairman Robert Stempel wrote to the San Francisco Board of Supervisors that a GM training video referring to a Japanese-made vehicle as "that little faggot truck" was an "unfortunate incident that does not reflect General Motors' policy toward lesbian and gay people." His apology could well have been prompted by the Board of Supervisors' threat to cancel a $500,000 contract with GM.

Unfortunately for the lesbian and gay community, Pete Wilson defeated former San Francisco mayor Dianne Feinstein in the gubernatorial race, but she would prevail in the end, winning Wilson's coveted U.S. senate seat. That week, Queer Nation again appeared in the news. Demonstrators had repainted a California state flag in rainbow colors. Jonathan Katz, a spokesperson for the group, said the flag would be presented to Pete Wilson in January when he became governor, along with a list of demands from the community. Queer Nation, singing "Over the

Rainbow" and holding pictures of Judy Garland, hoisted a rainbow flag above the old State Building near the Civic Center in San Francisco.

The most striking aspect of this demonstration was that it had humor. The AIDS crisis had all but sapped the community of playfulness. Queer Nation reminded me of Harvey Milk. It reminded me of his Pooper Scooper law. Milk had believed that he could be elected mayor of San Francisco if he could solve the problem of owners not cleaning up after their dogs. He had gone so far as to plant some dog poop in the grass just before a television press conference that he had scheduled at a small neighborhood park. At the end of the press conference, he "accidentally" stepped in the poop to demonstrate the need for his law. Yet, while Queer Nation accounted for the first appearance of humor in years, there were also the first signs of the truly militant homosexual of Anita Bryant's fantasies. In New York, Larry Kramer, a founder of ACT UP, was calling for an anti-antigay terrorist group, and the line between civil rights and civil disobedience was being drawn.

One week after the Lavender Sweep, Abby Abinanti called to say that the Department of Social Services had denied the home visit, but that this denial had been expected. It was department policy. Their grounds were that Jesse was not available for adoption since his biological mother still wanted him. Somehow I must have thought I could be the exception to the denials, to the "policy." I was no longer sure that we had come so far. If we had to squirm through loopholes, was that progress? Yes, and no.

It was now late November 1990, the twelfth anniversary of the assassinations of Harvey Milk and George Moscone. The next night there would be, as there was every year, the memorial candlelight march that would duplicate the route taken on the day of their deaths. I had not attended the annual marches since that first spontaneous one.

I could not sleep, and I felt as if I had a fever, but when I took my temperature it was normal. I sat in the living room by myself while Cheryl and Jesse slept. The adoption proceedings and the extensive questions about my past had stirred images and memories long forgotten, fears long suppressed. This was the story that would not appear on the forms.

I was a poet, and San Francisco is a poet's city. I arrived in San Francisco from Massachusetts in 1976 with four hundred dollars, and took a room at the downtown Y. After a few months, I received a letter in the mail. The woman I loved had fallen into a coma and was dying of leukemia. I had been in love with her, but we had had a strained relationship. She had often spoken romantically of her own death; and she did not want to be lesbian. She did not want to lose her position in the horse world, where she was a show judge and taught riding to adolescent girls. She kept her relationship with me secret, almost hermetically compartmentalized from the rest of her life. Her friends were not even aware of our relationship. When her leukemia was diagnosed, I believe that she welcomed it.

Simultaneously, in the spring of 1977, Anita Bryant, best known as a singer of patriotic songs and the spokesperson for Florida's Citrus Commission, "found Jesus." Her then husband, Bob Green, using Bryant as a magnet, created a financial empire by organizing Save Our Children from Homosexuality, also known simply as Save Our Children. Bryant's first goal was the repeal of the gay civil rights bill in Dade County, Florida. The San Francisco community was highly involved in the fight against Bryant, sending money and bodies. I could do nothing. I was immobilized with shock and grief at J.'s impending death. Save Our Children took out full-page newspaper ads declaring homosexuals guilty of "a hair-raising pattern of recruitment and outright seductions and molestation" of children. The FBI's records on the subject were, again, simply ignored.

The city's gay community, in an attempt to help our people in Florida, held several fund-raising events, including an Anita Bryant look-alike contest and a "Moon over Miami" fund-raiser at the Castro Theater, San Francisco's landmark movie palace, where Armistead Maupin, a local gay writer and author of *Tales of the City*, kissed Mayor George Moscone on the cheek and introduced him as "the hunkiest mayor since Sunny Jim Rolph."

On April 29, 1977, a few months after her diagnosis and two weeks after her thirty-fourth birthday, J. died. I could never forget that Anita Bryant called homosexuals "human garbage," because I read this on the day when J. was cremated.

In the months to come, my depression gradually lifted, and I decided to attend the Castro Street Fair. How was it that I could be in such a large party crowd, and feel so isolated? I wandered up Castro toward Nineteenth Street. Harvey Milk was sitting on the collapsible platform of a dunking booth outside of his modest store, Castro Camera. He was a candidate for the Board of Supervisors from District 5, and I knew that he was the most charismatic of the gay civil rights activists. I watched as one by one the men came up and threw softballs at the metal target that would drop the platform and dunk Harvey into the water. When I saw what was pasted on the target, I could not resist. It was a picture of Anita Bryant.

I paid my dollar, stepped up to the line and took three softballs. Harvey Milk, soaking in the cool spring breeze, stared at me somewhat sadly. I threw the ball high and wide, and he smiled. I could not take my eyes from his. There was something about him. He had a special passion that went beyond the desire for personal fame and fortune. It became very quiet around the dunking booth. I had been the only woman to step up to the line, and the playful taunting of Milk had stopped. I tossed the ball up and down in my hand, and smiled at him. I gave it everything I had when I threw the second ball at that picture of Anita Bryant, but I missed. Harvey grinned playfully, swishing his long feet back and forth in the water. Keeping my eyes on his, I deliberately missed the target as I threw the last softball. I just couldn't dunk him, and he knew it. Harvey Milk laughed, but a large strong blond man stepped up to the line seconds later and hit the Bryant photograph dead center with terrific force. I stood and watched as Harvey was dunked at least a hundred times.

Despite the phenomenal number of baptisms that Harvey Milk experienced that day, Anita Bryant and Save Our Children won in Dade County, Florida, by an overwhelming margin. Anita Bryant returned in her monogrammed Rolls-Royce to her Biscayne Bay mansion, where she was enthusiastically greeted with her favorite hymn, "Victory in Jesus." She then danced a jig.

The day became known as Orange Tuesday, and the vote sent

six thousand people into the streets of San Francisco. Harvey Milk had designed a march route for just such occasions, which included leading the marchers out of the Castro and up the steep San Francisco hills toward the Fairmont Hotel and Grace Cathedral. He literally marched out the crowd's anger.

Days after Orange Tuesday, on June 22, 1977, Robert Hillsborough was stabbed to death in San Francisco by four boys who shouted, "Faggot! Faggot!" as they watched him die at their feet. His mother, Helen Hillsborough, filed suit against Anita Bryant and Save Our Children for creating the atmosphere of hate and violence that led to her son's death. Robert Hillsborough had been a gardener. That year at the Gay Freedom Day Parade, which occurred just a few days after the Hillsborough murder, hundreds of people spontaneously laid flowers on the steps of City Hall in his memory. I stood beside the seated statue of Abraham Lincoln near the City Hall steps, and watched as the mound of flowers piled higher. I will never forget the name of Robert Hillsborough.

On July 2, 1977, five teenagers grabbed Charles Lewis, a gay man, and while the two females held a cocked gun in his mouth, he was held over a garbage can and raped by two of the three males, who shouted, "Anita is right! Anita is right!" He escaped with his life. Anita Bryant's response to this news, and to the murder of the gardener Robert Hillsborough, was "There is a homosexual murder every day in San Francisco. . . . My conscience is clear." Anita Bryant had given new meaning to dancing on the graves of the dead. She published a book entitled *The Anita Bryant Story: The Survival of Our Nation's Families and the Threat of Militant Homosexuality.*

San Franciscans were not taken in by Anita Bryant. In November of 1977, Harvey Milk was elected to the Board of Supervisors. He was forty-seven years old, and a visionary: He thought in terms of the community as a whole, and how the lesbian and gay population fit into that whole. He thought in terms of coalition, and his dream for our community extended beyond San Francisco to the nation. His election horrified the gay political clubs, who saw him as an intruder, a radical, and a terrible image problem. The truth was, he had not stepped into line the way they wanted him to: He was not aligning only with the middle class, but also with people of color and the union rank and file. Yet outside the tight-knit circles of lesbian and gay political clubs, the community as a whole was thrilled by his election. Hope surged. I remember casting my ballot, pushing the pin through the number beside his name half a dozen times to be sure it would be recorded.

Harvey Milk was an effective legislator. By April 1978, just four months after his election, he had mustered the needed votes from the Board of Supervisors, and proudly stood by as Mayor George Moscone signed the gay rights ordinance into law.

Then came California state senator John Briggs with Proposition 6, which declared that all lesbian women and gay men should be fired from California's public schools in order to protect the children from recruitment and rape. Briggs, grabbing for power on the heels of Anita Bryant's national campaign, went too far, and it was fortunate for the gay community that he did. The Briggs Initiative stated that heterosexual teachers would also be fired if they voiced the opinion that lesbian and gay teachers should be allowed to keep their jobs. Briggs and Bryant upped the ante at every turn, with Bryant now in a fund-raising frenzy. Using "Bible-based techniques," Bryant was preparing "counseling centers" for the treatment of "sexual perversions and moral problems. . . . With God's provision," she said, "we will establish intensive treatment facilities on ranches or farms which will, hopefully, be contributed for this purpose." It was not clear if the "ranches or farms" would be voluntarily occupied, or if they would be connected to the police arm of the states. That June, Anita Bryant called for a national "pray-in" on Gay Freedom Day, and in her newsletter explained that our day was "the most despicable and outrageous thing that has happened in America. It is time the Christians of our country unite to fight back spiritually and legally to stop this contagious immorality." But still there was hope. The July issue of *Ladies' Home Journal* revealed that a poll of Colorado, Indiana, Missouri, New York, and Florida teenagers had selected Adolf Hitler and Anita Bryant as the two people who "have done the most damage to the world." If Anita Bryant wanted attention, she had gotten it on a national scale.

In the background, in the politics of San Francisco, someone else desperately wanted attention. His name was Dan White, and he had been elected to the Board of Supervisors along with Harvey Milk. Dan White was an immature individual who should never have been elected to public office. As an adolescent, he had been a racist schoolyard bully. This did not prepare him for dealing emotionally with the rough-and-tumble world of San Francisco politics, which had at its core the art of compromise. He was being surpassed at every point by the flamboyant and effective leadership of Milk. Dan White was seething with envy and rage. He had been the only supervisor to vote against the gay rights ordinance, and he warned of a coming backlash against our community.

When Briggs launched his campaign, J. had not been dead six months, and I was student-teaching at Lowell High School, the public school for the academically gifted in San Francisco. Every day, when I stood before my class of adolescents, I was conscious that I was lesbian. It was ridiculous, and I knew it, but I could do nothing about it. No one at the school knew I was lesbian, and J. was dead, so my sexuality seemed inconsequential because I did not believe I would love anyone again. The truth was, at that point, it was easier to be in love with a dead woman. Nothing could be taken away. No one could do very much. No vote or judge's ruling could affect me.

A few days before the vote on the Briggs Initiative, in the eleventh-grade creative-writing class I was teaching, a student referred to "faggots." I found myself rising to my feet and asking, in my perfectly detached and rational teacher's voice, "Does anyone know where the word 'faggot' comes from as a reference to gay men?" From my tone, I might as well have been asking who stole fire from the gods for humankind.

The class was silent, and some of their mouths were hanging open. "Gay men were used as kindling sticks," I said, "which are also called faggots, for the fires that burned the witches to death. Many of the witches were lesbians or single women who owned property, which was then confiscated and given to what were thought of as 'real' families."

No one moved. It was so quiet in the hot and sunny classroom.

"I will not tolerate anti-gay remarks, or ethnic slurs of any type, in this classroom," I said.

And that was it, I thought. Back to creative writing. But a tall, red-haired boy raised his hand and said, "I want to say something." No one moved. I thought I was about to be challenged.

"You've all known me for my whole time at this high school," he said, "but you never knew my father. I want you to know that my father was black, and that I've been listening to you say 'nigger' when there's no blacks around for too long."

I could not understand at first why he had chosen that time to speak, but then I realized it was his invisibility that he was addressing, and he was tired of paying the price. The boy did not appear at all black, and so his ethnic background had been invisible. He had passed, the way I passed every day, but he had the courage to break his silence.

It would have been the perfect opportunity for me to out myself in the classroom, to say "By the way, your teacher is lesbian," but I could not. It was believed that Briggs would win; J. was dead; I could barely feel or think beyond the next few hours; and Anita Bryant was organizing ranches that would not be run by Roy Rogers and Dale Evans. I had no emotional resources left, and I did not want to lose my livelihood, too. From my years of being in the closet, I knew the depth of racism and homophobia in the power establishment. My family on the East Coast, although they had the usual cultural biases, had never been people who had expressed racist or homophobic beliefs, yet they knew only the vaguest details of my life. The lesbian and gay community itself was youth-oriented. This was the pre-AIDS world, and the community had no real comprehension of death except by suicide or homicide. There was absolutely no one with whom I could talk. I thought I saw J., or heard her voice, in the middle of the night. When I finally fell asleep, I dreamed of her. I felt unstable. It was impossible for me to join the grass-roots, face-to-face campaign against Briggs, to do things like go to my bank and give the teller a little card that said, "I'm gay. Please vote No on 6."

I believed I was powerless and emotionally incapable of confronting the enormous power base of the Briggs campaign. I knew that Briggs had been an effective fund-raiser, receiving substantial contributions from, among others, San Francisco Chartered Bank of London and ARCO, the Atlantic Richfield Company. Signs were being posted in the city that read, "Fags, Queers and Other Perverts STAY OUT." It was fairly certain that many of those posting these signs were not people from San Francisco. People were driving into the city in the middle of the night and going "hunting." When the gay community attempted to keep his initiative from appearing on the ballot, Briggs cried out against "repression" and "censorship." This is a tactic often used against the community, and one that successfully confuses the usually supportive liberal establishment.

In the midst of this, Tom Ammiano formed the Gay Teachers and Schoolworkers Coalition. He was the first gay teacher in the country to challenge a school board. He was instrumental in lobbying the board to include positive representations of gay lifestyles in the school system's "Family Life" curriculum, an extraordinary feat considering the political climate. He was slim, Italian, articulate, and passionate. He was also very funny, and used his gift for humor as a shield and weapon. I watched him on television, in the newspapers, deflecting attack after attack: "Love your shoes. Hate your politics." Although I could come up with a dozen good reasons for my silence, I felt like a coward for not standing beside him. From what I had seen, lesbian and gay public visibility was a red flag taunting death, and I was afraid to die.

Briggs attacked the gay community with amazing viciousness, declaring "This is not a civil rights issue" and warning his audience that only Proposition 6 could prevent "homosexuals from having access to your children. That's the issue: Do you or do you not want to give homosexuals access to your children?"

Briggs, who was not from the city, stood on the steps of City Hall and declared San Francisco to be "the moral garbage dump of the nation."

Shortly after his election, Harvey Milk made a tape in which he said: "This is to be played only in the event of my death by assassination. I fully realize that a person who stands for what I stand for . . . an activist, a gay activist, becomes the target, or potential target, for somebody who is insecure, afraid, or very disturbed themselves. Knowing that I could be assassinated at any time . . ."

Harvey Milk teamed with Sally Gearheart, a professor of speech at San Francisco State University, to lead the opposition to the Briggs Initiative. They debated patiently and articulately, publicly asking President Carter to extend his call for human rights to the millions of lesbian and gay people in the United States.

At eight o'clock on the evening of the election, I sat with my roommates in front of the television set, waiting for the returns. At the time I lived two blocks from Castro Street. The tension was almost intolerable. We did not believe Proposition 6 would be defeated. We were not even sure if it would lose in San Francisco. The newscaster announced, "From our exit polls, it looks as if Orange County has voted against the Briggs Initiative."

I did not immediately understand the significance of this statement, but my roommate, the lesbian daughter of a fundamentalist preacher from Southern California's Orange County, explained immediately that the Briggs Initiative had lost. Orange County is the most conservative county in the state. If Briggs lost in Orange County, the young woman said, he'd lost everywhere. We immediately went to Castro Street, and on to the "No On 6" headquarters. People had come out of their apartments and the clubs, and were embracing in the streets. Some were weeping. The community had not had such a victory since Harvey Milk's election, but this was even more spectacular. It was statewide. Coalitions had been built. My heart opened as I watched Harvey Milk take the stage at the campaign headquarters. I believed in this man, and I wanted to stop the ghettoization of my life. I would begin by coming out to my own family.

Proposition 6, the Briggs Initiative, was defeated on November 8, 1978. Nineteen days later, on November 27, 1978, Supervisor Dan White strapped on a concealed and loaded gun, put extra bullets in his pocket, and climbed through a basement window into City Hall in order to bypass the metal detector. He first assassinated Mayor George Moscone, then crossed to the opposite end of City Hall, where he assassinated Supervisor Harvey Milk. He pumped three bullets into the mayor, and five bullets into Harvey Milk. The last shot was fired into Harvey's skull with the gun almost resting on his temple.

Within hours, word came down the street that everyone was to come at nightfall with a candle. As the darkness covered San Francisco, I walked the two blocks to Castro Street. I could not tell how many people were there. I passed my hand over the top of the candle flame, and my skin got too close to the fire. As I pulled my hand away I looked up and saw that I was in the midst of thousands upon thousands of lights shimmering in the darkness. It was so quiet, and then we began to walk. People stood and watched as we passed, many with heads bowed, their hats in their hands. There were occasional whisperings, but mostly it is the soft sound of shoes on the pavement that I remember, and the distant beat of a slow drum at the front of the procession. I warmed my hands on the clear glass cup that held my white candle. It was a dreamlike walk, a nightmare that was not frightening because I was not alone and the murder was not really unexpected. I would have been surprised if Harvey Milk had not been killed.

I was in the last wave of the march. As I neared City Hall, I could hear the speakers, whose voices traveled through the silence and bounced off the Civic Center façades, wavering and dissolving above the reflecting pool. I knew the sound very well. It was the sound of hearts breaking. I was no longer alone in my experience of death. As I rounded the corner into the Civic Center, I heard the unmistakable voice of Joan Baez singing "Kumbaya." I turned left toward the Polk Street steps of City Hall and stood near the statue of the seated Abraham Lincoln. It was impossible to hear Baez and not feel a spasm of grief. As her final note dissolved, we lifted our candles, and the sound of weeping mixed curiously with birdsong from the trees. I cried in the new way I had learned to cry in private. It took less energy, was far less difficult, if I simply let the tears roll out, and didn't bother with all of the accompanying heaving of shoulders and agonizing. I looked for the first time at the faces of the others from the procession, and I saw that it was not just a lesbian and gay crowd. There were straight people, and children, and elderly Irish and Italian ladies wearing veiled hats, their patent-leather purses in one hand, candles in the other. I was thinking that I had never heard birds sing at night, when there was a sensation of moving light to the left of my head. I turned and saw that the statue of Abraham Lincoln was illuminated by candlelight. The mourners had placed their candles carefully on his seated form, which leaned forward as if listening very closely to the words of a petitioner. The candles were on Lincoln's shoulders, his hands, and his knees, and wax rolled across his face and cheeks. I placed my candle near his foot.

In a Gallup poll conducted between December 1 and December 4, 1978, just a few days after the final dispositions of the bodies of George Moscone and Harvey Milk, Anita Bryant was ranked seventh as the woman most admired by the adult American public, even more popular than Queen Elizabeth II of England. I slammed shut my closet door.

Bryant and Briggs did not succeed to the extent they had wished, but they left a legacy. They were commanders in the fundamentalist army that established the political and financial power base from which the most ardent premillennialists could launch their attacks. (The premillennialists believe that if you are not "saved" by Jesus Christ, you will be destroyed during the Second Coming, while all the saved are lifted up off the earth during the obliteration of the unsaved. This anxiously awaited event is called the Rapture.) The right's financial advisers discovered that demonizing lesbians and gays was an extraordinary fund-raising tool, even better than a photograph of Teddy Kennedy. It was becoming clear that money was the bottom line, and that there was a fortune to be made.

By 1980, the Republican party had coopted this newly politicized group and made their deals. By 1990, Bryant and Briggs had been replaced by Pat Robertson, Jesse Helms, and the Traditional Values Coalition. There was always someone, whether a Prayer Warrior or a candidate for the presidency, pushing to the front of the line to attack gays. They believe with fervent conviction that lesbians and homosexuals must be stopped at all costs, for two reasons: With our talk of civil rights, we are interfering with the saving of souls that would otherwise be qualified to take part in the Rapture; and we are a threat to the American family. But these radical fundamentalists are not the ones who send cold blasts through my psyche. That distinction belongs to the political operatives who do not even believe what they are saying, but are simply following orders and building a voter base.

It was now 1990, but still the bashers came into the city at night in pickup trucks, screaming, "Dyke!" and "Faggot!" and sometimes beating us to death. So much had changed; so much had not.

The hours dragged by and dawn flickered gray along the horizon on the twelfth anniversary of the assassinations of Milk and Moscone. I went into Jesse's room, tucked the covers under his chin, and sat on the little couch against the wall. His room was very small, no more than six by twelve feet. Above his bed was an original drawing called "Star Baby" by the artist Maggie Wingfield, which pictures a little boy against a blue cosmic backdrop. Upon his head, he is balancing the magical star baby. On the next wall was a small, brown-framed drawing of two brown-and-white hound-dog puppies. This picture had hung on the wall in Cheryl's childhood bedroom. Above the bureau was a picture of my father and Jesse in an embrace.

Asleep, Jesse stretched his arms above his head. He cupped his hands like the boy balancing the star baby on his head. Behind my thankfulness at having the chance to adopt Jesse was rage at a system that would expect me to understand it was "just department policy" to declare me so irrelevant to his life that the agency would have to be ordered by the court to come to my home. I also knew that these motions to compel home visits were being denied in other parts of the state.

The wave of love I felt for Jesse skidded into a wall of fear at the thought of how vulnerable I might be making him by my presence in his life. At a time when I thought I would be pulling closer to Cheryl and Jesse, I felt myself moving away, as if somehow that would protect them.

I had helped to put this little boy into the position of having two mothers in a heterocentric world. I now had a choice. I could deny my feelings for him and his for me, and, with some vaguely heroic notion of protecting them by my absence, go away from the two people I loved most in the world; or I could make myself visible and do whatever I could to smooth the way for him. I could never deny him. It was impossible. When I thought of it, the feeling of grief far surpassed that which I had felt at J.'s death. I would begin by becoming visible. I would start by joining that night's memorial march for Harvey Milk. What I could not do from fear, I could do for love.

I quietly shut Jesse's door, and stood for a moment looking at the framed picture in the hallway, which hung there to protect it from fading. It was the only place in the house that did not get direct sunlight. In her will, J. had left me Jean Cocteau's artist print of the young and angry poet Rimbaud. He is holding a book in one hand, a green branch in the other, his Catholic confirmation ribbon tied around his right arm. Framing the portrait of Rimbaud, Cocteau had written in French: "He has set fire to the hypocrites. He has destroyed the games."

That night, the air was clear and brisk, as November evenings can be in San Francisco, and the fog hung high upon Twin Peaks, overlooking the Castro. I stopped short on the corner of Noe and Market streets. I had almost stepped on the strangest thing. At my feet there was a stenciled sidewalk drawing. It was a perfect likeness of Harvey Milk's head, but with a halo. His hands were raised up beside his face, which had an expression of mock surprise, as if he were about to be baptized in the dunking booth. I looked more closely and saw that red paint has been dabbed on the centers of his palms to represent stigmata. Across the top of this elaborate stencil, which was about two feet by two feet, was the question

WHAT WOULD HARVEY THINK?

About what? I wondered. Further along the sidewalk was another stencil:

## A THOUSAND
## MILITANT HOMOSEXUALS
## OF LIGHT

Anita Bryant's myth of the militant homosexual was becoming a reality, while she herself had fallen into obscurity in Eureka Springs, Arkansas, singing two shows a night at the Grand Duchess Ballroom of the Four Runners Inn. Anita Bryant closes each show with "God Bless America" and the "Battle Hymn of the Republic," but although his mother will never forget her, she probably does not even remember the name of Robert Hillsborough, the gentle gardener murdered for being gay at the height of her hate campaign.

The crowd was growing at the corner of Castro and Market, which had been renamed Harvey Milk Plaza. Members of the Lesbian and Gay Freedom Day Marching Band arrived carrying brass instruments, drums, and woodwinds, the large white plumes on their hats motionless in the twilight. They clustered behind a motorized cable car. I knew that this was for the most part a new crop of musicians. Years ago, Cheryl had marched in the band, playing the bass drum. She had loved the band—they had let her play any instrument she wanted, because, she thought, they were so excited to have women members. Most of the original musicians, including their director, Jon Sims, were now dead from AIDS. The band had not marched in the candlelight memorial since the night of the assassinations, when only the drum had beaten.

Lesbian and gay police officers stood at the perimeter of the gathering crowd. The women officers' hair was perfectly moussed and trimmed; their uniforms were snug, their guns resting in the holsters strapped to their hips. The guns looked very big to me, and I thought it was funny that the policewomen moved as if they were physically enormous. It was a typical cop walk that I had only noticed before in men.

It became clear that this would not be the usual few hundred marchers. I saw Tom Ammiano, and I wanted to congratulate him on his election to the school board. Yet I felt discomfort at approaching him when I remembered my inability to stand beside him as a lesbian teacher many years before during the No on 6 campaign. I moved into the crowd, and found myself beside the Kosmic Lady, an eccentric San Francisco personality on the level of the Emperor Norton. She was explaining global and galactic *glasnost,* personal and planetary *perestroika* (Gorbachev was still in power), when I saw Gilbert Baker walking across the street, directly toward me. He wore a dark, conservative winter coat and white tennis shoes. He had left his crown of thorns at home for the evening. His hands were in his pockets, and he was smiling like a very happy bad boy. He walked beside Cleve Jones, who had been Harvey Milk's City Hall aide. Cleve was now himself one of our most effective spokespersons, having brought to fruition his original vision of an epic quilt memorializing those dead of AIDS, which became known as the Names Project.

The march began, and the atmosphere was charged. The Lavender Sweep had energized the community. Banners announced the presence of the Asian Gay Association, the Harvey Milk Democratic Club, ACT UP, and Queer Nation. The marchers now numbered close to a thousand. I walked the length of the march beside Gilbert Baker. All along the parade route, various individuals came up to him as if to pay their respects. A number of the very young who were marching with Queer Nation knew who he was, and although he was almost forty they thought of him as one of them. And why wouldn't they? His political cartoon of Pink Jesus had driven the Prayer Warriors into a frenzy at the GHOST demonstration, and had captured much of the press's attention. Gilbert Baker is from Kansas, the son of a judge, a fan of Barbra Streisand, and a Vietnam-era veteran. He believes that all art is exhibitionism because it is about making a private dream real. He believes that the Queer Nationals are angels.

"What does it mean, 'What Would Harvey Think?' " I asked him.

"It's the battle between the assimilationists and the queers, between those of us who could never fit in a closet, and those of us who can pass."

He looked at me, and I knew he was thinking, "Like you."

We walked beneath the freeway overpass, where someone had

hung a banner that read, EVERY SOCIETY HONORS ITS LIVE CON-
FORMISTS AND ITS DEAD TROUBLEMAKERS. Gilbert pointed to the
sign and said, "Harvey Milk was not endorsed by a single gay
political club. He was considered too radical. Too dangerous.
You need to remember that."

We rounded the corner into the street near City Hall and I saw
that the police officers had stopped marching outside the crowd.
They had joined the procession, become part of it. This was very
moving because the assassin, Dan White, had been a policeman
before he became a supervisor. I had never forgotten the FREE
DAN WHITE T-shirts that some officers had worn, but at that
moment, watching the lesbian and gay officers join the march, I
knew that it was indeed possible to work within the system.

The procession passed the statue of Abraham Lincoln. Several
young people, who were children at the time of the assassinations, were ceremoniously placing their candles on Lincoln's
shoulders and near his feet.

"This is a beautiful tradition, isn't it?" I asked a young Queer
National, identifiable by her leather jacket covered with yellow
stickers. She stared at me blankly and put her hands in her
pockets. She seemed shy for someone with an earring through
her eyebrow and the word LABIA emblazoned across the back of
her jacket.

"It's a tradition?" she asked.

I realized that our history needed to be told again and again,
with many voices. I decided to come out of the closet as a writer.
It was, in truth, a way to make up for my silence in the past,
especially during the John Briggs attack on teachers. I hoped that
by the time I finished, I would be able to answer the question
"What would Harvey think?" and I would be able to forgive
myself for staying closeted in the workplace while he was alive,
when the one thing he asked us to do was to come out.

The next evening, it was my turn to put Jesse to bed. He was
wearing his blue-and-yellow Superman pajamas and carrying his
Paddington Bear.

"You read *Peter Pan*," he said imperiously.

Jesse could not get enough of *Peter Pan*. He was especially fond of the Mary Martin version, which he called the "people *Peter Pan*," but he had a special place in his heart for Disney's cartoon Peter, who was so adept at sword fighting. We had the videotape and audiotape of Disney's version, with the accompanying book. We also had the sound-effects book; you press the pictures along the side as you read, and so create the sound of Captain Hook's laughter, or the clash of swords to accompany the words.

This night, Jesse wanted the "big book," an elaborately illustrated original 1911 version by Sir James Barrie, through which we were slowly making our way. Sir James said that each night, Mrs. Darling would sort through her children's minds, setting them up afresh for the next day, occasionally stumbling across an odd name or object. I knew that Jesse's mind was full of swords, pirates, and wild animals, and I could see, as I read to him and his eyelids became heavy, that another world where life and death were not real was touching upon his, pulling him into its adventure.

I stopped reading at the place where Mrs. Darling falls asleep, just before Peter comes to the nursery to retrieve his shadow. But Jesse whispered, "More Peter, please," and so I continued to read until Jesse's head fell forward and locked into a child's trance.

She dreamt that the Neverland had come too near and that a strange boy had broken through from it. He did not alarm her, for she thought she had seen him before in the faces of many women who have no children. Perhaps he is to be found in the faces of some mothers also. But in her dream he had rent the film that obscures the Neverland, and she saw Wendy and John and Michael peeping through the gap.

# CHAPTER IV

# The Neverland Cap

IT WAS NIGHT, and there were hundreds of them, on the auditorium floor and in the balcony of the Women's Building in the Mission District. The Queer Nationals raised their arms and snapped their fingers in a room where flat head-sized tinfoil stars were attached to the dark draperies on the raised stage, where silver flecks sparkled in the high ceiling. Pairs of bare light bulbs glared from above, surrounding an awkward, massive Bad Deco lighting fixture meant to represent a lotus, the flower that is supposed to induce dreamy languor and forgetfulness. But this lotus was inverted.

The room smelled of hair spray, Dippity-Do, spray paint, and wheat paste. I was surrounded by a moving wall of black leather jackets adorned with bright yellow stickers. QUEER. DYKE. FAG. LABIA. The inverted triangles, pink for the boys and black for the girls, which the Nazis had forced homosexuals to wear in prisons and concentration camps, were now converted to symbols of pride. WE RECRUIT. WHAT CAUSES HETEROSEXUALITY? It was Dada made accessible, the impossible commingling of lesbian identified male-to-female transgenders and militant butch queens. The "granola dykes," once sequestered in separatist women's communities, planned actions alongside "lipstick lesbians."

The facilitators, a cross-dressed girl and a round-faced young man wearing pink berets called the meeting to order.

"Every society honors its live conformists and its dead trou-blemakers," the young girl announced.

Hundreds of fingers snapped in the air, Beat gone Queer.

Gilbert entered the room, wearing flowing silk trousers and a long, androgynous shirt-dress of the flags of the world. He took a seat in the middle of the room, his air that of the indulgent uncle visiting with candy in his pockets.

The facilitators asked if there were any law-enforcement officers, surveillance agents, or media representatives present. They apparently expected an FBI agent to raise his hand.

As the meeting progressed, the Vibe Watchers circulated through the room. If you felt frustrated or angry at what was happening, you went to a Vibe Watcher to work out your feelings. It was within the Vibe Watchers' discretion to stop the meeting to process the problem. I watched as the emotionally charged gathered solicitous empathy from the Vibe Watchers, only to return to their seats and rejoin the meeting.

Sitting on the edge of his chair in the front row, every power of concentration crystallized in his eyes, was the young art historian, Jonathan Katz. His body language was that of a large powerful cat, and his mind was constantly moving. I could actually see this in his eyes and jaw. I could see that he would stop at nothing. He was an intellectual dedicated to revolution. As each person rose to describe his or her focus group, his eyes were riveted on them.

"We're forming a group to protest the comedian Gallagher and his jokes about gays and AIDS. He said he wouldn't burn flags, but he might burn a couple of fags. We're zapping the promoters of his gig."

Two women took the floor. "We are from LABIA, Lesbians and Bi-Women in Action. We are going to sponsor another Girls' Night Out. Men are welcome. Now. For those of you who don't know, last time we did this we went to a Union Street club and *gasp!* danced together. The bartender called the police, and when we got outside we were surrounded and we almost had a riot. I guess they didn't like our dance steps."

It was clear from the reaction of the group that this would be a heavily attended action.

A young butch queen in a leather jacket, with long blond hair and a small, tasteful earring hooked through his eyebrow, announced the DORIS (Defending Our Rights in the Streets) SQUASH (Super Queers United Against Savage Heterosexism) Look-alike Contest. "DORIS," he said, "can be male, female, transgender, butch, or femme."

Their young voices seemed to be coming from another reality, from a clubhouse that adults never entered.

"The Art and Propaganda Committee will be meeting on the balcony, and PUC will be in the back room discussing Pete Wilson's inaugural. The Swish Squad is under the balcony. Queer Planet is planning an action to protest the exclusion of queers by Amnesty Heterosexual."

Amnesty International had been renamed. By the end of the next year, they would have revised their policies to include homosexuals imprisoned solely on the basis of having had gay sex.

VIVA announced that they would meet to discuss reworking the ads on billboards, which they did with great creativity in the middle of the night. The Pollack Squad was not into creative alteration, preferring basic paint splattering on what they perceived to be offensively heterocentric, racist, or sexist images on billboards. I was immediately struck by the high level of consciousness concerning sexism in the young men.

As each speaker took the floor, my eyes came back to Jonathan, who was turning their words over in his mind like political Rubik's Cubes. He would be capable of revolution or destruction. I would later learn that he was thirty-two years old; as a much younger man, he had read *A Passage to India*. He believed it was essentially a book that proved the ultimate chaos of the world, a book that said there is no order, there is no plan, no divinity, that all stands in chaotic relationship. Since there is no plan, Jonathan believed that those who can make the best claim win, and that the seizure of power rests in the politics of chaos.

Jonathan took the floor. The movement at the back of the room stopped.

"I would like to request two hundred dollars to purchase flags and banners for the PUC action in Sacramento on Inauguration Day, and for a bullhorn."

"Give him the money," I said. I wanted to watch him. I wanted to see what he would do. He was clearly from a privileged class and had not lost that sense of entitlement that often vanishes when homosexuality becomes clear. Upper-class homosexual men are often the forces behind the scenes, but Jonathan would never stay behind the scenes. His charisma was powerful, and it was clear that some Queer Nationals thought it was destructive.

A femme woman in a red cloche hat blocked his request. Anyone could "block" anything, which meant that the request or action would not be undertaken. There was silence in the room.

"The person with the bullhorn has a louder voice than others at actions," she said.

Was she responding to that sense of entitlement with which Jonathan could overwhelm? He received his two hundred dollars, but no bullhorn. This brief moment encapsulated the main internal battle in Queer Nation. There could be no leaders. No one person's voice could be louder than another's. The Femmes, a focus group of females and males, had been formed to counter what they saw as masculine white male dominance at meetings. They made a chart listing behaviors that were masculinist in one column, with alternative, femme behaviors on the other side.

| | |
|---|---|
| Long, loud, forceful presentation. | Think of talking at the kitchen table, not giving a speech. |
| Speaking again before others speak. | Think what we miss when we don't hear from everyone. |
| Me, me, me. | So, la, ti, do. |

Jonathan again took the floor, pitching a visibility action called SHOP, Suburban Homosexual Outreach Project, which would take place at a shopping mall in the white suburb of Cupertino. It would be a fashion show of "queer types." The excitement was clear, and Jonathan appeared gratified at the response, yet here and there throughout the room I could see him being watched by those suspicious of this articulate man who moved through the world with what to them was an aura of imperial manifest destiny.

Jonathan, the product of privilege, had never held an actual job. He came from a long line of scholars and rabbinic figures. His family had a strong Zionist background; his grandfather Ben had run guns for the state of Israel before it became a state. The Katz family lived by a code of responsibility to social activism. They were, in essence, the "Yiddishe Kennedys." As I came to know Jonathan, I believe that he too had something to prove, to make up for the closeted years, which included his time as student-body president at George Washington University.

In a few short months, Jonathan Katz would be pictured and quoted in local newspapers and magazines, and many national ones, including *Time, Premiere,* and *Vanity Fair,* as a spokesperson for Queer Nation's internationally covered confrontation with Hollywood's biggest power brokers, including Michael Douglas. Jonathan knew that, while few people were truly interested in the very important court decisions concerning lesbian and gay civil rights, millions formed their opinions of the world while watching *Entertainment Tonight* and the television talk shows.

But for now, Jonathan was focused on what he believed to be the intellectual and cultural center of our society—the shopping mall—and he again pitched the SHOP action to Queer Nation. "We demand that we be able to walk in a mall as open queers. And we say, 'We're not like you. We don't want to be like you. Get over it.'"

The group began to chant, the snapping fingers punctuating the queer rap:

> We're here.
> We're queer.
> Get used to it.
> We're here.
> We're queer.
> We're fabulous.

The meeting broke into focus groups to plan actions. I joined the MTV zap group formed to protest the banning of Madonna's video "Justify My Love." The focus-group leader was a leather-jacketed girl with a sticker across her back that said, IF YOU DON'T LIKE THE NEWS, GO MAKE SOME OF YOUR OWN.

"This video had queer-positive images such as cross-dressing and male and female bisexuality," she said. "That's why it was banned."

A video hookup was switched on, and a videotape was played of the famous Madonna interview on *Nightline* with Forrest Sawyer, which had occurred a day or two earlier. At least one hundred of the Queer Nationals were jammed near the television. As the interviewer solemnly intoned the accusation of "suggestions of bisexuality," the snapping of fingers permeated the air. QN adored Madonna and hung on her every word as she explained that "Justify My Love" was an expression of her sexuality. *Nightline* then aired the video, which featured the Monroe-esque Madonna walking along a sterile white corridor at the opening of her sexual fantasy. When she declared, "I want to kiss you in Paris," the Queer Nationals gyrated and danced. I looked across the auditorium at the animated focus groups planning bizarre actions that would infuriate some, charm others, and probably make the news. It was another world, and in many ways, it was beyond gay.

Clusters of transgenders mixed freely with leather-jacketed advocates of civil disobedience, and a lavender-suited Santa Claus made a list of shifts for Christmas bell-ringing in front of Neiman-Marcus. All of the money collected by the Lavender Santas would be donated to a shelter for battered women and children. Even their choice of recipient for the money was unusual. Most of the Santas were men, yet it was to disenfranchised women and children that they were giving the money.

On the television screen, Madonna rushed down the corridor, playfully biting her thumb and shaking her hand in an Italian-girl gesture of hotness and pleasure. Everyone in the auditorium paused to snap in approval as one Queer National read the message she had put at the end of her video: "Poor Is the Man Whose Pleasures Depend upon the Permission of Another." Madonna, who has a profound understanding of drag, then appeared for the *Nightline* interview with bright red lips, her black dress conservative, the collar high, only a triangle of neck showing. Her hair was up like a Park Avenue matron's. The Queer Nationals were silent, almost reverent. Gilbert came up behind

me and whispered, "She's their Jesus." He smiled and wandered
away like the hookah-smoking caterpillar in Wonderland.

Madonna was rolling hot. "Why is it okay for ten-year-olds to
see, you know, someone's body being ripped to shreds, or Sam
Kinison spitting on Jessica Hahn? Why are we gonna deal with
these issues? Why is it okay? Why do parents not have a problem
with that? But why do they have a problem with two consenting
adults displaying affection for each other, regardless of their
sex?"

The snapping and cheers crackled beneath the inverted-lotus
light fixture, and I found my arm rising and my fingers snapping.
I quickly brought my arm down again. No one was looking at
me, but I felt ridiculous and, yes, fabulous! It was the Queer
Rapture.

❖

"They are irresponsible spoiled brats."

"They are destroying everything we've worked for."

"Seventy percent of them are HIV-negative, so they have time
for malls."

"They don't understand politics."

"We think of them as Heiress Nation."

"They are dangerous."

"They're French-kissing at the cable cars downtown. What
will the tourists think?"

"This isn't about civil rights. This is about exhibitionism."

"They just want to get their picture in the paper."

"They are destructive."

"They don't know their history."

"They are evil."

"Especially Jonathan. Jonathan Katz is evil."

This was not the radical right talking. These were certain
moderate gays and lesbians, and some progressives, who had
carved out neat little niches and performed innumerable tasks for
straight politicians friendly to gay rights. These were not, of
course, the people in the street confronting ten thousand Prayer
Warriors who had come to our city to exorcise us of our demons.
In truth, the establishment crowd could not do that and retain

their positions. Politics is based on compromise, and that is exactly what Queer Nation refused to do, and did not have to do. What would Harvey think?

I could not answer that, but I believe in going toward the energy, and as the memorial AIDS quilt grew like a wild blanket of death, and as lesbian and gay families had to fight the legal system to protect their children from the Traditional Values Coalition's hate policies, which had permeated state and national government all the way up to the President of the United States, there really was no place for me to be but in that room with Queer Nation. I did not think I was part of them, but I wanted to help by videotaping their actions. The presence of video cameras tended to put a damper on spectator violence and police overreaction.

While my friends would be watching Martina Navratilova play at the Virginia Slims tournament, and driving down to Palm Springs for the Dinah Shore Open, time-honored lesbian activities that I fully support, I knew that this year I belonged in that Cupertino shopping mall with the "evil" Jonathan Katz.

❖

All in black, I followed the Queer Nationals, through the eye of the videocamera, into the mall. Through the lens, everything was black and white and not quite so real; it was like a newsreel of a future time. Jonathan had been hit in the head by a security guard at the last mall action, and he had taken precautions against a recurrence, bringing a lawyer and having certain people designated "cop blockers" and "irate-patron blockers." His greatest concern was with the unprofessional police, who were apt to overreact and were not terribly clear on the Constitution.

The group carried a white banner with pink triangles and black letters: YEAR OF THE QUEER—1991. Perhaps the action was popular—it drew almost thirty men, and five women—because everybody was a star, and everybody would have a turn to walk down the glittering makeshift runway in the Vallco Fashion Park Mall, to confront surrogate parents and perhaps their own questions about beauty.

They sang "It's a Queer World After All" as we walked

through the track-lit funnel entrance into the center of the mall. The song drew mall patrons and salespeople from the stores and toward the action. The patrons' children were delighted, skipping alongside. The parents weren't sure what to do, but followed. Young straight couples, hand in hand, stood staring, their mouths literally open. I watched it all from the safety of the black-and-white video.

Smiling yet stunned soft white faces turned toward the show. The mall's Christmas décor of greenery and miniature white lights provided a festive setting and the high ceilings of the cultural cathedral echoed the singers' voices as the Queer Nationals took the escalator down to the lower level.

The parents sensed no danger because the event felt like a circus. Everything was out in the open. It was pretty and playful, and there were no secret dark alleys, just lots of junk jewelry and a rainbow of colors. The patrons walked with their children to the show area, and many stood along the balcony on the upper floor. As my camera bobbled and caught the images, I felt as if I were floating in a fishbowl.

Jonathan took center stage in a white dinner jacket, black trousers, and bow tie, a silk scarf from the 1920s around his neck.

"We want to help you identify queers," he said. There was confusion on some of the patrons' faces. Was this a homophobic hate group, or were these real homosexuals? There was no confusion on certain faces: the faces that belonged to the lesbians and gay men who worked in the mall. We could tell who they were, yet most of them were probably invisible to their employers. They could not believe their eyes, and they could not stop smiling.

Jonathan introduced the Go-go Boy, the Gym Clone, and then the International Male Catalog Boy. This role had been selected by John Woods, the only black in the group. I later learned that John was from a world the reverse image of Jonathan's. Born in 1963 in Murfreesboro, Tennessee, he was one of five children raised by his mother, who worked as a janitor for $11,000 a year. Until the ninth grade, he was a troublemaker. He was blind in one eye; the other children had called him "Four-eyes," "Cross-eyes." He compensated for the teasing by donning makeshift brass knuckles and becoming a tiny bully whose temper gave him strength.

His mother stopped asking him to go to the store to purchase groceries with food stamps because she knew that he was embarrassed. Then a teacher found him and helped him to discover his mind. He became obsessed with self-made men: Elvis, Sammy Davis, Jr., Howard Hughes. He read everything and was fascinated by the media. He practiced speaking, religiously exercising in front of *ABC Evening News*. He knew he would get nowhere as a poor black man with a slow Tennessee drawl.

John Woods wanted everything now, and he was not going to settle for anything less. And here he was, promenading as the International Male Catalog Boy in the Suburban Homosexual Outreach Project at the Vallco Fashion Park Mall, not another black person in sight. Through the lens of my camera, I had watched him on the train as he leafed through several catalogues. He later told me that he had been looking for an image that resembled him, but there was no one who looked black.

He said that when he went into the mall, singing, he felt weirdly empowered, and nervous. He wasn't sure what to expect. Now, as he turned and modeled his sweater, he became acutely aware that people were staring at him. The show must go on, he thought, but he felt conspicuous and vulnerable.

John Woods would remain with Queer Nation, and take charge of media. He would not give up the playing field to the white men. He would be the prime mover in bringing the homophobia and racism of the Boy Scout leadership to the center of national media attention, and would almost single-handedly force San Francisco United Way to reexamine its giving policies and finally to withdraw financial support from the Scouts. He certainly had no idea that this would happen only months down the line, as he took his final spin and left the runway to the raucous cheers of the other queer fashion plates.

Jonathan and John were to have a tense relationship. While they respected each other's work, they could not read each other, and it's hard to trust when you cannot imagine what it is like to see through another's eyes, to think through another's mind.

Jonathan introduced the Status Queen, the Transgender, and

the Guppie or Gay Urban Professional. "You may not pick him
out on the street, but we bring him here for your enjoyment."
The Country-Western Look, an Old Hippie, the Radical Faerie
Look . . . "Butch and femme combo. Camouflage skirt and
combat boots." The Luppie. "Notice the power drag. The brief-
case. She's never without it. It's welded to her hand. . . ." The
Beautiful Lipstick Lesbian. The Castro Clone. "Notice the mustache, Exhibit A. The jeans jacket, Exhibit B. The black hanky
in the back pocket. What does that mean? Permanently in the
time warp of the seventies, he never wants to leave the Castro.
And so it took special encouragement to bring him down here to
Vallco." The New Clone. "He's never seen without his whistle,
his leather jacket, the black bandanna. The leather belt and blue
jeans. That's the outfit, and it's the only one. Makes dressing real
easy."

The crowd was riveted, smiling, leaning over the balcony to
get a closer look as the models cheered each other on.

"What can we say about Tracy? She's got the best plastic
jewelry in the West, and she's a plumber!

"Finally, the Untyped Fag."

Nondescript in every way and wearing a sweatshirt, a young
man stood in the middle of the circle and raised his hands to the
patrons in the balcony suspended above our heads.

"I want you to know you might think you can identify who's
queer and who's not," he said, "but you can't. We're your
friends. Your brothers. Your sisters. We're your children. But
we're afraid to come out to you because we're afraid you might
reject us. But you shouldn't reject us, because we are deserving
of your love, as you are deserving of ours."

He pulled off his sweatshirt and revealed a Queer Nation
T-shirt. The other models cheered wildly, and a few heads
bobbed approval from the balcony.

"Now," said Jonathan, "We're going to show you what two
girls and two boys kissing looks like so the next time you see it
in public, you don't stare and you don't say nasty things."

The kiss-in began. My camera spent very little time on the
kissers, but instead scanned those watching. Always, no matter
how often I saw them do it, the kiss-ins twisted me into a knot,

because it was then that the demonstrators' vulnerability was highest. They could not see who was behind them, and it was the kiss that inflamed the homophobes, and the kiss seemed endless to me. Why did they have to do this? Unfortunately for my nerves, although New York usually did a nice polite peck, San Francisco went French. If onlookers shouted or groaned in disgust or horror, the Queer Nationals kissed even more deeply. Just when it seemed they would kiss forever, Jonathan waved to the patrons and said, "Thanks for watching. We love you."

A young male shouted at Jonathan from the balcony, "Hey faggot!"

Pointing his finger at the teenager, and looking oddly dashing in his elegant evening wear in broad daylight, Jonathan shouted, "That's *Mr.* Faggot."

The Queer Nationals dispersed throughout the mall, handing out the literature they had designed for the action.

### HETEROSEXUAL QUESTIONNAIRE

"What do you think caused your heterosexuality?"

"Most child molesters are heterosexual. Do you consider it safe to expose your children to heterosexuals? Heterosexual teachers, particularly?"

"Is it possible that your heterosexuality stems from a neurotic fear of people of the same sex? Maybe you just need a positive gay experience."

The patrons received copies of "How to Recognize a Queer," which was a take-off on a recent tabloid article advocating electroshock and cow prods to "cure" suspected gay teens, and the "Gay Look-alike Checklist," ostensibly created to alert heterosexuals when they were inadvertently appearing gay in their hairstyle and dress.

Jonathan went into Sears and handed literature to the salespeople. This was against the shopping mall's rules, but he was a pure escalationist. He went to the electric power tool department and handed a hot-pink sheet to a salesman, whose eyes filled with tears.

"Thank you for coming," the salesman said. "No one's ever come here."

The salesman was a closeted gay man, and the handout Jonathan had given him was by far the most controversial. Security guards had tried to confiscate it without success.

PARENTS, ARE YOU ABUSING YOUR CHILDREN?

Is your heterosexism filling your child with painful shame and self-hatred? Did you know that more than one-third of teen suicides are because the child was convinced by her/his parents that her/his sexuality was shameful and wrong? YOU LOVE YOUR CHILD! Make your daughter know that you will always love her— no matter who she loves. Make your son understand that you will stand behind him always and rejoice in his love and happiness— whether he finds it with a woman or a man. DON'T LET HOMO-PHOBIA TAKE YOUR CHILD FROM YOU!

I filmed one infuriated middle-aged man crushing the pink paper into a little ball and throwing it on the floor, his face red, his arms trembling. The women, however, most often read the paper, folded it, and slipped it into their purses, looking thoughtfully at their children.

On January 2, 1991, at the next Wednesday's Queer Nation meeting, the SHOP action was given a standing ovation, a reaffirmation of the Year of the Queer was made, and an emergency activation and phone zap of Pete Wilson's inaugural committee was announced. The focus group sponsoring the action was called Indignant Queers, or simply IQ. Unbelievably, governor-elect Pete Wilson's inaugural galas would include a high-profile performance by Gallagher, the comedian who said in his act that as a good American, he would "burn fags, not flags." His repertoire had since expanded to include spraying the audience with Silly String and saying, "This is AIDS in a can. Now you don't have to fuck a fag to get it."

The zap group's flyer listed three phone numbers: the inaugural committee, Wilson's campaign headquarters, and his San Francisco senatorial office. As the uproar escalated, Wilson's press liaison, Dan Schnerr, said, "We were made aware of Mr. Gallagher's act after the selection had been made. We have made it clear to Gallagher through his management that gay-bashing is not appropriate entertainment for our event." The Queer Nationals thought the statement hilarious, as it implied that this type of "entertainment" would indeed have an appropriate milieu.

Jeff Brooks, aka Sister Rosetta Stone, or the Oracle of Oakland, introduced his mother, Olive, to the group. Olive Brooks was seventy-four years old, her attire careful, a blue coat, new perm, black clutch lying neatly in her lap. Jeff had his arm around her shoulders, and she smiled shyly. The Queer Nationals burst into snaps and—in deference to her presence, I suppose—applause and cheers, so there could be no doubt by Mrs. Brooks that she was highly welcome.

As the applause for Mrs. Brooks died down, a young man named Robert White stood up and walked to the front of the room. With military passion, he said that he was about to ship out to the Middle East, on alert for the Persian Gulf War. He said that regardless of our thoughts about war, we needed to remember that there were a lot of queers willing to fight and die for us because they loved us. This was a strange moment in Queer Nation's history, because it revealed the fact that there was no one political point of view within the group. The only requirement for membership was self-selection and the declaration of queerness, which could in fact accommodate any sexuality.

It was announced that Barney Frank, up-front gay member of the United States Congress, had sent a thank-you note for his Queer Nation T-shirt, which his lover had appropriated. That was the last light moment of the meeting; then the tone became fractious.

SHOP was charming, said a man in leather and pearls, but a real action involved arrests. Others disagreed, saying visibility was important, not arrests. There was a shouting match: Was this a direct-action group, or a cattle call for Oprah? The Femmes were furious that only macho actions were considered revolutionary.

The young man with long brown hair and an earring in his

eyebrow announced that ACT UP/New York was planning "Days of Desperation," which would coincide with President Bush's State of the Union Address. They would attempt to shut down Grand Central Station and all arteries entering New York City. They wanted Queer Nation to endorse their action. Fingers snapped and heads nodded in approval, although the granola dykes and the opera queens were somewhat tentative. With the war coming, the FBI was broadcasting, through the media, descriptions of possible saboteurs and potential catastrophic terrorist attacks on large American cities. To advocate closing down all arteries into New York City was not in the category of playful.

A large man—he had appeared the week before in a strapless gown and feather boa, and now was wearing standard leather and stickers—rose to his six-foot-two height and suggested forming a focus group to shut down all international phone lines for one day. This was greeted with only moderate interest. He followed up with the announcement that ACT UP/San Francisco would be doing its own "Day of Disaster" on January 15, 1991, the deadline for Saddam Hussein to pull out of Kuwait. They would attempt to shut down all Bay Area Rapid Transit trains running in and out of San Francisco. There was a look of amazement on the faces of the gym clones, the status queens, the luppies, and the lipstick lesbians as it was announced that this would be "big CD." "CD" stands for civil disobedience, which involves arrest.

The focus group DORIS SQUASH announced that they wanted to take over all media, including radio stations and talk shows, and make them talk about queer issues. The disco queens, gym teachers, and country-western cowgirls giggled.

Queer Peace announced that on Bush's war date, they would be participating with other antiwar groups in an attempt to shut down San Francisco's Federal Building. Queer Peace would have responsibility for the Polk Street side of the building, which would be a "queer safe space." It seemed that some antiwar protesters were wildly macho heterosexuals who did not take too kindly to protesting alongside drag queens.

Jonathan asked those who would be attending the PUC action at the governor's inaugural to wear bulky clothing so that they could smuggle in literature, which they would then be able to pass out to the crowd. This sounded very exciting to the Sweater Queens and the Radical Faeries.

These announcements, which amounted to a militant wish list, were made in the open to a room of well over four hundred people. There were now so many people that the balcony was full. To think that there was no one in the room who would report these activities to the police was unbelievable. The Queer Nationals put their names, their phone numbers, and the locations of strategy meetings (usually someone's home) for each focus group on the Queerline, which anyone could call. It would be surprisingly inept of the police if they were not monitoring it.

Incongruously, a queer bowling party was announced, and then legal witnesses were recruited to observe actions and testify, if necessary, in civil or criminal trials. The agenda was chaotic. I felt a deep concern for the Queer Nationals, especially the younger ones, who seemed to be getting swept up into something that could easily explode. There were members of the Revolutionary Communist Party (RCP) and the Revolutionary Workers League (RWL) now attending the meeting in an attempt to co-opt Queer Nation, as they had so many other grass-roots gay groups. I was worried that the joy of visibility, the adrenaline rush of singing "It's a Queer World After All" in a mall was being lost. Not only was the agenda chaotic, but it was difficult to discern whose agenda it was.

A new focus group was formed. It was called Sybil, after the most famous case of multiple personality. Sybil, of course, had no focus, and would meet on the sidewalk. This was an oddly appropriate way to end the evening.

I drove home. Cheryl and Jesse were already asleep. There was an open piece of mail on the kitchen table. On January 14, at nine o'clock, the motion to compel a home visit would be considered by the court. Strangely enough, I felt nothing. I had shut down.

Later, in the very early morning hours, a bomb exploded at the deserted Women's Building, destroying the front doors, which were fifteen feet from the auditorium where Queer Nation and ACT UP met.

❖

At the Queer Nation meeting on January 9, I watched as a woman in a trench coat crawled from under the stage and took a seat in the auditorium. The woman on duty for the Women's Building announced that multiple bomb threats specifically for our group had been received. It was their duty to warn us, so that anyone who wished to leave could. They had not used a bomb dog, and the bomb team had not been there, but Officer Sally DeHaven, the woman in the trench coat, happened to attend the meeting that night at the urging of out-of-town friends who wanted to see what Queer Nation was all about. DeHaven, the permit officer at Mission Station, was known to the people who ran the Women's Building, and they had asked her to search the room. The meeting began and the facilitators asked, as usual, if there were any law enforcement officers, surveillance agents, or media representatives present. Sally DeHaven identified herself and told the Queer Nationals not to leave unattended bags on the floor, because they were prime hiding places for bombs.

Then across the aisle from DeHaven, and directly behind me, Officer Lea Militello rose to identify herself. I remembered seeing her at the Harvey Milk memorial march, where she had joined the marchers rather than stay on the perimeter. She was now in plainclothes, and her presence, along with DeHaven's, was coincidental. This was true, but you could not possibly have convinced the radical elements in the room of it. Militello had previously attended a meeting uninvited, to address a bashing of some Queer Nationals. She had come in full uniform, gun and baton on her hip, and the Vibe Watchers had found it necessary to stop the meeting. The presence of the police in the room infuriated those planning civil-disobedience actions, because police department directives make it necessary for any police officer, on or off duty, to report a crime in the making if she should become aware of it. I'd say that shutting down international phone lines or all BART trains, taking over the federal building, or aiding and abetting the shutdown of all major arteries into New York City might fall into that category.

Lea Militello stood and said yes, she was a police officer, but this was supposed to be Queer Nation, an all-inclusive group.

"I'm queer," she said, and she had a point. The group was thrown into bitter confusion.

Lea Militello was also the police department's liaison to the lesbian and gay community, and she held a degree in criminal justice. She was thirty-two years old, and had received the Medal of Valor and three Police Commission commendations. She and her female patrol partner had been awarded the Medal of Valor in 1983 for subduing without incident a robbery suspect who had made several attempts to stab them both. One Police Commission commendation was for disarming a man dressed up like Santa Claus who had threatened to kill some kids. She described him to me as "a nut who happened to have a hatchet and a shotgun." Lea Militello was five feet six inches tall, and she kept a Garfield sticker on the butt of her .357 magnum. She had had many occasions to pull her gun from its holster, but she had never had to shoot. She was proud of this. She came onto the force the year after Harvey Milk and George Moscone were assassinated. When it became known that she was lesbian, she received what she referred to as "gifts" in her mailbox. Only members of the force had access to these mailboxes. Among the "gifts" had been used condoms, and dildos slathered with K-Y jelly. Occasionally, women officers would be cut off on the radio, and so would be unable to call for help if they needed backup. This was no longer simply insulting behavior, but behavior that could result in death. When Willis Casey took over the department, Lea worked with a group of officers to put together an antidiscrimination policy that included sexual orientation, and she helped to revolutionize the minority-sensitivity training of police officers. The old training had consisted of taking new police officers to gay bars. She had worked closely with the new chief; AIDS training went from a fifteen-minute block of time to five hours. She had just celebrated her ninth anniversary with her partner and was the nonbiological mother of their young son, Ryan. Ryan's birth had been the most important moment in her life, and the three of them would be featured in the Mother's Day issue of *Redbook* magazine the next year.

At the moment, Officer Lea Militello was determined to be accepted as a queer activist, albeit an activist within the police department. It was true, however, that she would never participate in civil disobedience. It was from within the system that she would work. Since Queer Nation described itself as a group with the goal of promoting unity among all people, no one could technically be excluded, including police officers.

For the first time, I spoke at a Queer Nation meeting.

"I'm not worried about those in this room who identify themselves. They're familiar faces to us anyway. It's those in this room who are not identifying themselves that we should be worried about." I was referring to the Revolutionary Workers League as much as to the FBI. Snapping fingers, more dialogue. The young woman in charge of the building returned to announce that another bomb threat had been received, and she wanted us to know, so that we could have the option of staying or going.

"I want you to know," she said, "that these cops are staying here, even if they have to stand in the lobby, unless you guys have a focus group that knows how to defuse bombs."

The granola dyke's mouth was slightly open, the clones shuffled their combat boots, and one transgender looked thoughtfully at a bobby pin she was twisting nervously in her long fingers. John Woods watched carefully, but said nothing. He did not view police as sell-outs to the state, and he himself had no intention of ever being arrested. As a young black homosexual male, he found nothing romantic or attractive about arrest.

Jonathan was on the edge of his seat. He looked as if he were about to fly, and he seemed terribly happy. The presence of a police officer identifying herself as queer posed a fascinating intellectual problem for him. Here it was at his feet, delivered by the ideal social laboratory of San Francisco: The proof that since there is no plan, the seizure of power rests in the politics of chaos.

No one left the room, and the fight continued. I joined Gilbert by the door. He had his hands in the pockets of his long wool coat, and he was smiling sadly.

"It's a setup," he said.

"What?"

"All of a sudden: bomb threats, obvious police presence at the meetings, the Gulf War is about to erupt. See? No matter what happens, the group is destroyed. It's clearly split."

DeHaven stood and said she would wait outside. She had not

meant to disrupt the meeting. If anyone wanted to talk to her about procedures at the department, she would be outside. Militello reluctantly followed her out to the lobby. It was agreed that there would be a mediation for all those deeply concerned about the police presence at the meeting.

There was a line for the Vibe Watchers as an angry dialogue followed, during which some factions stated that anyone who goes to work for the state is not queer. They did not know their history. They did not know the fierce battle that the lesbian and gay community had undertaken in order to get representation on the force, which was the only way to stem routine police violations of civil rights. Gay men had been regularly hounded and rounded up. After a drunken bachelor party in 1979, off-duty policemen carrying beer bottles had decided to go to Peg's Place and "get the dykes." When the men were warned by the woman at the door that she would call the police, they announced, "We are the police and we can do what we goddam well want to," after which they shoved and punched their way into the bar, throwing the bar's owner onto the floor in a headlock and wreaking general havoc. Ten years had passed, and this generation had no memory of these once commonplace events.

Queer Nation was then asked to endorse and contribute five hundred dollars to an undisclosed action. They were asked to simply trust that the action would be worthy of their endorsement, but they could not be told what it was. Many of the Queer Nationals were uncomfortable with this request, and the feminist femmes went into patriarchal overload.

Marty Mulkey was angry and frustrated, his long hair flying, the earring in his pierced eyebrow catching the light. He demanded to know, "Am I the only one worried we've stopped being a direct-action group and instead have become an encounter group? The Phil Donahue show? ACT UP and QN were founded around CD. If you don't do CD, what do you do?"

Two voices encapsulated the argument:

"Go to the malls!"

"This is a war, not a fashion show!"

In the end, QN voted to endorse an action being kept secret even from themselves, and to contribute five hundred dollars to it. No one had blocked because they did not want to deal with the in-your-face queer machismo of the proposal's promoters.

Queer Peace (Perverts to End Armed Conflict Eternally) was an exuberant, youthful group. They announced a "Kiss-in for Peace" at dawn at the federal building on January 15, President Bush's deadline for Saddam Hussein to pull out of Kuwait. They would be joining other groups, including Bay Area Pledge of Resistance, the major local antiwar organization. Many at the QN meeting were uncomfortable, silently worried about their friends and family in Israel, their brothers and lovers in the military. They did not go to the Vibe Watchers, but many thought of Robert White, the self-avowed Queer National who was now in a ship headed for the Gulf.

As I left the meeting, I picked up a stapled handout from the information table by the door. The top sheet read, in bold letters, DO SOMETHING. Inside, there was the schedule of protests against "George Bush's Oil War." "In the event of an emergency (WAR), meet at 5:00 P.M. on the day the war starts at Fifth and Powell, Chevron headquarters. The day after the war breaks, at 6:30 A.M., shut down all major buildings, roadways, financial centers in the City." Flyers and pamphlets were beginning to appear on the tables that had nothing to do with any actions created or endorsed by Queer Nation, and as I had suspected, no Queer Nation focus group was identified on this handout.

In the lobby, Lea Militello was on edge as we came out of the meeting.

"Well, Officer Militello," I said, "if you're going to be a part of Queer Nation, they'll probably want you to go on an action. Would you like to go to a shopping mall?"

"I'd love it," she said, and she kissed me on the cheek. I'd never been kissed by a cop. LABIA contended that if the police had been "hunky guys" there would have been no problem with their presence at the meeting.

I decided not to tell Cheryl about the bomb threats. I did not want to worry her, and I had no intention of leaving the meetings. It seemed to me that there was something very crucial happening in that room, and even if it frightened the horses, I would not be a deserter.

❖

I was at home, on the phone, waiting for the War Memorial Building personnel to find out if Donna Hitchens's Superior Court swearing-in ceremony was still to be held. Desert Storm had begun at four o'clock, and Donna's ceremony was scheduled for five. I looked through the picture window. On the sidewalk across the street, driving back and forth, back and forth, was a five-year-old Latino in a motorized military jeep decorated with tan camouflage. When had they changed the children's war toys from the green camouflage of jungle warfare to the sand-colored camouflage of the desert?

Yes. As of four-thirty, the ceremony was still to be held. If Donna was going to go ahead with the swearing-in ceremony, then I would attend. I owed her too much, and it was too important a moment in the lesbian civil rights movement, to not attend. Cheryl and I had planned to go together, with Jesse, but we decided it might be wiser if she stayed at home with him. I remembered the DO SOMETHING pamphlet; five o'clock was also the time its authors called for the streets to be taken over.

The streets seemed oddly deserted as I drove near the War Memorial Building, which was across the street from City Hall and one block from the federal building. I parked many blocks away, on the opposite side of Market Street, a main artery through the city. If the roads were blocked by demonstrators, I would be able to leave.

I used the entrance to the Museum of Modern Art, housed in the War Memorial Building. The ceremony would take place in the building's Herbst Theater, where the U.N. charter was signed in 1945. The theater itself was elegant, with flowing red velvet curtains and an elevated, moderately sized stage. The strange silence of the streets outside gave way to classical music played by three women musicians, two violinists and a cellist. Members of the San Francisco Sheriff's Department, in tan uniforms and gold badges, stood in the aisles of the theater. It was an all-woman group, courtesy of Sheriff Mike Hennessy, a strong advocate of lesbian and gay rights. The first six rows were cordoned off for dignitaries, mostly judges. Supervisor Roberta Achtenberg

and her son, Benjie, were there, as were Supervisor Carole Migden, Del Martin and Phyllis Lyon, school board vice president
Tom Ammiano, and Abby Abinanti and her partner, attorney
Cheryl Sena. There were no leather jackets, except mine. It had
been a difficult choice, but I thought I would be safer on the street
wearing leather, since I had decided to attend the Queer Nation
meeting later that night. I was wrong. The leather jacket would
end up targeting me.

The lights dimmed in the theater, and the musicians carried
their music stands and instruments into the wings. It was five-
thirty, and President Bush was now on the air. The participants
took their places on the stage; prominent among the standard bar
association people was the dignified African-American judge
John Dearman, the first black to become presiding judge of the
Superior Court. Judge Dearman did not seem to be affected by
what was going on outside the theater. He later told me that his
grandmother Rosie Banks had taught him to concentrate only on
what was happening right before him, and this night the lesson
served him well. He explained to the audience, with a strange
look of personal amusement on his face, that judges never received any applause, any recognition, and that he wanted us to
applaud for each and every Superior Court judge who had chosen
to attend the ceremony, and that he wanted each judge to stand,
face the audience, and take a bow. Twenty-three of the twenty-
nine Superior Court judges were present, and slowly we worked
our way through each one. It was as if Judge Dearman were
making the judges acknowledge us as much as having us acknowledge them. It was an excellent turnout considering the
outbreak of war and the fact that Donna Hitchens's election had
caused shock, and to some degree, panic, at the court.

Just after Donna's defeat of the incumbent, there had been a
meeting attended by twenty-four of the Superior Court judges.
Judge Carlos Bea gave a presentation showing where the incumbent had made mistakes in his campaign. It was pointed out to
Judge Bea that he himself had not won by a significant margin.
The campaign literature of the judge whom Donna had defeated
had made a very big issue of his family, displaying his wife and
children in what seemed, for a judicial candidate, an exaggerated
manner that hinted of a coded signal. Donna's campaign litera-

ture featured only pictures of herself and an impressive list of endorsers. Her strategy had been to call for diversity on the bench. The appointed incumbent had been yet another white male district attorney. Donna made a point of saying that there was nothing wrong with white male district attorneys, but that there also needed to be representation for women and minorities. Judge Dearman, the son of a Texas sharecropper, had not attended Judge Bea's strategy presentation, but he had watched the hysteria from the sidelines and thought it verging on comic as the black judicial robes flapped through the halls like dark birds flying into mirrors.

After Judge Dearman concluded his presentation of the twenty-three judges, and acknowledged the significance of Donna's election, Barbara Brenner, Donna's former law partner, took the stage. She explained that Donna had wanted the event to proceed as planned, but that everyone could say whatever they wanted to say. She talked of the way in which Donna embraced rather than tolerated difference. She spoke of Donna's propensity to mix up the San Francisco and New York Giants. I was firmly in the room. The street could wait. The street would always be there, but not this moment. I was certain that Harvey Milk would have loved it.

Judge Mary Morgan, the partner of Supervisor Roberta Achtenberg, and Benjie's co-parent, prepared to swear in Donna. Mary Morgan had been appointed to the municipal court by then governor Jerry Brown. She told of the courage it took to go into a courtroom in the early seventies, as Donna Hitchens had, with the words "Lesbian Rights Project" on your letterhead.

Donna took the oath from Judge Morgan as Donna's partner of fifteen years, Nancy Davis, their two young daughters, Kate and Megan, and Donna's mother and stepfather looked on. Donna then put on her black judge's robes. The audience, almost every seat taken, rose to its feet in a standing ovation. It had been such a long, sometimes brutal journey. She and Nancy had been forced to go to trial, with Roberta Achtenberg as their lawyer, for the first second-parent adoption in California. Now Donna Hitchens would sit in that very same courtroom, not to battle for her family, but as the judge.

Yet this was a difficult moment for Donna. She told us that she felt the ceremony was self-indulgent and superficial in terms of the outbreak of war, but that it was one of the most important nights of her life, and for her community. Her election, she said, was not just about her, but about San Francisco. She spoke of her deceased father, Walter, of his ability to question authority, of his unconditional love for her, of his willingness to take risks. His influence had contributed to her improbable election to the Superior Court, which was not the traditional career path for a forty-five-year-old working-class lesbian whose coalition politics, beginning with the African-American civil rights struggle of the early 1960s, had always involved communities that had been marginalized.

When the ceremony concluded, I watched as people greeted Donna, and then I went upstairs to the Green Room, the scene of many civic receptions in San Francisco. It has a balcony that overlooks Van Ness Avenue; from it one can see for many blocks. As I entered the Green Room, I heard the roar of chanting, dulled by its movement through the granite walls of the building. I made my way to the balcony, which is framed by massive pillars. Much to my surprise, there were several middle-aged women in black cocktail dresses with their arms raised, their fingers in V-shaped peace signs. For a moment, I thought they would burst into "Don't Cry for Me, San Francisco." Their husbands, who included certain prominent Superior Court judges, stood uncomfortably in the arched doorways behind them, glancing back into the reception room, hoping their colleagues were not noticing their wives. Over to the left, in the direction of the federal building, I could see what looked like flares or Roman candles being shot into the air, and there was the faintest smell of gunpowder. Passing by on the street below were thousands of protesters. Some of the men shouted up angrily to those of us on the balcony, "Into the streets! Into the streets!" Somehow I couldn't quite see these women taking to the streets wearing cocktail dresses and heels. Police and news helicopters shot bright spotlights down onto the moving protest. The helicopters seemed almost to be waltzing above the demonstrators, being careful not to collide, their lights like those of some Hollywood opening gone mad.

I left the balcony. Inside the Green Room, the judges and their wives—the ones not on the balcony giving the crowd the peace sign—mingled and nibbled on hors d'oeuvres with lesbian and gay civil rights lawyers, their voices refined and tinkling like champagne glasses clicking together. I asked a woman who seemed to be in charge if she knew where Donna was. The woman was tense, her attention torn between what was verging on chaos in the streets and the need to keep the cocktail party inside the Green Room as dignified as possible. She said that she believed Donna was in the hallway, greeting the children. I went to the hallway and watched as she greeted each child with the same special attention she had given to the dignitaries on the stage. As the last child walked away, I was alone with Donna. The children gone, her solid maternal stance dissolved. She seemed in shock, torn by the role she was forced to play that evening. Her youngest child had clung to her during the ceremony, and she was worried about how the war was affecting the children, not just her own, but the children upon whom the bombs were now dropping.

"I have to go inside now," she said. It was clear that the Green Room was the last place this woman wanted to be on this night.

When I left the War Memorial Building, I saw that the bulk of the demonstrators had passed. I could trace their progress simply by following the waltzing helicopter spotlights. They were headed up Market Street, toward the Castro. That meant it would be easy for me to cross Market and get to the Women's Building, where Queer Nation was scheduled to meet. Adjacent to the War Memorial Building is the Opera House. Three young men with bandannas covering their faces were using red spray-paint on its façade. I walked past as they slowly spray-painted the words THEY'RE DYING NOW. They saw me and held their paint cans poised in the air. They studied me, trying to determine if they should run. They were afraid of me, and I was afraid of them. That is war's legacy. I turned my head away, and they went back to work. As I passed the next building, Davies Symphony Hall, I saw that across the base of a piece of sculpture someone had scrawled the name John Lennon.

I drove to the Women's Building, avoiding the raucous street protest by watching the directions and angles of the helicopter beams, which revealed that the march was erratic, taking no particular route. The Queer Nation meeting was not being held this evening in its usual auditorium space, but rather in an upstairs room that overlooked the street. There were only thirty or so people present for the meeting. Many were prowar, having strong pro-Israeli sentiment; some had relatives in Israel who were in terrible danger from Saddam. The people who were at this meeting formed a circle and shared their thoughts and feelings. It was the most civilized thing they could have done, yet there was a great divergence of opinion. Among those present was John Woods, who was now the group's media contact and editor of the weekly *Queer Week Newsletter*. He was worried about his brother, who was in the Gulf on the *Ranger,* an aircraft carrier, but he supported his brother's military mission. John believed that there were a lot of people in this country, including people in Queer Nation, who did not have an appreciation for what they had here.

"A lot of queers are more worried about their hairspray. They don't even know where their hairspray comes from, or what's involved in making hairspray, or patent-leather shoes, or whatever else they're wearing," he said. "We take a lot for granted here. Saddam Hussein has to go. He's killing his own people. He used gas on them. We have no choice. The man has nuclear weapons, and he's going to use them if he has to. What about the Kuwaitis?"

A young man confronted John. "Kuwait is an oil-rich country. A country of feudal, racist, sexist homophobes." The implication was that John, because he is African-American and gay, was supporting a country that hated him.

"They're still human beings under fascist military attack," said John, "led by a Hitler who might attempt to destroy the world with nuclear weapons."

I did not participate in the debate. I was exhausted and chose to sit on the windowsill overlooking the street. Above the Women's Building, there was the sudden clipping sound of helicopter blades and the wide beam of its waltzing light. I went downstairs and outside to watch the march pass. It was a predominantly straight group, but the lesbians and gays were certainly creative and visible, carrying queerly humorous signs: MONEY FOR HAIR CARE, NOT FOR WARFARE, PERVERTS FOR PEACE, and SURRENDER DOROTHY. I started to walk with them, halfheartedly, but I was really headed for my car. The only thing I was still certain of was that I wanted to be home with my family. I got to the intersection of Valencia and Eighteenth streets, and saw that the traffic had been stopped for several minutes. The drivers appeared frustrated. There was a gap in the march, where it was very thin. I saw that there were four children, no more than eleven or twelve years old, strolling through the intersection. They did not seem to understand that they were walking against traffic. I stepped into the street, held up my hands and shouted, "It will only be a minute or two more." A white pickup truck, a blond man driving and a dirty-haired woman beside him, came up on the wrong side of the street and started to gun the truck across the intersection. The driver and his passenger were in their late twenties. The children were just at that moment passing by, and I stepped in front of the truck. "Wait. There are children. Just another minute," I said. I felt angry at the parents who were so foolish as to allow their children on the streets this night.

The woman in the truck had a beer can in her hand. She took a swig and yelled at me, "What the hell good do you think this will do?" I said nothing; as I saw the march was almost completely past, and that the helicopters were indicating that it had veered again, this time toward the Bay Bridge, I turned away from the truck and started to walk back to the sidewalk. Suddenly, the driver of the truck slammed down on the gas, and turned the steering wheel directly for me. I moved as quickly as I could, but the truck's fender slammed against my upper right arm and threw me to the ground. I heard the man scream, "Dyke!" I could only surmise that it was my leather jacket, which had become the insignia of queer radicals, that had inspired him. The street tar felt hard and the color seemed so much blacker than I had ever thought it could. It seemed to have glitter in it. I looked up and saw the taillights of the white pickup truck receding down Valencia Street. There were only stragglers in the march, and they kept on walking by. The motorists at the front had seen what had happened, but they did not move. I looked up and was trying to pull myself to my feet when my eyes caught those of a woman passing by. She said to her two friends, "Wait. That woman's been hit." I felt almost dreamlike as I realized that I was the woman who had been hit. They helped me to the sidewalk and asked if I wanted a ride to the hospital. I could tell my arm had not been broken, just very badly bruised. I thanked them and went to my car.

I went home and joined Cheryl in front of the television set. A former U.S. military officer said, "War is very hazardous." I started to laugh—too much, I suppose, because Cheryl looked at me strangely. I did not tell her about being hit because I did not want her to try and stop me from going to the street. I would never again, however, step in front of a moving vehicle unless I was willing to be killed.

I had trouble sleeping that night. I could not stop turning on the television set, even in the middle of the night. They were counting the bombing missions, which are called sorties. I went into Jesse's little bedroom and sat on the couch to watch him sleep. I could hear the television newsreader's voice. He was upgrading the number of sorties. It disturbed me, the use of this peculiar word. It sounded like a dance step.

The next day, I picked Jesse up from school. The children were outside, on the playground. There was a cement area where the children often drew in chalk. All over the building itself were chalk peace signs, the symbol from the 1960s, but on the ground were the pastel outlines of children's bodies. The playground supervisor explained apologetically that before they realized what was happening, the children were playing war and outlining each other's "dead" bodies in the playground. The ground was covered with little pastel-chalk death poses. I found Jesse and tried to behave as if everything was normal. I balanced him on my hip and we rubbed noses. His teacher told me that he had had a good day, that in the morning they had said the Pledge of Allegiance, and then they had joined hands and everyone sang "All we are saying is give peace a chance."

"Did you like that song, Jesse?"

"Farmer Dell," he said.

"Okay," I said. "Farmer Dell."

*    *    *

Later that evening, I met my friend Larry Janssen. Larry is a teacher, and a moderate kind of gay man. He looked at me in amazement, describing his own behavior as if he had been overtaken by an alien spirit. He had been walking home from work when he was spontaneously caught up in an anti-war protest. "Last night I walked for five hours through the city streets in my Italian leather shoes, and I took over the Bay Bridge wearing gray wool-rayon-blend pleated pants, a gray-and-black sweater, and white socks. Did you ever notice the ivy coming down onto the bridge? I realized where I was, and as I tried to get away, I kept slipping on the ivy because of my shoes. I found myself standing on the lower deck of the bridge, surrounded by people who looked like they had just stepped out of *A Clockwork Orange*. I avoided arrest because of my fashion statement."

We started to laugh. It was the type of laugh you have when everything is released and everything is so absurd that nothing makes any sense. We were sitting beside each other on some steps in the Castro, my arm throbbing. A friend stopped and said, "Israel has just been bombed. They're wearing gas masks in Tel Aviv, Haifa, and Jerusalem." Every time I saw a child in one of those gas masks, screaming and terrified, I thought of my own child and the place that he had opened up in my heart. The only way this horror could be happening was through demonization, through making an entire race evil, an entire people not human, and thus worthy of genocide, and it seemed there was no one on the face of the earth that day who was not demonizing someone.

That Sunday, Jesse and I were watching television when Cheryl came home from bowling and told me that one of the lesbian bowling teams, whose members happened to belong to the National Guard, had been called up to do battle with Saddam Hussein. When they returned home, however—if they *did* return home—they could be discharged as unfit for service, even if they were wearing Desert Storm medals. Randy Shilts, the respected journalist (he was the author of *The Mayor of Castro Street,* a biography of Harvey Milk, and of the consummate history of the AIDS crisis, *And the Band Played On*) had broken the story that the Pentagon had instituted a "stop loss policy." Stop loss meant that even if someone "confessed" to being gay or lesbian, they would still be shipped to the Gulf, not to be discharged until they returned. For me, the most startling piece of this scenario was that the lesbian bowling team had shipped out with great pride as a point of honor.

Jesse was standing in front of the television screen, trying to determine who was the bad guy. He could not tell the difference between the American and Iraqi soldiers. He made planes out of crossed Popsicle sticks, and began "bombing" his stuffed animals. He was playing, but there was tremendous anxiety in his play. I felt a terrible sadness as I watched him, as if he were being lost to something over which I had no power.

The next evening I came home with armloads of flowers, as if the flowers themselves might help to bring back my Jesse. The house was quiet, the lights dim. Cheryl was sitting on the couch and Jesse was beside her, holding a long brown feather and watching her intently. Cheryl was just finishing sewing together two green squares of felt. She cut two slits in the side and helped Jesse to slip the feather through the notches. She had made a hat for him just like Peter Pan's.

Ceremoniously she placed the Neverland cap on his head, and he was transported. It was a stroke of brilliance on Cheryl's part: I watched Jesse's anxiety dissipate before my eyes. He looked at me and said, "Wendy. Do you want to fly?" And so for the duration of the war, Jesse spent much of his time as Peter Pan. He decided that I was Wendy; Cheryl, of course, was Tiger Lily.

❖

Our motion to compel the home visit was granted, and the Department of Social Services was ordered to comply by February 4. Every day, I waited for word of the home visit. Every day, there was only silence. The deadline came and went, but the department never responded. I was beginning to hate its power over me. Abby advised patience, but I imagined right-wing plots, which is easy to do when you start paying attention to each and every attack.

The bomb threats were now almost routine at Queer Nation meetings, but instead of being frightened away, I became more dedicated to attending the meetings. Yet never did I identify myself as a member of Queer Nation. There were no actions that I really wanted to participate in, but I seemed to be waiting for something, and I had no intention of leaving regardless of what the mainstream gay community believed. At this point, ACT UP and Queer Nation were being held responsible for all of the destruction during the antiwar demonstrations, all humans in black leather jackets now being assumed to belong to one of the two groups. My reasonable friends with reasonable jobs and something to lose warned me that my reputation might well be destroyed if I continued to associate with the "brats," but I was convinced that these were the community's metaphorical children and that although they were often naughty, they were still ours. And then there was my own little problem: a level of rage building in me, around the adoption, that would be appropriate nowhere else. If I were a stepparent, I could simply fill out a form, pay my three hundred dollars, and be sent the official notification that the adoption had been granted. I was playing by "their" rules, exposing intimate details of my life, inviting "them" to come into my home and examine me. I was doing everything I was supposed to do, but there was no phone call. As my anger drew me closer to the Queer Nationals, it created a wall between Cheryl and me, because anger never nurtures lovers. There was even something I can only describe as an invisible, ghostlike barrier between Jesse and me, a barrier that I could not see, but that I suspected had always been there.

# CHAPTER V

# *Love Demands Everything*

GILBERT BAKER, aka Pink Jesus, had attired himself in jeans and a Rolling Stones tour T-shirt. In the basement storage bins in City Hall—or Silly Hall, as Harvey Milk had liked to call it—I helped Gilbert rummage for some banners in red, orange, and pink, which he had originally made for the inauguration of Mayor Art Agnos. This Valentine's Day would be the first day of official domestic partnership, when any committed couple, regardless of sexual preference, could be legally recognized by the City of San Francisco. It was the first time in the country that such a law had been passed by voter approval.

I hated it. As the law was written, there were absolutely no tangible benefits to legally registering. You got a piece of paper that said you were responsible for each other's living expenses, and that was it. Domestic partnership held no legal weight whatsoever in terms of health insurance, child custody, inheritance, or taxes. I thought it was a marriage sham for the untouchables.

The international press and an army of television cameras and photographers prowled City Hall, anxious to find lesbian and gay couples willing to be photographed. They would not have long to wait. All day, hundreds of couples registered. Ironically, stationed here and there on the galleries in City Hall, framed by blue-and-gold-burnished ironwork, were clusters of heterosexuals enacting real marriages. I had not realized that Valentine's Day marriages in City Hall were such a long-standing tradition. I had always looked the other way. Why would lesbian and gay people bother going through with what to me was a charade, especially when it was juxtaposed with these happy, heterosexual couples right in our faces, kissing to applause and blessed by the state.

I began to videotape. With the camera on my shoulder, the images were transmuted into black-and-white, which gave them that comfortable distance and gave me the feeling of being a faux journalist. I stood at the balcony of the second-floor gallery outside the mayor's office. The square rotunda rises four stories, with galleries on each floor. As I scanned the heterosexual couples in the process of taking their marriage vows, my camera caught on the image of Jean Harris, every salt-and-pepper hair in place, forty-seven years old, strong and athletic-looking. She stood directly across from me on the other side of the rotunda, in the shadow just outside the massive carved oak doors to the chambers of the Board of Supervisors. She walked to the top of the thirty-six sweeping marble steps that fan down to the first floor.

Jean was surveying the preparations for the domestic partners' celebration. Chairs were being placed at the base of the steps, flowers were being arranged, a sound system was being set up, and Gilbert was finishing hanging the banners. Jean scanned the rotunda, and her eyes went to the massive dome, which is over a hundred feet wide and weighs ninety thousand tons. When Harvey Milk and George Moscone were assassinated, Gilbert designed a poster of the exterior of City Hall, the spectacular dome lifted from its base at a ninety-degree angle, a wide shaft of light thrusting from inside the building into the sky.

Jean Harris seemed to be watching the light as it filtered through multipaned windows at the dome's base and flickered across the surfaces of the ornate scrolls, carved heads, and a rather remarkable amount of sculpted fruit. Harvey Milk had loved this building, and he had always encouraged us to take the main staircase.

Jean Harris was working at the time as an aide to Supervisor

Harry Britt. Jean Harris can easily be mistaken for a man, which is part of her charm. She is the only complete cross-dresser in the history of City Hall, and I have actually heard her say that heterosexuality is a learned response. It is hard to know if she really believes this or has simply learned the power of hyperbole. Her enemies call her the lesbian Al Sharpton; her friends, the lesbian Harvey Milk. I had sat with her in her City Hall office, the room where Harvey Milk had been murdered. It was his assassin's old office. Dan White had called Harvey into the room to kill him. The last thing Harvey saw was the Opera House across the avenue. There was no plaque, there was nothing to tell you that in that little room the course of history had been changed. I found myself looking for some sign of the brutal assassination—some mark on the rug, on the wall—but the decorators had covered up everything. I could, however, feel something in that room, but it might quite simply have been Jean Harris's rage.

"I wear a necktie because I want every man who sees me to know I got the necktie on, I'm after their power, I want their money, and I want their women. Okay? And I will wear the necktie and wave it in their face," she said. "When I enter their offices, I'm not some girl coming in with sensible pumps on and a nice little dress to be a nice, sweet lady, and just sit down and try to get the boys to be nice to me. They know right up front, I'm a dyke, I'm tough, I'm here, I want to know exactly what's going on, and if you've got the power, I'm gonna try and take it from you."

As a child, she was a ringleader, and her favorite game was "Ditchum." There would be two gangs, and one gang would go off and try to ditch the other gang. The goal was to capture every member of the gang that was trying to ditch you. A game of Ditchum lasted for hours. Jean Harris was still playing this game. Her expertise and tenacity would help to topple the sitting mayor of San Francisco, who did not understand just who Jean was.

In one of the candlelight vigils for Harvey Milk, Jean had been marching, holding her candle. She said, "I was cussing Harvey Milk out: 'I don't have a lesbian leader. Tell me what I'm supposed to be doing.' And I swear he was flying around overhead

as we were walking, and he said, 'No one's going to do it for you, Jean. Get into it yourself. Do it. You do it. You have to do it.' "
A spiritual giant or séance fanatic Jean Harris was not, but she began to obsessively watch *The Life and Times of Harvey Milk*, the Academy Award–winning documentary about Harvey's life. She had been, in essence, born again queerly. Perhaps my favorite moment with Jean was when she shouted into a microphone at the Harvey Milk Democratic Club, of which she was then president, "We're a kinder, gentler people, goddamnit."

I watched from the balcony as Jean leaned against the burnished gold ironwork of the balusters at the top of the marble staircase, her white shirtsleeves rolled up, a tie askew around her neck. Her legs rested against the gold carving of a roaring lion's head, trapped in the metalwork like the beings in the castle of Cocteau's Beast. She was looking at the marriage ceremonies, and then at nothing but the base of the staircase where Harvey Milk's body had lain in state beside George Moscone's, his mahogany casket strewn with white chrysanthemums and red roses.

Harry Britt walked out to the steps behind Jean, said nothing, and returned to his office, which was across the narrow hallway from hers. It was Harvey's old office. Harry had been there for twelve years; he had been appointed by then mayor Dianne Feinstein. Harry likened Feinstein to the queen of England after World War II, wanting only to do the right thing after the assassinations. Despite the fact that Feinstein and Milk were usually at odds politically, she a classic moderate and he a progressive, she wanted to appoint someone as politically close to Harvey as possible, someone who would carry on Harvey's work—even if that person opposed her policies—so that Dan White's bullets would not have won. Dianne Feinstein had been the president of the Board of Supervisors at the time of the killings, sitting, in fact, in her office beside Milk's (and across from Dan White's) when the five slow shots were fired into him. Her great dignity, strength, and sensitivity at the time of the assassinations held the city together and warded off a chaos of emotion and destruction.

In the tape-recording to be played only in the event of his assassination, Harvey Milk named Harry Britt among those he felt would be acceptable successors to his seat. In accordance with Milk's wishes, Dianne Feinstein appointed Britt. Harvey Milk had thought it would be George Moscone who listened to that tape; he never dreamed that the mayor would be killed along with him.

Harry Britt grew up in Port Arthur, Texas, where his principal role model was Liberace. He was a Methodist, and as a precocious fourteen-year-old he taught the summer vacation Bible school. There was a little girl in his class, seven or eight years old, a visiting Baptist. She was very naughty, and Harry considered her a discipline problem. She grew up to be Janis Joplin. They were probably the two most alienated children in Port Arthur.

The walls of Harry's office were covered with photographs of the first memorial march, of Harvey, of movie stars like Jane Fonda who had lent their star power to fund-raising for gay politicians in the days before all of their energies were recruited for AIDS fund-raising. The day after Harvey was elected, at seven-thirty in the morning, he told Harry that he expected to be killed. "This is the moment in his life of greatest triumph and fulfillment," Harry told me, "and he's thinking about getting killed. It shows you how close he lived to death and anti-gay hatred, and how distrustful he was, and at the very time he's telling gay people with every breath of his life to get involved in mainstream politics, he also understood—like a general sending his troops into war—that they may get killed."

Harry Britt had a deep disregard for those gay people who were "very skilled at ingratiating themselves to the masters." He called them "house faggots" and he felt that many straight liberal politicians kept them around when they wanted to be reassured that going the extra round for gay rights was not wise or possible until after the next election. To Harry Britt, Mayor Art Agnos fell into this category of straights.

It had taken twelve years for Harry to pass the domestic partnership ordinance, which Mayor Agnos did sign. Harry claimed that the mayor had not wanted to sign it if it allowed for nonresidents to register their relationships. The city attorney's office was worried about "lavender chapels" and yet another string of trivializing jokes on the late-night talk shows. Harry accommodated this concern, yet left a loophole. Out-of-towners, and city residents who did not wish to appear on an official list, could get the forms and have them privately notarized. For twelve years, Harry Britt had fought for domestic partnership legislation. He was not interested in marriage for himself, but he knew that there had to be a way legally to prove that we existed, and he vowed to remain in office until that legislation was enacted. For twelve years, he had watched Valentine's Day come and go, and he was finally victorious. Twelve years of hate mail. Twelve years of death threats. Twelve years of pondering, What would Harvey think? At fifty-two years old, Harry might now find it possible to achieve, with a clear conscience, his wish for anonymous retirement.

When Jean and Harry decided to hold the Valentine's Day celebration in City Hall, it was suggested by the registrar that because of the traditional heterosexual marriages that would be taking place, there would not be enough personnel available to process the forms of the homosexuals and others wishing to become domestic partners. It was suggested that perhaps we should wait for another day, perhaps the day before Valentine's Day. Or the day after. Valentine's Day had already been taken.

Obviously, these people did not know with whom they were dealing. Jean Harris and her protégé, Kurt Barrie, were adamant about our right to Valentine's Day, and they arranged for volunteers, identifiable by rainbow armbands, to work in the registrar's office.

I stood across the street from City Hall and videotaped the affirmation of partnership ceremony taking place on the steps between Doric pillars flanked on either side by colonnades. I happened to be among some straight men who appeared to be homeless as well as alcoholic. They were incensed, infuriated by queers getting married in a public ceremony. One man was particularly angry about a sign that a gay man was holding on the steps. The sign read GOD IS GAY.

"I'm gonna do somethin' about that," he said. His buddies agreed, and I followed them closer to the festivities, watching them through the video lens. The nature of the festivities stopped them, however. It was an interfaith service sponsored by the

Lutheran Lesbian and Gay Ministry. Among those listening carefully to the minister's words were a lesbian couple with their two-week-old baby. I was filming them as a carload of adolescent boys and girls drove by behind them, shouting obscenities. They were oblivious to the shouts, listening instead to the Song of Solomon.

Jean Harris appeared on the steps in a black tuxedo. She looked transported, oblivious to anything but the ceremony as she sang along to Cris Williamson's "Song of the Soul."

> Open mine eyes that I may see
> Glimpses of truth thou hast for me
> Open mine eyes, illumine me
> Spirit Divine

I was now on the top of the steps, filming the crowd. They were holding flowers, and twenty feet behind them another truckload passed by, this time packed with white males in their thirties. They slowed down to shout, "Faggots! Dykes!"

Jean Harris looked right at the truck as it raced away, but she did not seem to see it—no one did—and they continued to sing, joyful and wondrously oblivious to the catcalls, shouts, and gestures.

> "Love of my life," I am crying
> I am not dying, I am dancing;
> Dancing along in the madness
> There is no sadness,
> Only a Song of the Soul.

As the song ended, we were asked to link arms for a prayer. I stopped filming and happened to link arms with the man carrying the GOD IS GAY sign. As I looked up and across the crowd, I caught the eye of the man who was "gonna do somethin' " about this. He was seething, and here I was, arm in arm with his target. I was very happy he did not have a gun.

Jean's right, I thought. We're a kinder, gentler people, goddamnit.

\* \* \*

I followed a lesbian couple through the process of registering; as they finished, they were exiting the registrar's office, arm-in-arm. They had to pass by three men in their late twenties, street people, who had draped themselves around the perimeter of the exit doors for the sole purpose of snickering at the couples and gesturing at their backs as they passed into the rotunda. Again, the lesbian couple did not see or hear the hecklers. Was it that I was watching everything through the lens of the video camera, and so saw things that I would normally miss? I was beginning to think that a very powerful fairy had sprinkled some sort of magical dust throughout this magnificent building, and that it was protecting our people.

I followed the lesbian couple to the chambers of the Board of Supervisors at the top of the grand staircase on the second-floor gallery. The chambers are a jewel of carved oak; happy couples were seated on the benches, waiting attentively. Their arms were linked, and they appeared nervous and excited. They were of every ethnicity, shape, and age. They were so vulnerable, and I could still not understand why they were doing this. It was just symbolic, which to me was worse than nothing.

I returned to the second-floor gallery outside the mayor's office and focused my camera on the staircase. Gilbert was beside me; he gained the distinction of being the only one in a red ball gown. We stood on either side of a spotlight, which Gilbert carefully focused at the top of the stairs where each couple would stand in the pool of light.

Jean stepped to the microphone at the bottom of the staircase and, as she announced that "Harvey Milk is flying around in this rotunda right now," the doors to the chambers opened. The couples emerged and formed a line as a string-and-keyboard ensemble began to play "The Shadow of Your Smile." Just like a real wedding, I thought, down to the bad music. As they descended the stairs, Kurt and Jean took turns announcing the couples' names.

"Tom Ammiano and Tim Curbo." Tom, the vice president of the school board, and his partner of fourteen years, who was also a schoolteacher, descended the staircase. The cheers from the hundreds gathered at the bottom of the steps to witness the celebration echoed throughout the building. Down they came, the variety of human beings unbelievable, dressed in tuxedoes, dresses, leather, ACT UP and Queer Nation outfits.

I saw Jonathan standing at the foot of the steps, his arms crossed against his gym-toned chest, the words QUEER NATION emblazoned across his shirt. Along with other members of Queer Nation, he had walked dozens of precincts—including those traditionally ignored as being too conservative—on behalf of Proposition K, the domestic partnership ordinance. As the procession of couples continued, I realized that on some level it was like the fashion show in the mall, yet the fashion show never conjured anything like the massive wave of emotion that was building in me as the couples descended the stairs.

One man walked by himself down the thirty-six steps. His lover was dying of AIDS in the hospital, so he was taking the walk for them both. There were six straight couples, and one of these couples made the walk with their nine-year-old daughter. Two bleached-blond boys took the walk hand in hand, each wearing a T-shirt with the words MR. RIGHT. Another male couple descended slowly, arm in arm, one of the men appearing weak as he leaned heavily upon his cane. The applause washed over them, and the dying man smiled with such burning happiness that I was sure he felt no pain.

Two old fellows in their sixties, with rumpled baggy pants and John Deere hats, walked carefully down the stairs, their work-battered hands entwined, their eyes on their feet. They looked like they had just come off the farm. I looked beside me at Gilbert, who was now dramatically dabbing at his eyes with a white handkerchief.

"What's the matter?" I asked.

"Wedding," he said, dabbing away, and although he was camping it up, there were real tears in his eyes. Gilbert liked to pretend that he was solely a political cartoon, above the emotional fray, but that was a lie. I saw it time after time. What was true was what was happening inside City Hall, and the only reminder of the world outside was the words Gilbert had scrawled across a large paper heart that he had pinned to his faux cleavage: "This war is breaking my heart."

The names of the couples continued to reverberate as they descended the marble staircase, which had graced the presentations of kings, queens, and heads of state.

"Simone Dorman, Anne Dorman, and daughter Elizabeth Simone Dorman."

The family stood at the top of the staircase as their names were read. Anne Dorman held their blond three-year-old daughter in one arm, and as they walked down the steps, I was beginning to understand why these families were doing this. At the bottom of the steps, in the quivering light flashes of cameras, Anne took Simone's hand and kissed it. My eyes filled with tears.

"Gail Brown, Lucinda Young, and their daughter, Mara Young." Mara was a teenager. It is difficult for a teenager to be different from her peers in any way, yet she had walked down the stairs with her two mothers.

"Lori Feldman, Marcia Baum, and Baby Maya." Maya was less than two weeks old. The applause and love washed over them as they very carefully made their way down the stairs, and I realized that I was crying. These were not people used to grand entrances, photographic flashes, televisions, and a crush of press. Yet these were people willing to perform this very public act, which had absolutely no material or practical gain attached to it, in order to affirm their love.

Most of the people who descended those steps never have gone and never will go into the streets. They never have used and never will use the word "queer," or confront the Traditional Values Coalition or a President Bush who called them immoral and unfit to parent. They are our silent majority, and it was only in this way, only to express their love for each other, that they would perform such a public act.

As the last couple descended the steps, Harry Britt stood at the podium, flushed with emotion. "The voters of this city overwhelmingly acknowledged the right of lesbians and gay couples to come out of the shadows and to become publicly recognized as loving, caring, and committed people. What you have done by bringing your love to this place, and walking down these steps together, is truly an important moment in the life of the American family."

Then lesbian and gay leaders took the stage: Supervisor

Roberta Achtenberg, Tom Ammiano, Supervisor Carole Migden. Tom Ammiano announced, "I particularly liked the straight couples that came today. I approve of mixed marriages." Congratulating the community, and also taking the stage, were Supervisors Kevin Shelley and Angela Alioto, both the children of former mayors of San Francisco.

Jean returned to the microphone, dashing in her tuxedo, and introduced Judge Donna Hitchens as if she were the lesbian Socrates.

"I'm now gonna have her come up," said Jean, "and do whatever judges do at these kind of things. So welcome her: Judge Donna Hitchens."

We loved Donna Hitchens, and she could not stop the applause. She could only step from behind the podium briefly and applaud us. Donna Hitchens is a rare public figure, a source of wisdom and unconditional love.

"This isn't quite the intimate wedding our parents planned for us," she said, "but it is truly a joyous occasion. As I watched people come down the steps, there were tears. . . . Today, you signed a declaration that you share an intimate, committed relationship of mutual caring. Today is a day of public celebration of those relationships, and of your personal relationship. It is a day when most of you did not make your first commitments, but have recommitted to that relationship you have shared with each other over the last five, ten, fifteen, thirty, thirty-five years. So I'm here to wish you the best from the city and county of San Francisco, but to also say, May your closeness not diminish, but strengthen your individuality and your wisdom, the gift that you bring to others. Many poets have said that love asks nothing, but I submit to you today that love demands everything."

I bought carnations, roses, and candy, and threw my anger and cynicism in the car trunk for the night. I went home and handed the flowers to Cheryl. She held them in her arms, but she did not move.

"Why are you so far away from me?" she asked.

I told her I didn't know, but that I loved her and needed her to trust me, to know that I would always love her, but that right now, this was the best I could do. The adoption proceedings were cornering me emotionally.

"You're his mom," she said. "Don't you know that? Why do you care what they think?"

"I do."

"I don't understand," she said, but she put her arms around me anyway.

Our child's whisper reached us from the floor near our feet.

"I drank the poison."

Jesse was sprawled upon the rug, arms outstretched, eyes closed.

"What's he doing?" I asked, somewhat alarmed.

"Dying," she said, in a matter-of-fact voice. "He's been doing it all night."

"The poison, I drank the poison," Jesse whispered, pretending to swoon.

"He just watched Mary Martin's *Peter Pan*," said Cheryl. "Captain Hook puts the poison in Peter's milk, but Tinker Bell drinks it and begins to die."

I picked Jesse up, the imaginary poison pulling the life out of him as he sprawled Pietà-style in my arms. This guy is *dramatic*.

"I *do* believe in fairies. I *do* believe in fairies," I repeated again and again, as Cheryl clapped her hands and Jesse miraculously came back to life.

That was my first good night's sleep since the adoption process had begun. That day had been like no other. San Francisco's City Hall is a building filled with magic and history, built on top of a cemetery and fashioned after the Invalides in Paris, which houses the tomb of Napoleon. Given the power of certain places, given the obliviousness of the lovers and families to the taunts and ridicule of the ignorant on Valentine's Day, 1991, I cannot say with absolute certainty that Harvey Milk's ghost was *not* flying around in that rotunda.

# CHAPTER VI

# An Accidental Radical

THE LOS ANGELES case of Michele G. was made public.
She was the nonbiological mother of two children she had co-
parented with her partner. The two women had been together
since 1969. After many years, the relationship broke up, and
later, Michele G.'s partner, Nancy S., refused visitation rights to
Michele G. The court upheld Nancy S.'s claim that there was no
legitimate connection between Michele G. and the two children
who called her mother. The court declared Michele G. a "biological stranger." Bizarrely, the court stated that she should have
attempted adoption, despite the fact that the policy of the State
of California was to automatically deny such an adoption.

Abby Abinanti discovered that the attorney general's office
had never forwarded our order to compel the home visit to the
Department of Social Services, and the social worker assigned to
our case would be leaving for four to six weeks on a medical
leave. I could probably expect to hear from her by mid-May.
Again, my mind began to race. This adoption proceeding was
taking far longer than anyone had predicted. I knew that the
Traditional Values Coalition was all over Sacramento, fighting
the lesbian and gay civil rights bill, AB-101. Would mine be the
case that the attorney general would attack? Would the judge
who decided my case know nothing of lesbians besides what he'd

seen in the movies or read in a 1950s textbook on aberrant, pathological personalities?

I became fearful that the adoption would not go through, and although I did nothing to reveal it to him, it was as if Jesse knew somewhere inside his heart that something had happened. That week, I experienced what seemed a new level of love from him. He looked squarely into my eyes, and he seemed so self-assured, so solid, so certain of who he was. I remembered that moment at his welcoming ceremony when he was four days old. He had grasped the white carnation as if to acknowledge me before sinking back to the world of the newborn. He had made me his at that moment, and he had known who I was. I saw again in his face that same expression, which now seemed sympathetic. The problem was never with him. It was always with me. When I dropped Jesse off at school that week, he put one arm around my neck and his hand on my cheek. "Bye-bye, pretty head," he said. Children always think those who love them are beautiful.

❖

They looked very young to me, in their late teens and twenties, but I'm sure they felt quite old and that, at forty, I must have looked ancient. I watched them come to the Women's Building in San Francisco, to the land of inverted lotus eaters, from the most unlikely places as representatives of Queer Nation chapters. What had begun as a phenomenon of New York, San Francisco, and Boston, was now a truly national grass-roots media extravaganza. I was witnessing the surge of a great energy, and there could be no turning back. The genie was out of the bottle, she had no concept of compromise, and she never dressed down.

We heard from Shreveport, Louisiana, that they had held a Queer Pow Wow, and that New Orleans planned Queer Nights Out, plus their own shopping expedition. You could almost have expected chapters to crop up in Chicago and Boulder, Houston and Detroit, Cleveland and Atlanta. But Lincoln, Albuquerque, Tallahassee, and Salt Lake City?

Who were the Queer Nationals, and why did they make so many people so mad? I found a clue in Hook's question to Peter during their duel to the death: "Pan, who and what art thou?"

"I'm youth, I'm joy," says Peter. "I'm a little bird that has broken out of the egg." Sir James tells us that Peter's answer is of course nonsense, that Hook knows this, and that it is, in fact, proof to Hook that Peter has no idea who or what he is, "which is the pinnacle of good form."

If you tried to get someone to define "queer," the answers were as paradoxical as those descriptions and philosophical stances regularly attributed to Harvey Milk. If everyone I spoke to was telling the truth, Harvey Milk was an autocratic capitalist businessman, a socialist democrat, a Republican stockbroker, and an off-Broadway hippie producer. Now certainly our academics will create a massive body of critical thinking on Queer Ethics, identity politics, and the New Gay Order, as *The Village Voice* has described it, but I'm not sure that anyone will be able to say what in the world "queer" means. For me, it was simple. I remember my grandmother sitting on her flowered couch in Somerville, Massachusetts, blowing a smoke ring into the air and commenting with her musical brogue on the quality of a thought or event. "Isn't that queer?" Nana would say. By the way she tilted her head and looked through the window at the sky, she made the word beautiful, and the child that I was thought queer to certainly be something magical and mind-stopping.

Week after week, I attended the Queer Nation meetings, saying little, enjoying every moment. I felt like a doting aunt, filled with unconditional love, ignoring the fact that some of the kiddies were tying firecrackers to the kitty-cat's tail. Marty Mulkey was still disdainful about the apparent thrust of Queer Nation energy toward "getting queers in toothpaste ads," but I was old enough to remember when the first African-Americans brushed their teeth with Crest on American televisions, an event that had been debated with an intensity equal to the decision whether or not to blockade Cuba during the missile crisis.

Even the most militant advocates of civil disobedience had to smile at Judy Helfand's Arboretum Stroll in Golden Gate Park for which you were encouraged to "dress identifiably queer," and the notable Fabulous on the Ferry adventure of the bisexual focus group UBIQUITOUS (Uppity Bi Queers United in Their Overtly Unconventional Sexuality). Led by the performance artist Christine Carraher, UBIQUITOUS tour guide in full Cracker Jacks sailor outfit, they took the ferry to Sausalito, an upscale Marin tourist haven across San Francisco Bay. The kiss-in included demonstrations by opposite sexes, a first for Queer Nation.

Jeff Brooks, his mother Olive safely home in Indianapolis, organized an AIDS awareness event, Queer Nation–style: an inventive game-show parody, the *HIV Queel of Fortune,* which featured the "Daily Demo" instead of the "Daily Double." Irene Dick, an avid bicyclist, veteran of the SHOP action, and founder of a focus group for Queer Dungeons & Dragons players, was the evening's lovely Vanna White clone. Irene wore a tasteful garden-party dress with a poufed debutante skirt for the event. She also wore beige hose and tasteful pumps. Anything for AIDS awareness. Irene stood sideways in front of an enormous wheel and spun her arm as if it were a huge rotating pointer. As her arm moved, the crowd of several hundred shouted in unison, "Queel . . . of . . . Fortune!" Irene pointed at a category, and Jeff quizzed the panelists on their AIDS awareness. The questions included those concerning high-risk behaviors, which all involved not using a condom. If you got four questions wrong, Jeff pointed at you and said, "Sorry. You're dead."

John Woods was busy organizing QUEER SCOUTS (Queers Undertaking Education Enlightenment and Recruitment of Special Children Overlooked Under the System), and LABIA, led by its journalist cofounder Rachel Pepper, was romping through straight bars on Friday evenings. HI MOM (Homosexual Ideological Mobilization Against the Oppressive Military) was encouraging queers to form long, mediagenic lines in front of military recruitment centers, and so forcing the recruiters to fill out the lengthy application forms. Not only did this take up the recruiters' valuable time, but it was an ideal media event: Each recruit applicant identified himself at the end of the process as homosexual, and so was rejected.

With rhinestones glued to his Mickey Mouse hat, splashiest of all was Ggreg Taylor, who organized a "Lavender Tortoise" bus trip to Disneyland. The son of a double-A alcohol drag racer, Ggreg was never a motor head but always a trophy girl at the racetrack. The Lavender Tortoise excursion, an absolutely nonviolent group except in terms of makeup selection, was greeted at the Disneyland monorail by a golf cart crammed with men in blue suits accessorized with earphones and dark glasses. The monorail driver told Ggreg that there were two hundred security guards behind the scenes, apparently braced for a massive, confrontational gay rights demonstration. As Ggreg well knew, 750,000 lesbians and gays can march on Washington and get a back-page one-paragraph filler article in the national press, but if thirty-five drag queens get in a bus and drive to Disneyland to go on the rides, or to Jesse Helms's house to deliver a fruit basket, people notice.

I returned home from one of the Queer Nation meetings, quite happy and enthusiastic about what was now my main source of entertainment, distraction, and peace. Cheryl was sitting on the couch in the living room, her arms crossed. The lights were too bright, and I was surprised that she was still awake.

"What are you up to?" she demanded.

I was completely thrown by her anger.

"I went to a meeting," I said.

"That's all you do. You go to meetings. You never take me out anywhere. You come home when I'm asleep. You're like a man whose career is more important than his family."

"That is absolutely untrue." I dismissed her, and headed for the kitchen. It infuriated me that she compared me to a man. If I were a man, we wouldn't be having these problems.

"You don't spend enough time with Jesse, either," she said. "This has been going on for too long."

"Don't be ridiculous," I said, but she played her high card and said, "I don't want you to adopt Jesse."

I became furious, full of panic.

"What are you talking about?"

"I know what you're doing," she said.

"I went to a meeting. I knew you'd do this. Biological-mother chauvinism. You all do it."

"Don't analyze me."

"Why are you so angry?" I demanded.

"You're angry all the time," she said. "The only reason you want to adopt Jesse is so that you can leave me and go have your exciting life and still have rights to him." Her eyes filled with tears and she began to cry.

"That's not true!" I said, and it wasn't, but what was true was that we were both becoming paranoid from the stress of the adoption process. She experienced me as tossing her emotional crumbs, and I was resentful and jealous of her legal status with Jesse.

"I'm sorry I said that," she said. "You can adopt him, even if you are going to leave me."

"I'm not going to leave you," I insisted.

"I think you already have," she said, angry again. On one level, it was true. It was how I dealt with this feeling of being an impostor, not a real mother, not a real family, just a biological stranger.

"You don't understand what I'm feeling," I said.

"No, I don't. There's nothing I can do to make it better. Are you seeing someone else?"

"No. I've never done that. In fact, I've never felt more alone in my life."

"I'm here for you, but you choose over and over again to be somewhere else," she said, her anger rising.

"Then don't threaten me with Jesse," I said.

"I'm sorry. I just don't understand."

"I know."

"You're not planning on leaving?"

"Not at all."

"It's the adoption?"

"Yes, Cheryl."

We were quiet.

"I do love you," she said. "I want our family to stay together." We held each other, and I told her I loved her, but my mind was stuck on those two words: biological stranger.

❖

However diverse Queer Nation's focus groups were, however varied their dress and political agendas, everyone, myself included, was about to be forged together into one consciousness that would feature orchestrated rage, and a queer musical rendition of *West Side Story* in the arrest holding pens in the basement of the Hall of Justice.

On the Queer Nation information table on the evening of April 10, 1991, there was a green Day-Glo flyer announcing, "Queer Psycho Killers Strike Again!" Apparently, a movie entitled *Basic Instinct,* about to be shot in the city, featured deranged bisexual women and lesbians. I was certain that it was some two-bit pornographic film company trying to make a quick buck. LABIA decided to have an early-morning informational picket at the Rawhide II bar, where the film was shooting the next morning.

Pam Bates, a plumber by trade and a veteran of the women's movement, organized the demonstration. Pam, a handful of other women, and a few men arrived at the Rawhide early the next morning, the typical April gray sky slit with light battling its way out, as if God were shouting, "Roll 'em!" but no one was quite listening, since it was San Francisco and the cappuccino machines were just heating up.

Pam and her friends sipped coffee from foam cups, and when people stopped to inquire about the action, she said, "Oh, they're making a homosexual movie in there and it has lesbians and bi-women as the bad guys, once again." That was about it. Pam also chatted with a woman from the film company who approached her. The woman, who seemed extremely nervous as she scurried away from Pam, then had an animated conversation on her little portable phone. Shortly after that, the police arrived with almost thirty metal barricades for twelve practically silent protesters. The point was not to chant and shout, but to show actual lesbians, many in their work clothes for their downtown jobs. Pam smiled and waved as she watched the police, who had a certain amount of trouble putting together the barricades. She suggested that perhaps they should have a special course on barricade assembly at the police academy.

The film crew began to arrive. The police had to move the barricades to let them through. Then they moved the barricades back. Then they had to move them to let through the equipment. Had to close the barricades. Open the barricades. Move the barricades. The sound of metal scraping across the sidewalks made for an odd, contrapuntal background noise as LABIA and Queer Nation members strolled along the sidewalk, pausing now and then to carefully remove by fingertip the little stray balls of Styrofoam that always seem to float on top of one's coffee. The film crew and police worked feverishly to place barricades all the way to the end of the block. What were they expecting? Could it be that working on a movie depicting diabolical lesbians and bi-women had caused some irrational fears to sprout up among the crew?

Two more crew members, burly white males, arrived.

"Ah, for crying out loud . . . Just what we need is a bunch of queers."

"Is this some faggot group?" asked his buddy, as if the women were deaf and could not read lips.

"Are we a faggot group?" the women asked each other.

"Fag-dyke, maybe," ventured one Labian in a business suit.

The action at the Rawhide was definitely femme. No one shouted or threatened. There was not one moment of confrontation. Passersby were spoken to only if they stopped and asked what was going on, and signs were tasteful: TESTOSTERONE KILLS—NOT LESBIANS. Just as the police finally got the hang of the barricades and got themselves into position, the picketers checked their watches and headed off to work. Some went to downtown insurance offices and advertising agencies, others to community organizations that service AIDS patients, others home to cottage industries. Pam Bates, a member since 1979 of the Plumbers and Steam Fitters Local 38, strolled down to the union hall to see if there was any work.

It was a lovely day, the slits of light in the gray sky now broken open into wide bursts of sun. The police opened the barricades, the police closed the barricades. The crew talked on walkie-talkies and portable phones. They looked around the corners, looked to the tops of the surrounding buildings. They were alone, they were anxious, and they drank too much coffee, according to one of the caterers who was also a member of Queer Nation.

"The cocksuckers think we're being unfair to them," responded a Teamster working on the crew, when asked why

Queer Nation was protesting outside the bar. This was reported by the respected film critic Daniel Mangin. Their choice of "cocksucker" as a descriptive noun for the mostly female group was, as Mr. Mangin noted, ironic. Mr. Mangin also noted that virtually every positive portrayal of lesbians is censored, or de-lesbianized, by Hollywood filmmakers because test audiences don't like it unless the lesbians die in the end, which raises the test audiences' comfort level.

Supervisor Roberta Achtenberg thought it "patently absurd that they are doing this in our backyard."

Supervisor Carole Migden asked, "Why are we always cast in a perverse light?"

Supervisor Angela Alioto, a practicing heterosexual, found the comments of the film crew uncalled for, and suggested that they be "required to take sensitivity classes." Supervisor Alioto always had the most Californian solutions, but the Teamsters and the film company did not seem terribly interested in sensitivity training. What they were interested in was keeping secret the shooting schedule.

Things just didn't get off to a good start.

*Queer Week* reported "Dykes on a Rampage," and a banner headline in the gay *Bay Area Reporter* parodied the tabloids: LESBOPHOBIC PLOT THICKENS. We got two new words out of this, and hope to see them in the next *Webster's Collegiate Dictionary:* "lesbophobic" and "de-lesbianized."

Jonathan Katz would soon become the Queer Nation spokesmodel (to use Ggreg Taylor's word) in the fight against Hollywood Homophobia. Hollywood homophobia means depicting lesbians and gays as violent and perverted, and refusing to show positive images of lesbians and gay men unless they die in the end or become straight. Jonathan had been out of town delivering a paper on Jasper Johns and Robert Rauschenberg to a lesbian and gay studies conference. His paper was entitled "Culture and Subculture: On the Social Utility of Queer Artists in Cold War American Art." He had lectured at the Art Institute of Chicago, the National Museum of American Art, and Harvard. Jonathan had been awarded the first predoctoral fellowship in lesbian and gay studies given by the Smithsonian National Museum of American Art. He would soon be portrayed by media unfriendly to militant homosexuals as an ignorant, anti-art, neo-Nazi Brown-shirt and the Jesse Helms of the left. Across the back of his leather jacket he had slapped a yellow Day-Glo sign with black lettering that said MILITANT HOMOSEXUAL; this probably helped out the media effort. Jonathan was also a vegetarian opposed to killing any kind of living thing, but the media didn't report that. (In fact, when I last visited him, there were ants all over the sugar bowl, and he was carefully spooning sugar from *around* their swarming little black bodies. I marveled at this sensitivity in one so militant. That evening I mentioned this to my downstairs neighbor, Terry, who was sitting at my kitchen table watching me prepare Jesse's favorite dinner of Kraft Macaroni and Cheese Wheels. Terry smiled and said, "Wait until Jonathan's got mice all over the kitchen. Then tell me what he does.")

Back in the City of Costumes after the academic lecture circuit, Jonathan called Mark Pritchard, who had agreed to be the media contact for HASH. HASH, or "Homosexuals Against Stereotypes in Hollywood," was the new focus group of Queer Nation, formed specifically to protest the filming of *Basic Instinct*. At their first meeting, at the Café Macondo, Mark had reluctantly taken on the task of media contact, although he was already being deluged with media phone calls for the Street Patrol, the Queer Nation version of the Guardian Angels. Rather than being red like the Angels', the Street Patrol's berets were "absolutely fuchsia." Mark was a member of UBIQUITOUS, a Texan, a practicing Lutheran, and a closet fancier of Broadway musicals. One of his hobbies was keeping track of fundamentalist rising stars and recruiting events, which he enjoyed infiltrating. I remembered him as the Queer Nation spokesmodel when Larry Lea's ten thousand Prayer Warriors had come to the city on Halloween to exorcise us of our demons. This diabolical-demon thing was getting old. Mark thought the film company was doing the same thing as the Prayer Warriors: coming to San Francisco to use it as a backdrop for their fantasies, and doing so with impunity because they had money. He knew, however, that the movie would not take place inside a building like Civic Center Auditorium, with guards at the doors shouting, "No costumes!"

The point of coming to San Francisco was to exploit the exterior shots. "It's a fragile thing, a movie," said Mark, smiling.

Mark's phone number was on the Queerline as the contact for activists interested in protesting *Basic Instinct*. John Woods was busily faxing out his news releases concerning the upcoming protests, listing Mark as the contact. (John, a systems analyst–programmer by day, and our International Male Catalog Boy for the Suburban Homosexual Outreach Project, was probably the only member of Queer Nation with a bachelor's in business administration in information systems and marketing.) John did a very good job, and Mark was now swamped with media calls, with which no one else wanted to deal. When Jonathan called to ask what he could do to help, Mark crowned him media contact, and the advocate of the politics of chaos began to play with Hollywood. Jonathan knew that because his adversaries were among the most powerful names in the movie industry, this could be the World Series of Queer Nation actions.

I had been amused, feeling somewhat above the whole scene until I found out that this was not some two-bit pornographic film company. It was Mario Kassar's Carolco Pictures, and he had paid the screenwriter three million dollars, the largest sum ever paid for a screenplay in the history of the industry. The movie would be distributed by Tri-Star, the world's largest distributor. The director was being paid five million dollars, and the star of this twisted-sister concoction was Michael Douglas, who would receive fourteen million dollars to fend off diabolical lesbians and bi-women. Why was Michael Douglas, a socially conscious, Academy Award–winning producer and actor, starring in what *Newsweek* would call a "Kiss Kiss, Slash Slash" tale of the biologically strange?

GLAAD, the national Gay and Lesbian Alliance Against Defamation, was a group known for its reasonableness. Day-Glo stickers were not among their accessories. The San Francisco cochairs, Jessea Greenman and Holly Conley, had read the script and found it tremendously homophobic, but until I had personally read the words on the page, I decided to reserve judgment. I was, however, certainly getting a bit testy about the whole thing.

\* \* \*

The Gulf War was over, the Communist empire had fallen apart, and it looked as if no Democrat had even the vaguest chance of unseating President Bush who at the time had 90 percent approval ratings. In other words, there was no news. And then the Goddess visited upon the people "Queer Nation versus Hollywood," and *Entertainment Tonight* found it good. And the *Hollywood Reporter* followed. And soon, the slick magazines, television, newspapers, and radio followed, and they too found it good to multiply all the way to Dan Rather, Bryant Gumbel and the paper of record, *The New York Times*.

The last time my name had been in the news section of a newspaper was when I was ten years old in 1961 and it was announced in the weekly *Somerville Record* that I had won the Albion Street Playground's Tall Tale Contest. That actually gave me a record of more hard press coverage than most of the other Queer Nationals. I don't think that justifies categorizing me as a "media whore." It was not that Queer Nation had some brilliant, masterminding, media-savvy whiz kid behind the curtain. It was, quite simply, that if one was willing to publicly say "I am queer," and actually had the nerve to pose the question "What causes heterosexuality?" people noticed.

❖

Being the mayor of San Francisco has been described as a job similar to herding cats. Carved in marble above the dark-paneled entrance doors on the second floor of City Hall are the words THE MAYOR. On April 15, 1991, a few days after the Rawhide informational picket, I sat in a blue leather chair in the lobby of the mayor's office, waiting to interview him. Eight-armed brass chandeliers with bare light globes illumined the elegant lobby, which opens onto a balcony overlooking the Civic Center plaza. There were eight desks in this area, and at one of the desks near the back of the room, a heavyset woman was having an animated conversation, her long dark hair falling over the telephone handset. She was talking to someone who was obviously furious.

"There's nothing the mayor can do. There's nothing any city can do to stop a demonstration. . . . Why don't you meet with them? . . . You'll get backup from the police whether you've met with the group or not. As soon as any demonstrators show up, you'll have police coverage free of charge. . . . I'm not minimizing this. The mayor's hands, and my hands, are tied."

The woman hung up the phone, and it rang immediately.

"Robin Eickman," she said. I realized she was the executive director of the Film Commission, the go-between for Hollywood producers and the city.

"I told you this would happen, Alan," she said. ". . . Even if I went to him, what can he do? There's nobody here who can stop that process from happening. The mayor cannot stop people from exercising their civil rights."

There was no doubt she was talking about *Basic Instinct* and the LABIA/Queer Nation action at the Rawhide. Now, wearing a tasteful, ladylike ensemble from Saks Fifth Avenue, I looked quite different than I had when I attended Queer Nation meetings in my black leather jacket, so I suppose I sufficiently blended in with the dark woodwork and blue carpeting.

"Look," said Eickman, "have there been any death threats? . . . Then I cannot get you round-the-clock police. If there are any death threats, let me know."

I was stunned. Pam Bates and Judy Helfand were not in the business of issuing death threats. Not even Jonathan would go that far. He wouldn't even kill his ants. It was true that Jean Harris had once given Ggreg Taylor and his friends a carton of raw eggs to throw at a tour bus that was slowly rolling through the Castro, its occupants madly snapping pictures of the hand-holding lesbians and gay men. But death threats? It really wasn't a community tradition.

The mayor appeared and escorted me into his office, all Persian rug, polished wood, flags, and a prominently displayed oil painting of fruit. Embroidered in black onto the breast pocket of his white shirt was the image of San Francisco's City Hall. The man was utterly charming. He opened a drawer and showed me his childhood baseball mitt, and there was a San Francisco Giants baseball on the mantel. Also displayed on the mantel was the musketlike pistol that his grandfather used as a Greek revolutionary, and a very old lantern that ran on olive oil. His parents had used it when they first came to this country. In a glass cabinet were hat blocks. Agnos's father had made a living blocking men's hats and shining their shoes.

"This is the only baseball glove I've ever had in my life," said the mayor, giving it a few good hits.

"But I bet it's nice and broken in," I responded.

He smiled and settled down into a chair beside me, choosing not to isolate himself behind the massive wood desk. He reminded me of a very aggressive, competitive boy who had been highly disciplined and taught impeccable manners. He was extremely bright, and extremely careful of each word he said to me.

"I never dreamed—I still can't believe—I'm the mayor," he said. "I walk into this fancy office and say, 'Holy cow.' "

And it *was* startling that he had become the mayor of San Francisco. Art Agnos did not even speak English when his father brought him to grammar school.

There were those who claimed his support for gay rights was based on political expediency, and there were lesbians and gays who counted him among their closest friends. For whatever reasons, the mayor had been a long-time supporter of gay rights, believing homosexuality to be an innate quality, or as he referred to it, "biological instincts."

"Now, there is no scientific evidence for that," he said, "and the reason for that, in my view, is that society is afraid to find out. Just imagine what it would mean if suddenly there was scientific, irrefutable evidence that gay and lesbian people are born that way, not manipulated that way by the traditional stereotypic kinds of definitions that 'make people that way.' The domineering mother, the weak father, and all that baloney. I don't believe it. I think the fundamental issue is that gay people were made that way by whoever makes us, and whatever your God is.

"I believe that one of my boys, or both, could wind up being gay when they reach that point when they are aware of their feelings. They may already be. Who knows? It is a natural, God-given, or nature-given, biological instinct. And so, I want to create a world, like every parent, where my children will have a happy, well-adjusted, successful life, and part of that is creating an environment where they're not going to be discriminated against because of their sexual orientation."

How could this be Jean Harris's homophobe? Harry Britt's plantation owner? I thought I'd test a button, and I questioned him about his stormy relationship with Queer Nation, and told him that many of the Queer Nationals were not the horrid monster brats they were being portrayed as. He studied me carefully. He was very angry that some Queer Nationals had redecorated his house one night in pink toilet paper, and had drawn explicit sexual chalk drawings on the driveway, under which they had chalked the words QUEER REFUGE. The media, and the mayor's press secretary, at first thought the action had been done by homophobic right-wing elements, the type of people who had commonly attacked Agnos's home in Sacramento whenever he tried to push through gay rights legislation in the Assembly. He was most upset about his two young sons. It was difficult to explain to them why gay people were turning on him. The mayor also wanted no more talk of sanctuaries and refuges for a while because he wanted to downplay the city's reputation as anti-war—any war, anywhere. San Francisco, under the auspices of Harry Britt, had recently declared itself a refuge for conscientious objectors to the Gulf War. No politician aspiring to statewide or national office wanted to so much as seem opposed to that war. And the jokes had started. The "Bored" of Supervisors was depicted in cartoons as a pack of monkeys declaring "sanctuary for people who hate their parents, and sanctuary for anorexic overeaters . . ." The Chamber of Commerce was complaining that conventions were being canceled because of the refuge declaration, and the mayor went on record as being opposed to yet another declaration of sanctuary, which he thought frivolous. This had infuriated some activists.

The action at the mayor's house was not a unanimously agreed-upon (thus, "official") Queer Nation action. The idea took shape spontaneously among a few people at the end of a meeting the previous month. When the press found out it was an action by a rogue element of Queer Nation, they compared it to the Nazi burning of the Reichstag, an analogy a bit extreme for pink toilet-paper streamers.

"Well, as it was introduced and brought to my attention," said the mayor, "they said that they wanted a sanctuary for gay and lesbian people in the city, and to have signs put at the city limits that would indicate that. I thought that this was a frivolous kind of act in the face of all of the work that I know needs to be done to advance the gay empowerment movement and to produce tangible results like domestic partners, like a family policy, like parental rights.

"I thought that a symbolic resolution on gay refuge diverted energy. We already are a sanctuary for gays. Does anybody have any doubt? I mean, that went on the books. I think this was a political exercise for Queer Nation because it was sexy and fun, and quite frankly, sometimes these groups divert a lot of positive, productive energy for issues that really have no input, and no output. What does it mean? Who's ever going to extradite someone from San Francisco? It will become Johnny Carson's latest joke, David Letterman's latest joke. And frankly I love this community and I have worked so hard with this community for the reasons we talked about earlier, that I don't want to have to spend the next two years arguing about and defending those kinds of issues because it's a side issue. And I resent the community leaning that way. Now, some of these Queer Nations, these young people, are also working out their own liberation. Oh, they get mad when I say that, too."

The mayor was very angry, pacing along the red Persian carpet, and so I tried to break his momentum.

"No LABIA members decorated your house," I said. "How would you like to be part of a group called LABIA?" I laughed, but he didn't. I liked him. I liked that he had an image of City Hall embroidered over his heart. I liked that he kept his baseball mitt in his drawer.

"If one of my sons comes to me and says he's gay, I'll say that's fine, and I'll help him find a nice man," declared the now enthusiastic mayor. I had never heard a straight man make such a statement. We talked for another hour, and as he escorted me to the door, he put his hand on my shoulder and said, "Sometimes I just can't believe I'm the mayor."

Neither could Harry Britt or Jean Harris. There was so much old baggage between Britt and Agnos, who had supported Nancy Pelosi over Britt in a race for the U.S. Congress. In 1976, Art Agnos had also committed the unforgivable sin of capturing a seat in the State Assembly in a race against an unknown, ponytailed camera-store owner named Harvey Milk. Harvey's campaign posters had read HARVEY MILK VERSUS THE MACHINE.

Yet, before she won her seat on the Board of Supervisors, it was Art Agnos who had appointed Roberta Achtenberg to head the Mayor's Task Force on Family Policy, an act that had rallied (to no avail) anti-gay groups whose "family values" were threatened if lesbian mothers could actually head mayoral task forces on the subject. Agnos's goal had been to create a level playing field for all minorities in the city, and the record shows that it was his administration that brought lesbians, gays, and people of color into positions of real authority in City Hall. He had, however, dispensed with the usual community liaisons, which was a disastrous mistake that cost him his bid for a second term. When you're herding cats, especially San Francisco cats, you can never have too much help, you can never have too many ears.

It was true that Mayor Agnos was headstrong in accomplishing what he considered to be important and tangible results, and that he had a deep disdain for anything purely symbolic. Intellectually I understood, but I had been taught by the lesson of Valentine's Day that the symbolic offers hope, which is the first step to real change. On the other hand, I also knew that if something went wrong with my adoption, I could ask Mayor Art Agnos to stand beside me at a press conference, and he would be there.

I drove home, up and over Bernal Hill. Bernal Hill is the poor man's Nob Hill, and boasts a spectacular view of San Francisco and, to the west, Candlestick Park, where the 49ers win game after game in football heaven. I parked and admired the sun streaming through the gray clouds with a scattering of blue. The rays created what looked like bright spotlights on San Francisco Bay.

The mayor had told me, "I look for people with Peace Corps hearts and linebacker eyes." I imagined myself like Joe Montana, with black smudges under my blue eyes, being the guy on the team whose job it is to watch and see where the attack is coming from, and to be ready for it at all times, and to defend against it. I was trying to get in touch with my inner Evita, an odd and elusive thing, but necessary, since it was now clear that in the process of becoming Jesse's legal mommy, I was also becoming something of an accidental radical.

# CHAPTER VII

# Grain by Grain, Frame by Frame

GILBERT BAKER was living with Dennis Peron on Seventeenth Street in the Castro district. Dennis had been one of Harvey's campaign field lieutenants, and his living room was a crossroads for every variety of human being. Oftentimes, Gilbert did not even know the names of some of those passing through the house. The local news droned from the television set as Gilbert presided over storytelling time. He was fresh from a meeting with San Francisco's society ladies. There was some contention over the banners he was making for the Black and White Ball, which depicted a waltzing man and woman, very Fred Astaire and Ginger Rogers. The society ladies wanted Gilbert to hang the banners symmetrically between the massive colonnades of the War Memorial building.

"And so I told them that if they didn't let me hang them off-center, it would look very Hitler. Very Third Reich. They just died." And of course, they let him hang them as he wished. He absolutely loved the society ladies, remarking, "It's nice work if you can get it." One day, he was setting off Roman candles in a faux war demonstration near the Civic Center, the next day he was decorating the buildings for a huge, extravagant society event. The irony was lost on him.

San Francisco's Black and White Ball is held every other year as a fund-raiser for the symphony. Society comes out for this ball, which takes place simultaneously in several Civic Center buildings and venues. Yet all are welcome who can spare the price of a ticket, and dancing in the street is free. This year, the theme was "Dancing in the Dark." The Swigs and Gettys would be in attendance, and Gilbert wanted to take Cheryl and me as his guests. I had no desire to go, but I did not want to be impolite, and so I told Gilbert I would ask Cheryl later, but that I did not know then that it was the type of event she would enjoy.

I was sitting on the couch, and on an overstuffed chair beside me sat Cleve Jones, who was enjoying Gilbert's pontification about the glory of his decorations versus those of the designer from Macy's, who was doing the Opera House. Cleve was an old friend of Gilbert's from Harvey Milk days, when Cleve was Harvey's protégé. Cleve had helped Gilbert to dye the cloth for the first rainbow flag. Now, at thirty-six, he described himself as "one of the grand old ladies of the movement." Cleve owned one suit, and had never profited financially from the gay rights movement, yet he had the privileged aura of someone who had seen private visions become part of world symbology. The Names Project Memorial Quilt, commemorating those who had died of AIDS, had been Cleve's brainchild, and he had traveled all over the country and the world as an emissary for compassion for those dying of this disease. Gilbert had helped to design the Quilt, but the Quilt itself was a gift from Cleve's memory of childhood illness. Before he was born, in Brazil, Indiana, his grandmother and great-grandmother made a quilt with dragons, ties and bows, totem poles, and coats of arms. Whenever he was very sick, his mother or grandmother would bring out the quilt, and he would trace with his finger the images they had sewn. Cleve's childhood comfort had translated into the most heartfelt communication device from the gay community. When the Quilt arrived in a city, public funding would suddenly become available for those suffering from the disease and those at risk. The Quilt had made open discussion of AIDS possible in the black Methodist churches. Cleve's greatest moment was when he met Rosa Parks, the now elderly black lady who refused to give up her seat on the bus to a white man and so triggered the 1955–

1956 Montgomery bus boycott and the ultimate collapse of legal segregation. On the sidewalk outside of a Detroit church, flanked by twin boys in choir robes, Rosa Parks handed Cleve a quilt panel commemorating the AIDS deaths of a mother, daughter, and granddaughter who were members of her congregation.

The Quilt made dialogue possible where the word "AIDS" could not otherwise have been spoken. Cleve had laid the now massive Quilt upon the White House Mall in 1988, and when President Bush, who had refused to acknowledge it, flew over the panels stitched by mourning parents, children, and lovers, Cleve had pointed at the President's helicopter and shouted, "Shame!" It was Barbara Bush, not George, who had darkened the lights in the White House living quarters and placed candles in the windows as part of the AIDS vigil.

Cleve was HIV-positive, but without symptoms. I hesitated, then asked him if he had ever imagined his own name sewn onto a panel. "I get asked that so many times," he said. "I have left specific instructions. I assume that at the time that I die, if I die of AIDS, that there will probably be a lot of quilts for me from different Names Project chapters. I have left specific instructions that any panels that come in with teddy bears on them are to have the teddy bears removed. I hate them, the association of homosexuals with teddy bears." What an odd man, I thought. What an odd thing to think about. Teddy bears. He looked up to the ceiling. "I don't care. I know many people who have designed their own quilts before they died, who have made their own in the last weeks of their lives. One man flew out here from Washington from the hospital. Was put on a stretcher, put on a plane, brought out here, brought into the Names Project, on a stretcher. He wanted a quilt that would match identically the one he had made for his dead lover." Cleve sat forward and leaned his tall, thin frame toward me. His voice was a whisper. "I spoke to one man who was in there very, very sick, and I said, you know, 'What are you doing here?' And he said that he had to be remembered, and that all of his friends had already died, and his family was gone, and there was nobody left in his life to make that panel with his name on it."

Cleve settled back into his chair. He had the habit of speaking with you intimately one moment, and then seeming to have no idea of your existence the next. His latest project was attempting to fund a community building on the boarded-up site of a burned-down church. The building would store the now enormous Quilt and act as a one-stop clearinghouse for those with AIDS. Some street activists hated the Quilt, seeing it as a symbol of weakness and a waste of money, and in the night they would spray-paint the boards on the building site: CLEVE JONES AND THE TEMPLE OF DOOM. Cleve was not terribly worried about this. He understood that for some, to accept the Quilt was to accept the hand of death on one's own shoulder, its bony finger then pointing only inches from one's face, a little trace of ridicule in its fleshless skull. Some could not live if they did not rage, and the Quilt was not about rage. When I asked Cleve what he thought of Queer Nation, he smiled and said that it was a crowd, a scene, a clique with dress codes, with its own vocabulary and affectations. Worse than all that, I think, Queer Nation made him feel old. "But I love them," he said, "because they are a generation of militant gay and lesbian activists that many of us were not sure was going to come along." Yet Cleve was irritated that Queer Nation did not seem to know their history, which was true. At one meeting, Jonathan announced, "We're going to take the California state flag and paint a rainbow over it!" Jubilant at this new idea, no one in the room knew that beside me sat Gilbert Baker, the creator of the rainbow flag, who had indeed done a rainbow job on the state flag at least ten years earlier.

"The second meeting I went to," said Cleve, "someone was talking about how they were proud to be part of the first generation of gay people to confront the police."

That was sadly humorous considering New York's Stonewall Rebellion so many years before, and San Francisco's White Night Riots, which were a response to Harvey Milk and George Moscone's assassin receiving a manslaughter conviction, a virtual slap on the wrist.

Mayor Agnos had shown me the intimate anteroom beside the main mayoral office. He had shown me where George Moscone had sat, where Dan White had sat, where George Moscone's body had fallen after the bullets hit his head; and he showed me the private exit door through which Dan White had fled, racing across the second-floor gallery, a crazy figure passing beneath the massive clock and carved figures of History and Progress, brushing past the burnished ironwork, past the roaring lion heads caught forever in golden metal. Did he hear his heels hitting the marble floors, and was it a satisfying sound, as he pushed open the oak door to the supervisors' chambers and pumped five bullets into Harvey Milk's head?

Cleve, who was Harvey's aide, was on the steps outside City Hall when someone shouted that the mayor had been shot and killed. Cleve had run up the rotunda staircase to the supervisors' offices, and had reached the door in time to see the coroner turn over Milk's body. Harvey Milk's head was bloody, blasted, his face bright purple. In Cleve's mind, this disfigured head would hang forever, a Technicolor nightmare.

In the small bathroom behind the chambers, Cleve had vomited, and when he had gathered himself together, he realized that the red he was seeing in the sink was Harvey's blood. Dianne Feinstein had knelt beside Harvey's body to take his pulse, and found that he was dead. When she removed her hand, it was covered in blood; before she made the announcement of the assassinations, she went into the little bathroom and washed the blood from her hands.

Using a temporary-insanity defense, Dan White's attorneys had successfully argued that Mr. White had been eating too much junk food, specifically Twinkies, and that this had resulted in irrational mood swings. Junk food had been responsible for Dan White loading his gun, putting extra bullets into his pocket, and climbing into City Hall through a basement window to avoid the metal detectors. Junk food had also been responsible for Dan White's reloading his gun after assassinating Mayor Moscone so that he would have sufficient bullets ready to assassinate Harvey Milk. White's claim of temporary insanity had been successful, and came to be known as the Twinkie Defense.

The afternoon of the verdict, I got off the streetcar at Eighteenth and Castro and saw Cleve, Del Martin, Phyllis Lyon, and Sally Gearheart, their arms linked, their faces shocked, the bright lights of the television cameras focused on them. I got closer and found out that Dan White would walk the streets a free man in five years. That night, police cars were set ablaze at the Civic Center, and the doors to City Hall were smashed. Cleve, who was only twenty-three years old at the time, had stood on a corner, shouting, "Dan White was a cop. Dan White was a cop!"

Cleve was questioned by the grand jury investigating the riots. The grand jury asked Cleve how he had gotten from the Castro district to City Hall that night. They were trying to determine if he was guilty of inciting to riot. Cleve asked to leave the room to consult his lawyer. He had a cigarette and returned ten minutes later to answer the question. "Mr. Jones, how did you get from the Castro district to City Hall on the night of the riot?"

"On foot," responded Mr. Jones, in perfect deadpan.

Shortly after Dan White was released from prison, he killed himself, and Cleve had felt pity for him. Yet Cleve remembered vividly one disturbing story that had come out just before White's release: Dan White spent his time in prison jogging with Sirhan Sirhan, the assassin of Bobby Kennedy.

When Dan White killed himself, the first thing Cleve thought of was a drag queen who had recited a poem just after the assassinations. The words were no longer exact in Cleve's memory, but their meaning was etched forever: "I promise you. I promise you this: If you get off for insanity, you will go insane."

Cleve draped himself on the couch in Dennis Peron's living room and watched Gilbert with amusement. The national news was now on, and Dan Rather announced that Michael Collins, one of the Apollo astronauts, had said that gays should not be permitted to fly to Mars because they might upset the rest of the crew.

"I demand to go to Mars!" said Gilbert with mock outrage.

I wondered how this news was affecting Peggy Sue and Rachel Pepper, LABIA members who were trying to get NASA to name some of the thousands of geological features on the planet Venus after lesbians.

Cleve took a drag from his cigarette, and watched as a young man loped through the living room. He was a piercer, meaning that he decorated himself with various metal objects in various locations, some rather intimate.

"Show Phyllis your tongue," said Gilbert.

How forward of Gilbert, I thought, but the young man complied. He stuck out his tongue, and I saw that, right in the fleshy middle of it, he had a large detailed silver metal skull.

I was not so much revolted as fascinated. How could this possibly be held in place? "How long is the post?" I asked in my best journalist's fact-finding voice.

"Nine-sixteenths of an inch," he said with some pride.

Cleve took a good long look at him and said, in a quiet, even voice, "Why don't you just go all the way and get a lip plate?"

I could barely control my laughter as Cleve and the young man studied each other with absolutely unreadable expressions, until the man walked away. Cleve Jones is a funny, bitchy, sometimes imperious queen with a Quaker's heart, and a green and blue tattoo of the world on his upper left arm.

Yet another news story captured the room's attention. His Holiness the Dalai Lama was in San Francisco. Six monks from his monastery had that day begun constructing a seven-foot mandala of colored sand, each grain to be placed by hand. The Dalai Lama himself had come to place the first grains of sand in the Kalachakra Sand Mandala at the Asian Art Museum. The mandala was the Wheel of Time, and it represented compassion. On one side of the city, grain by grain, for three weeks, the monks would create this remarkable sand painting, while on the other side of the city, frame by frame, *Basic Instinct* would be shooting.

"Cleve was beaten out of the Nobel Prize by the Dalai Lama," said Gilbert, and just as I was about to follow up on that, the piercer boy with the skull clipped through the middle of his tongue waltzed through the room, making a wide circle away from Cleve.

That night, I casually mentioned the Black and White Ball to Cheryl. I had not really thought she would want to go, but I felt guilty for my self-absorption of the past few months, and thought I could get a few points for at least bringing it up. Cheryl fixated on the idea, and for the next three weeks, preparations for THE BALL became her major household theme. I couldn't believe it. I had had no intention of going. On a very deep level, I hated it. It was an absolutely heterosexual event, the kind of thing that always made me feel as if I were from Mars—or, if LABIA had its way, Venus.

The Black and White Ball. Cheryl wanted it, and Cheryl generally got what she wanted. I had to go. Cheryl had never forgotten that she had not been able to attend her high school prom with the girl she loved, and so we would be taking care of Cheryl's adolescent scar with the psychodrama of "Dancing in the Dark" through the Opera House, through Symphony Hall, under tent pavilions, and in the middle of the street under gigantic mirrored glass balls suspended from cranes. Cheryl insisted that we help Gilbert prepare the banners and flags at the Dream Center, his sewing workshop in the Fillmore district. Cheryl referred to Gilbert as the Decoration Committee. Cleve would also be going, so I pretended that the ball was part of my endless "research." There was something horrifying to me about six thousand heterosexual couples waltzing on the Opera House stage, or about being surrounded by drunk straight males who had lost their dates at two in the morning, their brains pulsating with Commander Cody & His Lost Planet Airmen. But it was making Cheryl so happy, and Gilbert was so excited, and Cleve was going to wear tasteful diamond stud earrings. So I dragged myself through the preparations with as good a semblance of excitement as I could muster. It was, after all, just a dance. Cheryl had to work out her high school prom, and I would oblige her. The problem was, while she was readying for a peak romantic experience, I had a secret that I kept absolutely hidden from everyone: I was afraid that the straight people would laugh at us.

# CHAPTER VIII

# What Goes Around,
# Comes Around

MARK PRITCHARD messengered the *Basic Instinct* script to me. I was very curious as to what a three-million-dollar script looked like, but I would have to wait, because I had to go to Jesse's pediatrician, and then on to San Francisco State University, where I was teaching creative writing. So I put the script, in its large yellow envelope, in my teaching bag.

Now that the Department of Social Services had acknowledged the motion to compel the home visit, more requests for information had arrived in the mail. I would need written statements testifying to my parenting abilities from Jesse's nursery school teacher and his pediatrician, Dr. Jane Phillips. The department wanted to be sure that there were no signs that Jesse was experiencing child abuse or neglect. It was distressing that the state would request official documentation stating that I was not abusing my child. Dr. Phillips, who is heterosexual, called me into her office as she filled out the form, carefully noting each time she had treated Jesse. Dr. Phillips had cared for Jesse since his birth, and she had had many contacts with the three of us.

"I do these forms all the time, you know," Dr. Phillips said. "Everyone who adopts has to fill them out."

My palms were sweating. I felt as if I were hiding something, but I wasn't. It was simply that I had hidden for so much of my life.

"This isn't such a big deal," I assured her. "I just want to be able to cover Jesse under my health insurance."

Dr. Phillips, each bobbed hair in place, the kind intelligence never leaving her eyes, finished filling in the form. She folded it, put it in an envelope, and handed it to me. "That's not why," she said.

"What?" I asked her, and I felt alarmed, as if I'd just leaned into the darkness against something unknown.

"That's not why you're adopting him," she said. "You're adopting him because he's your son, and you're his mother."

She was not from my world, but Dr. Phillips understood, and that gave me great hope.

I went to the university and, after class, to my office. I opened up the yellow package holding the script. For some reason, the *Basic Instinct* people thought we did not have the script. They sent out press releases that said we had not even read it, that we were fanatics, censors.

It was late afternoon and the April light filtered through the window onto my desk. Here are some highlights of what I read:

The bisexual woman, at the point of orgasm, ice-picks to death in a rain of blood the aging male rock star she has tied to the bed with a long white scarf. The scarf is silk, of course, since this *is* San Francisco.

The lesbian character tries to kill the straight cop who is threatening her relationship with the bisexual ice-pick murderess, but dies when she crashes her Ferrari.

Flashback. The lesbian character, as an adolescent, slashes her little brother's throat. The script calls for a close-up of the lesbian character at approximately thirteen years of age, braces on her teeth, followed by another close-up of a black-and-white glossy police shot in which a little blond boy is lying in a pool of his own blood, his throat slashed. Reason for the killing? The adolescent lesbian has no idea. Did it on impulse. Daddy's razor just happened to be nearby. Lived on a farm. (You'd have to ask the writer, Mr. Eszterhas, to explain the subtext.) She is lesbian and instinctually hates males, even helpless little boys whose soft white throats are irresistible to the twisted sister if there's a razor on hand, especially Daddy's razor.

Throughout the movie, Joe Eszterhas called for thematic music: the Rolling Stones' "Sympathy for the Devil." The light was waning, and I carefully placed the screenplay back into its yellow envelope. Joe Eszterhas is a writer of pulp thrillers with lots of blood and betrayal. He stated, in regard to *Basic Instinct,* that gays must simply accept the fact that, like every group, some of us are deranged.

No major studio will touch a film script with a heroic lesbian or bisexual protagonist unless she dies at the end, goes straight, or is left alone, frustrated and frantically masturbating in the dark. It is, however, all right to make movies about gay men and AIDS. Gay men are the lost boys, and they will die. Hollywood is a place where many of the greatest living performers must stay closeted or they will become nonentities. They must never appear in *People* magazine with their true families. If they do come out, their destruction will be polite and sympathetic, and perhaps there will even be work for them behind the cameras.

Years ago, in the Boston underground of the late sixties, when the left hated gays as much as the right, it was impossible for me to find lesbians who were not into strict butch-and-femme role-play, which is just fine if that's your style. Other lesbians, the ones who could pass, lived in very private, protected circles. And so I went to a club called the Other Side, where drag queens lip-synched to Billie Holiday and Judy Garland. I liked the drag queens. They accepted me. One night I was excited when I saw a beautiful woman; I asked her to dance. In the middle of an elaborate step, she stopped and said, "You think I'm a woman, don't you?" I sighed, and we sat at a table together. She showed me how she made realistic breasts from bags of birdseed, and asked if my Alice-in-Wonderland hair was naturally blond.

There was a thin, very dark-skinned black drag queen named Eddie, and an equally thin, blond, Irish drag queen named Brendan. They were wearing Japanese kimonos that night. They were not lovers, they were best friends. Brendan always said, "Eddie's not black, and I'm not white." They were sitting with their arms around each other's shoulders. Eddie had just been raped by a soldier. "If you're being raped," said Eddie, "the most important thing is to relax. Completely relax." I listened to him with great respect. His eyes were enormous, brown, and glassy. I had never known anyone who had been raped—or at least, this was the first time I heard anyone talk about it. Then Eddie saw my face, which held shock like a piece of soft clay that had been punched once and squarely. The idea of living without love was too much for me. The idea that my love was a perverted, ugly thing, and that each pulsation of desire was another step toward hell and eternal damnation was too much for me. When you're young, you cannot have the sophistication that allows you to dismiss the tirades of priests, teachers, politicians, and peers. Each distorted image thrown in your face pushes against the trapdoor of suicide, which swings relentlessly.

Eddie extended his long, thin, black arm, which was decorated with jewelry stolen from Filene's. He made a big circle with his arm, his longest finger, white at the tip, marking the air as he spoke, oracular and clear as ice.

"What goes around, comes around. What goes around, comes around," he said. "And I want you to remember that, baby."

I don't know where Eddie is today, if he is alive or dead, but I still love him. I am now so much older, and sophisticated, I suppose. So much has changed in the world, so much has not. Driven to despair by isolation and fear, one-third of all teenage suicides are lesbian, gay, or bisexual.

As I left the university that day, the three-million-dollar *Basic Instinct* script heavy in my bag, I passed Angela Davis. In her Black Panther days, she was on the FBI's Ten Most Wanted list, and had the distinction of being the most wanted woman in America. She no longer wore her hair in her trademark Afro. It was now very long, with elaborate dreadlocks. She was impressive, unbent, certain of her vision, defiant in the face of doubters. She taught a course at the same time as I did, in the same building. Sometimes she would take her class out onto the lawn, under the trees, and I would watch through the window as the blackbirds dove down and tried to pluck strands of her hair for their nests. Sometimes she'd brush them away with long black fingers, sometimes she would let them steal a thread of a dreadlock. Angela Davis was living proof that one could retire, alive, from radical activism.

\* \* \*

At home, I put the script on the kitchen table, took my scissors, and snipped the script into pieces. I was very careful, very methodical.

"You making a sword, Mama Phyllis? I wanna make a sword." Jesse made a Peter Pan dagger almost every day, so I got him his red Mickey Mouse safety scissors and some construction paper.

"I'm making a press packet, Jesse. Can you say 'press packet'?"

"Press packet," said Jesse.

"Very good."

I felt very clear about this forty-five-million-dollar film, about the fact that it was being made in San Francisco, and about the fact that it was starring one of the most powerful actors in Hollywood. The well of emotion had transformed into calculation. I excerpted the most outrageous scenes and arranged them on sheets of paper. It would only be a matter of time before I visited Joe Eszterhas. The visit could take place on his turf. It would make no difference. What goes around, comes around, and I was going to come around. I felt no self-pity, no self-doubt. They were gone, like birds chased out of tall grass. Thank you, Eddie, wherever you are.

The phone rang. It was Jonathan, and he had the shooting schedule for *Basic Instinct*. We would now know where they would be shooting exterior shots, and what scenes they would be shooting. Mayor Agnos had ordered the Film Commission to release the schedule as public information, and he had issued a statement in which he said, "It is unfortunate to know that a movie is being filmed in which people who are often the victims of violence are portrayed as the perpetrators of violence. On the other hand, no city should be in a position of censoring a movie script. Nor should we be giving a Jesse Helms–like seal of approval to programs or scripts. I hope that a peaceful public outcry in response to this movie helps to educate the public and the film industry about the lack of positive Hollywood depictions of gays and lesbians." The *Basic Instinct* people used only the part where the mayor warned against censorship and a "Jesse Helms–like seal of approval." The man who had fought for gay rights for his entire political life now appeared to be collaborating with the film industry. This willful decontextualization of the mayor's statement, in combination with the mayor's unwise invocation of Senator Jesse Helms against people Helms regularly attacked for their very existence, finished off the mayor with the street activists, who were galvanized against *Basic Instinct*.

I went to Jonathan's to deliver the script excerpts for the press packets, and to give him a copy of Sun Tzu's *The Art of War*. Jonathan was wound tight. His phone rang constantly. The media would not let go of the censorship issue, while a meeting was being brokered by Harry Britt's office between the activists and the film company. Jonathan was frustrated with the censorship tactic, and I noticed that the ant trails in his kitchen were becoming remarkably complex.

"I am entirely within my rights to physically prevent this movie from being made," said Jonathan. "Not only is this my right, it is my responsibility to my community. For this community, there is no contest between freedom of speech, and freedom of life and liberty. And this film affects my freedom of life and liberty. And I am in a war, and in a war, ugly things happen. Ideological purities get muddied."

He carefully stepped over the ants and poured another cup of coffee, checking inside the cup for any dark, scrambling inhabitants.

"Want a cup?" he asked.

"No thanks," I said, trying to decline graciously.

"It is my responsibility to take the hits," he said, "and to prevent this community from undergoing further violence. To send a message to Hollywood that we're not going to take it anymore, to send a message to the press that we mean business, and to prevent this film from being made."

Jonathan read through the excerpts from the screenplay, and he put them down on the table as if they were kryptonite.

"You know who calls me, every day? Sometimes more than once?" he asked.

"Who?"

"Joe Eszterhas."

Joe Eszterhas called Jonathan Katz every day. Remarkable.

Eszterhas was feeding Jonathan information, and Jonathan was telling Joe what Carolco, the film company making *Basic Instinct,* was telling the community representatives. The film company was leaving Joe out of the loop. Joe was angry because he found out that the director, Paul Verhoeven, had brought another writer onto the set. Joe did not trust Verhoeven with his material. When Joe and his wife and children saw Verhoeven's *Total Recall,* Joe said he had felt the need for "a mental enema." Joe thought he was being set up to take the fall for *Basic Instinct;* he called Supervisor Harry Britt's office to say he would be interested in a meeting. He did this without telling Carolco or Verhoeven. Joe was very angry. Joe, or one of his operatives, had leaked a letter to the *L.A. Times* encouraging Carolco to meet with gay community leaders, and saying that it was important that not only he, but also Paul Verhoeven, attend the meeting. Now there was a problem. The writer of the screenplay was calling for the meeting, and the publicists were twisting in the wind.

"What does Joe say to you?" I asked Jonathan.

"He says he sympathizes. Wants to have the meeting with the community leaders."

"Do you trust this?"

"Phyllis. He wrote the script."

Whether or not to trust Joe Eszterhas was not Jonathan's focus that evening. Jonathan wanted to escalate. He knew that if we did not escalate, we would become impotent picketers, all but ignored in a few days, a minor irritant.

"Do it with mirrors, Jonathan," I said.

"What do you mean?"

"In the daytime, mirrors, reflecting the sun. At night, flashlights and glitter. The movie lights will adjust to the reflections, will seek out our lights and try to balance them. The film itself will be useless because of the erratic lighting."

"And noisemakers," said Jonathan. "Whistles and horns for the soundtrack." The whistles would have a strong subtext for our community, since it is with whistles that we signal each other in the night if we're about to be attacked by fag-bashers or dyke-bashers.

Jonathan was thrilled. It could work. We could really affect the filming and cost them some money, which he knew was their real interest. He grabbed the phone, called the Queerline, and left the following message for all those who would call in to find out about the protests: "Please bring flashlights, glitter to throw, and noisemakers." The exact transcript of the Queerline messages would soon be immortalized as Exhibit A in *Basic Instinct* v. *Queer Nation, an unincorporated association, and DOES 1–300*.

"Glitter," said Jonathan, with a reverence usually associated with finding the key to the Lost Covenant. "Glitter is so queer."

On April 23, attired halfway between Saks Fifth Avenue and Lenny's Leather Emporium, I went to City Hall to interview Supervisor Roberta Achtenberg. I walked through the metal detectors and up the rotunda staircase. There were dozens of people setting up lighting equipment for what I thought was some type of photographic shoot. I turned left and walked down the hall to the supervisor's office.

Roberta Achtenberg was born in 1950. Her parents owned a mom-and-pop shop in Inglewood, California. The cornerstone of her political philosophy of lesbian and gay civil rights was that to be pro-gay is to be pro-family, a position that strikes at the very foundation of institutionalized homophobia.

On this particular day, she was very tense. She was trying to secure passage of a policy that would allow city workers who were domestic partners to register themselves and their children for health benefits. This was the only tangible thing that could be gotten as a result of domestic partnership, and she succeeded in getting it.

Roberta had recently appeared with Supervisor Carole Migden on the cover of *Image* magazine. Beside their photograph were the words "Lesbian Power." *Image* is a full-color magazine insert for the *Sunday Examiner,* which has a circulation of almost half a million. Roberta had been asked by the interviewer if there really was one lesbian community, and she had responded: "There is some level of shared experience, life experience and some appreciation of history that you do have in common with other lesbians that makes you feel a sense of commonality or belonging that you don't share with other people. . . . It doesn't mean we all have the same view of solid waste disposal."

Roberta loved the picture on the magazine's cover, but the thrust of the story was supposed to have been about lesbians taking political power. Instead, after a few paragraphs about politics, the article had explored lesbian sexuality.

"Sex-positive articles are okay with me," said Roberta, "but it was like putting Mayor Art Agnos on the cover of a magazine with the text being what heterosexuals do in bed."

I had been told that on the night of Roberta's election victory, Officer Lea Militello, in plainclothes, had been glued to Roberta's side. I suspected that Lea had been on duty, her magnum strapped under her arm, so I asked Roberta if, during her campaign, she had experienced death threats.

Roberta paused. She tapped her fingers on her desk.

"Sure," she said. "Well, when it first started happening, I got very worried about my son. I kept thinking, you accept that for yourself and your partner. We're adults. We know that life can have these things in store for us. So you accept it, and go on with your life. If it happens, it happens."

In order for a lesbian woman or gay man to run for supervisor, did she or he have to accept the possibility of assassination? Sure. The way Roberta had said it, as if it were a given, was very strange, but I had never received death threats, and this could very well just be how one must react.

"It's one thing to accept that danger for yourself," she said. "It's another to imagine that the life of your child, an innocent being, could be in danger because somebody's a crazy person who wants to do something to you. I don't know. We had the cops come and do a security assessment of our house. They did additional drive-bys. Changed the telephone number. I was escorted by a police officer for all my public functions for a while."

"Lea Militello was with you?"

"You bet she was. And that had been going on for about three weeks before that. I started getting death threats about three weeks before."

She looked out the window. Her jaw was tight. She had just

gotten a call that day from a national magazine. She looked at me and knew I would understand.

"The magazine's representative said, 'Would you be willing to talk about your situation?' Excuse me? I live my life. I'm inside my life. Right? You feel the same way. Other people look at you and your partner and your child as a curiosity, as if it were something odd or unusual. When I was sworn onto the Board of Supervisors, I knew all of the politicians would be there. I knew my community would be there. I wanted to acknowledge my partner, Mary, for all the things that she had done. I wanted to recognize my son, Benjie, who had been a total trooper. I wanted people to see my sisters who have always stood with me, and my brother-in-law. I wanted the inside of my life, which feels to me like I imagine other people's lives feel to them, to be clear."

Benjie had sat in her lap when Roberta took her chair on the Board of Supervisors. Cheryl and I had sat at the back of the chambers, hand in hand, watching the parade of powerful San Francisco politicians, including Dianne Feinstein and Congresswoman Nancy Pelosi, two strong supporters of lesbian and gay civil rights. In Roberta's speech that day, she spoke of her son. "Benjie is a true San Francisco kid: He understands that having two moms is not the only legitimate form of family."

That night, Roberta and her partner went out to dinner at the Hayes Street Grill, where they bumped into Nancy Pelosi and her husband, Ron. Nancy told Roberta that she had observed something very important that day.

"I admire Nancy Pelosi," Roberta told me, "but I think people like her, people like Art Agnos, or like any other person who fits into the mainstream category, might have only an intellectual appreciation of what it means to live our lives. It's another thing to be inside someone's home. I think she had never experienced before in an emotional way my feelings about my family. What she was saying is that she felt the same way about Ron and her kids as I do about Mary and Benjie."

I interpreted Pelosi's remark slightly differently. I think that for one moment, as Roberta spoke, the congresswoman had experienced what it would be like to not be the norm, to live in a world where having a partner of the opposite gender was considered exotic, odd, and marginal, where your child might be considered a curiosity for having opposite-sex parents rather than two moms.

Roberta Achtenberg is not a person I would ever describe as warm and charming. She has a hard edge to her, a lawyer's mind, a brusque style. She understands that the art of politics rests upon the ability to compromise. Yet when there is a breakthrough in lesbian and gay civil rights, when justice even in its most modest form finally prevails, and when in celebration of that victory she speaks of her child, her partner, her community, emotion forces its way through a very narrow opening she cannot conceal, and her eyelid twitches slightly until tears force their way into her eyes—but never fall while the news cameras are rolling. When this happens, and I have seen it happen several times, I sit and wait to see what she will do with that roaring force, if it will break her apart. But she always gathers the power back into herself, like the trick camera work that reverses the progress of a storm and lets you watch it recompose itself into a fist of light on the horizon. To be pro-gay was to be pro-family: Achtenberg would never compromise those words.

When I left her office, I took the elevator to the ground floor. As I was leaving, my attention was caught by what I now realized was a movie crew at the top of the rotunda stairs. They were setting up a scene only fifty feet from both Supervisor Achtenberg and Supervisor Carole Migden's offices. I ran up the staircase and demanded of a crew member, "Is this *Basic Instinct*?"

"No. It's a thriller, with Kim Basinger and Richard Gere."

"What's the title?"

"*Final Analysis.*"

"It's not about killer lesbians and bi-women?" I was suddenly enraged, without a trace of that calculating persona that had been visited upon me so mercifully while at the university.

"What?" asked the crewman.

I looked a bit too intense. I imagine I looked, oddly enough, like a potential killer lesbian.

"Is this movie about killer lesbians and bi-women?"

"No!" he said, and he laughed as if he had never heard anything more ridiculous. But then he smirked and said, "And what would you do if it was?"

*And what would you do if it was?* It was such a clear challenge.

I knew one thing: There were things I could do that I could not if I were an elected official. Somewhere, at some point in time, I was determined to see Hollywood images of lesbians that were not psychotic, homicidal, or suicidal. By the time the Jesses and Benjies of the world were old enough to go to movie theaters, they would be able to see images of women like their mothers who were not sadomasochistic, murderous, man- and boy-hating nymphomaniacal perverts. There was no turning back for me. My son was going to have a choice of images, and if they called us censoring Brownshirts and put us in a beauty contest with Jesse Helms, so be it. Jonathan was right. The key was to escalate. Force the issue into the headlines. But it had to be done carefully. *Basic Instinct* was our best opportunity, and the war between the writer and the director would play into our hands.

That night the focus group HASH (Homosexuals Against Stereotypes in Hollywood) had a meeting to determine their next course of action. Jonathan, John Woods, Pam Bates, and Mark Pritchard were quite impressed that the film company had agreed to a meeting with community representatives from Queer Nation, Supervisor Harry Britt's office, and GLAAD, the Gay and Lesbian Alliance Against Defamation. The film company scheduled the meeting for three-thirty in the afternoon on April 24. They had been particularly solicitous, trying to make absolutely sure that everyone central to the conflict could be at the Hyatt Regency at precisely that time. Tensions had diffused. Perhaps they wanted to listen, could make some compromises.

Tanya Tandoc and Marvin Greer just happened to have volunteered to be that week's facilitators for the Queer Nation meeting, and their names and phone numbers were on the Queerline. At the HASH meeting, they noticed a man in a suit. Marvin, who had a round baby face, was suspicious, but then again, Marvin was always suspicious so eventually he would be right. But Tanya thought the man in the suit was queer. He had longish, curling hair, and he was standing with one hip jutting out, one hand on his hip. The meeting started with the usual check-in. When they got to the suited man, he presented the group with an order to appear in Superior Court on the fourth floor of City Hall the next day at three-thirty P.M., exactly the same time as the meeting at the Hyatt on the other end of town, which was supposed to address some of the community's concerns. The court hearing was requested by *Basic Instinct*'s makers, who wanted a temporary restraining order issued against any demonstrations. The man in the suit left, leaving rage in his wake. The meeting with Carolco was a setup. HASH immediately disbanded and regrouped as GEFFEN: Gay Extremists Fighting Fascistic Entertainment Normalcy. Any future court papers would have to read "*Basic Instinct* vs. *GEFFEN*." Geffen happened to be the last name of one of the most powerful and respected men in Hollywood, who had come out as gay, and who was a generous fund-raiser for both AIDS and lesbian and gay civil rights.

I appeared the next day at the City Hall courtroom in my own radical motif: I was now clothed completely in black, but with no stickers. The value of costume had become clear to me. This was going to be a show, a performance. There were about ten of us who wanted to witness the court proceedings in City Hall. We were accommodated, and I received permission to videotape from Judge John Dearman, who had sworn in Donna Hitchens the night the war broke out. He himself did not listen to the arguments, but remained in his chambers behind the courtroom while his research attorney talked to both sides. She would then go to him with her recommendation. What could be going on in Judge Dearman's mind? Judges are elected, and a coalition headed by the gay community had just defeated a sitting judge. His courtroom now had radical queers pitted against Hollywood.

I videotaped the *Basic Instinct* lawyers mercilessly. Long, quiet close-ups of their noses. My camera had practically become part of my shoulder.

Because Tanya and Marvin were the week's facilitators, they sat at the defendants' table, representing Queer Nation. Tanya Tandoc was twenty-one years old, the daughter of Kansas physicians; her father was Filipino, her mother German. Tanya watched *Star Trek* every day; she became quite grouchy when she missed it. (She missed a number of episodes over the next two weeks.) A cellist, she had once played the "Spring" movement from Vivaldi's *Four Seasons* in Chartres cathedral. Marvin, on the other hand, was into his espionage motif, looking for twists of plot and searching for listening devices planted by three-hun-dred-dollar-an-hour lawyers. Marvin fancied himself a sort of queer 007.

The *Basic Instinct* lawyers argued for the temporary restrain-ing order, and the Queer Nation lawyer argued against prior restraint, since there as yet had been not a single incident of interference with the filming. Judge Dearman's research attorney listened to both sides, occasionally looking up to my camera to smile.

She said to the *Basic Instinct* lawyers, "Let me just ask a question. My understanding was that the film producers were going to meet with the groups in the community to discuss their specific objections to the filming, and I guess the script. I'm wondering: Is that still planning to go forward?"

The lawyers mumbled into their ties.

"I was just thinking," she added, "that if these demonstrations were in some way a response to the fact that they may have felt they were shut out from any kind of meaningful discussion . . ." Her voice trailed off as she waited for their response. Perhaps the *Basic Instinct* lawyers *did* have little microphones in their ties, because they persisted in mumbling into them.

The research attorney thought it odd that the company had refused for over two weeks to meet with the community, and then, after getting the court date and time to hear arguments for the temporary restraining order, had quickly arranged a simulta-neous meeting with the community to discuss our concerns.

"We welcome their input," said the *Basic Instinct* lawyer.

"Not!" said one of the observing Queer Nationals.

As the lawyers spoke, I could see that Tanya was getting worked up, full of holy fire, very Joan of Arc, carrying the torch of all the queers. She was practicing speeches in her head: "We're your sisters, your brothers, your children, your aunts, your li-brarians." Tanya had an ongoing fantasy about librarians. Mar-vin, a member of the queer Street Patrol, was memorizing the lawyers' faces, looking for moles and any other identifying marks to be remembered when he prowled the perimeter of the movie set after dark in his fuchsia beret.

The research attorney went to Judge Dearman's chambers, and I stopped filming. I'm not sure what came over me, and I was as surprised as everyone else when I stood up and gave a dramatic reading and synopsis of the most offensive scenes, which I had brought with me. My voice was just loud enough to be heard in Judge Dearman's chambers, but not so loud that it could be considered disruptive. It just carried well. The Queer Nationals were giggling on the court benches, and it was clear that the *Basic Instinct* lawyers had not read the script, because the scenes were making them terribly uncomfortable. "Magna cum laude pussy," a line from the movie, and the ability of said "pussy" to speak, was perhaps not something they had gone to law school to represent.

I was really starting to enjoy myself. "Here's another good one," I said. "Michael Douglas's character baits Roxy, the lesbian character whose lover, Catherine, he has just slept with. 'Tell me something, Rocky. Man-to-man. I think she's the fuck of the century, don't you?'"

The courtroom doors flung open and Supervisor Carole Migden stood in the doorway.

"Oh, look," I said. "It's Supervisor Migden, come to see what's going to happen."

Supervisor Migden was a powerful woman and the quintessential Democratic party insider, holding the positions of chair of the San Francisco Democratic Party Central Committee and chair of the California State Democratic Party Platform Committee. She stood for a moment in the doorway. The woman knew how to make an entrance, and she remained in place just long enough for everyone to take in the blond hair, each strand welded into place, and the tasteful light brown power suit with her trademark shoulder pads. Once she was satisfied that her presence had been felt, her high heels clicked across the marble courtroom floor and she took a seat at the back of the room. Peter Altman, an activist carefully dressed in a button-down shirt, swiftly joined her at the back of the courtroom to explain in whispers what was going on. Carole nodded her head as Peter spoke, but with a quality only a displaced New Yorker can conjure up, her eyes were fixed and staring at the *Basic Instinct* lawyers. Their squirming was slight, but observable.

Judge Dearman, wearing a casual fireside-chat sweater, wandered out of his chambers, perhaps to find a pencil, perhaps just to take a look around.

"Oh, look," I said, "It's Judge Dearman." I gave a little wave and the Queer Nationals sat up nice and straight.

It was obvious that the *Basic Instinct* lawyers were not familiar with this court because one of them searched frantically for the judge in an attempt to rise and look fabulously respectful. He couldn't find the judge, who was only ten feet from him, because this judge was African-American and wearing a sweater. When he finally realized which person was Dearman, he turned away and sat down quickly, his papers flying from the table, his tie askew. Something about the judge had made him terribly nervous. Judge Dearman smiled and meandered back to his chambers.

"Oh, here's another one," I said. "The lesbians are having sex and snorting cocaine in toilet stalls in a converted church while everyone stops to watch Michael Douglas fondle the bi-woman's butt on the dance floor of a gay club."

Supervisor Migden smiled. We all smiled, except the *Basic Instinct* lawyers.

The research attorney returned. The temporary restraining order had requested that demonstrators be kept six hundred feet from the filming. Judge Dearman had granted the TRO, but the required distance was to be only one hundred feet, for the safety of the demonstrators during car-chase scenes. Glitter was cited seventeen times as a banned weapon in the court documents, making this the first queer restraining order. It was historically ironic that the order was requested by a movie company. In the 1930s, a common phrase describing "conversion" to homosexuality was "go Hollywood."

Across town, at precisely the time that the court was hosting Queer Nation versus *Basic Instinct*, Joe Eszterhas was riding the elevator that scales the inside of the elaborate atrium at the

Hyatt Regency, the same elevator that Mel Brooks used to film *High Anxiety*. Joe Eszterhas saw everything in terms of thriller plotting, betrayal, and twists, twists, twists. One can sit in a room imagining stories of elaborate betrayal for only so long before one's brain cells align accordingly. Joe's tactic was to betray first, to get in the first twist and be the manipulator, perhaps to ensure that he would never again experience the humiliation of his childhood and adolescence. Joe has one plot. First act: Establish the one you love the most, the one to whom you are closest—your lover, your husband, your father. Second act: Your lover, your husband, your father turns out to be the ice-pick murderer / the concentration-camp guard / the neo-Nazi. Third act: In order for the world to be safe, you must kill the beloved or make a pact with the devil—the classic Bram Stoker Dracula plot.

In his plots, it is always the one who is closest who enacts the betrayal. Who is closer to the screenwriter than the director? Who has more control? No one. Three million Joe had gotten, the highest amount paid to a screenwriter in the history of the industry. He was a great artist. He knew it. This was no popcorn movie. This was the greatest commercial script of all time. It would earn him his place beside Arnold Schwarzenegger, Sly Stallone, and Dostoyevsky in the pantheon of violent fantasy. But this director, Paul Verhoeven, would try to destroy the script. He was the enemy. He was Dutch, but he sounded German. Did he sound to Joe like the people who ran the repatriation refugee camp in Hungary, the one six-year-old Joe had been in with his parents before emigrating to America? Joe's mother, whom he loved so dearly, would work in America as a typesetter, her head over the fumes of melting lead each day. This job would turn her into a paranoid schizophrenic who saw rays coming out of the walls at Forty-first and Lorraine in Cleveland. It was terrifying for the boy. One moment she was there, but in the next she was inhabited by a mad, hallucinating stranger claiming to be his mother.

The first thing Joe heard from Paul Verhoeven's mouth was, "Vell. How can we put more tits and ass into this?" Then they discussed actresses. Joe had seriously believed that Meryl Streep would like to play the role of Catherine, the bisexual ice-pick murderer. Joe had watched Paul laugh—was he laughing at him?—and say, "When is the last time you've seen Meryl Streep's tits, yah?"

Michael Douglas had sat watching this little spat, along with Irwin Winkler, the original producer, who would refuse to work with Verhoeven. They were in Winkler's living room in Beverly Hills. As their discussion continued, Joe began to fight with Verhoeven, and Joe heard Paul say, "I am the director, yah? I am right and you are wrong, yah?" Verhoeven seemed to be pushing his face up into Joe's, and Joe threatened to come across the table at him. Michael Douglas had said, "Gentlemen. Please." You had to love Hollywood.

For their meeting with community representatives, including Harry Britt, Jonathan Katz, and Pam Bates, Carolco had provided a very nice selection of fruits on which to nibble. Joe sat with the community leaders and activists, and he listened. He watched Verhoeven from the corner of his eye. Joe said he had not realized that what he had written could hurt the community. He had not realized that there was so much censorship of positive portrayals of lesbians. He would be able to make some changes that would address the community's concerns and the script's insensitivities without significantly changing the plot or rendering useless anything filmed so far.

Paul Verhoeven and his producer Alan Marshall were enraged. Joe was not defending his script. The meeting had not been intended to discuss changes, but to explain to the community representatives that a filmmaker's only responsibility is to himself and to his artistic vision, and that if his vision happened to demonize a particular group, that was unfortunate. Somebody had to be the bad guy, but to make up for it, they would make a nice movie about queers. Next year, maybe. Jonathan shot that argument down in a flash, explaining that he was there for one reason, and one reason only: to discuss *Basic Instinct*.

It became clear to Jonathan and Pam that the meeting was supposed to be a public-relations stunt, but Joe Eszterhas was turning it into something else. Joe asked Rick Ruvolo, the aide from Harry Britt's office, if he would like a copy of the script. Joe handed it to him, and he would see that moment forever in slow motion: Rick snatching the script from his hands, and Verhoeven and Marshall in shock. Joe agreed to produce changes in a few days, and Verhoeven got an agreement from the community representatives that they would not reveal the contents of the script. The filmmakers still did not believe we had read the script. They were so far away from our world that they had no way to project themselves into it, or to imagine that there were closeted lesbians and gays all over Hollywood and on every movie set who were only too happy to provide us with every bit of information we needed.

Jonathan gave a press conference after the meeting, along with Jessea Greenman from GLAAD.

"Some queer kid," he said, "some baby dyke from Oklahoma who sees this film, could be pushed closer to the epidemic suicide among queer youth. I think Joe Eszterhas cared about that."

When Jonathan said the film company would have blood on its hands, he meant it literally. When asked if there would be any violent confrontations by Queer Nation, Jonathan told the press that Queer Nation did not exist, that it was a fictional entity, that it had no control over the actions of enraged individuals. The news that night featured one Allen Miller, a *Basic Instinct* spokesperson, who was asked if it was true that the writer wanted to revise some of the script. He confirmed this and added, "There were some things that could be changed."

This was a first. The writer had listened to the activists and had agreed with them on some points. The phones rang incessantly, Hollywood reeled, and Joe Eszterhas came down with a fever.

Two hours later, at the weekly Queer Nation meeting, there was a hand-lettered sign in both Spanish and English on the door to the Women's Building.

CAUTION. Due to the sensitive issues
involving the movie *Basic Instinct,*
possible infiltration by parties hostile to
Queer Nation could happen tonight.

Discretion and caution are strongly
suggested. DO NOT TAKE CANDY FROM
STRANGERS!

Mark Pritchard, in his positively fuchsia beret, stood at the door to the meeting, asking anyone he did not recognize to name three Queer Nation focus groups. Marvin, also in his beret, prowled the room, looking suspiciously at everyone. Jonathan sat tensely in his seat. He looked as if someone had taken hold of the back of his neck and was squeezing with full force. Jonathan had been advised that if there was any delay in the shooting of the film, he could be held responsible in civil court, and the film company would be able to personally sue him at the rate of at least $50,000 a day. Most of the Queer Nationals laughed this off, since they owned nothing and did not plan on amassing fortunes, but it was a real problem for Jonathan, who someday will inherit some of his family's money.

The Queer Nation meeting began, and in order to flush out hostiles and infiltrating media, a kiss-in was called. This was Marvin's idea; he was particularly proud of it. There were a certain number of very shocked faces as a member of the same gender planted full lips against theirs for the queer taste test.

By ten o'clock, thirty demonstrators were at the Moscone Center film site, and Jonathan was busily handing out press releases and waving to both the videocamera operators of the police department and the professional camera operators for *Basic Instinct,* who persisted in filming the demonstrators. Any fears that Jonathan had were always completely disguised amid the heterosexual public.

One camera bore an ABC logo, but when we contacted ABC and asked why they were doing such extensive shooting of the activists, it turned out that it was a ploy on the part of the film company. The fake logo was removed.

Officer Lea Militello was pacing on the opposite side of the street, closely observing both the demonstrators and the police. When she saw me, she came over and put her arm around my shoulder several times, causing Marvin to give me a suspicious look, which he followed by slowly walking around us to hear what we were saying.

I alerted Jonathan to another police videotaper. He marched right on over there and caused quite a commotion as I took a video of him standing squarely in front of the camera, waving and shouting, "Hi! Hi! It's Jonathan!" The demonstrators then blocked the street, trying to get the automobile drivers to blow their horns and so interfere with the soundtrack, while a member of LABIA handed out little mirrors the size of a quarter.

Annette Gaudino took the little mirror, licked its back, and stuck it on her forehead. Annette is a twenty-five-year-old, ninety-five-pound Latina from New York City, and she, like Jonathan, believes in confrontation and escalation. Annette had had childhood cancer from the ages of four to eight. A tumor had appeared first in her left kidney. The type of cancer she had travels through the bloodstream, like leukemia, to the lungs and to the bone. One of her kidneys destroyed, a tumor would also be removed from her lung, taking part of the lung with it. Yet the greatest trauma had been that her parents, who spoke Spanish and very little English, had been unable to communicate to the English-speaking doctors. As a four-year-old child, Annette had to translate what the doctors were saying to her parents about her possible death. Neither she nor her parents were given counseling, and there was no mention of alternative treatments. Her anger at the health-care system led to her involvement in ACT UP, where she focused on issues of concern to people of color, trying to make AIDS education and treatment accessible to ethnic-minority communities, where the next death wave of AIDS would strike. ACT UP had led her to Queer Nation. She believed that distorted images of lesbians, gays, and people of color, both gay and straight, contributed to our second-class status. Annette Gaudino would become the national spokesperson and driving force behind the demonstrations and media assault when *Basic Instinct* was finally released. With only two hundred dollars to go up against the world's biggest advertising machine, the activists would counter *Basic Instinct* by naming their protest group Catherine Did It, and thus giving away the end of the movie. *Entertainment To-*

*night* would find it more than newsworthy, especially when Annette later announced that she intended to shut down the Os-
cars. This threat would inspire the comic genius of Billy Crystal
to compare the Oscar ceremony that he emceed that night with
*Cape Fear,* and would get Annette arrested by the LAPD in
what was certainly a preemptive strike.

Annette adjusted her mirror on her forehead. It began to driz-
zle as she promenaded for the police videotaper, who continued
to document the Queer Nationals, most of whom now had little
mirrors stuck to their foreheads in direct violation of the temporary restraining order. The car horns were blaring at the people
blocking the street, and everyone was filming everyone. I filmed
the people filming the demonstrators who then filmed me filming
them. A young policeman asked one of the LABIA members what
the mirrors were for, and she launched into an elaborate monologue on how since the beginning of time queers had been considered magical people, and that the mirrors represented the queer
third eye. The policeman listened very carefully, as Officer Lea
Militello stood with her hands in her pockets a few feet away,
amused at LABIA's recap of revisionist queer history for her
straight fellow officer, who would now probably give her little
presents of sticky-backed mirrors in a friendly gesture. Another
straight cop, who was also listening intently to LABIA's explanation of the mirrors, turned to his partner in confusion and said,
"What did she say?"

His partner confidently replied in a Bronx accent, "She said it
was cultural," and they both nodded respectfully at the mirrored
ones. Lea Militello rolled her eyes up into her head as demonstrators sprinkled each other with glitter, which they called fairy
dust, and others arranged aluminum-foil headbands in their hair.
This was happening on Fourth Street.

Sun Tzu teaches the art of misdirection, of decoy. It had only
taken fifteen minutes to disconnect all of the film company's
lights along Third Street and plunge the set into darkness. Filming was delayed four and a half hours that evening.

The papers that afternoon had again reported that the *Basic
Instinct* people believed we had not even read the script. I sent the

script, excerpts highlighted, along with Joe Eszterhaz's suggested improvements, to Rob Morse, a columnist at the *San Francisco Examiner*. I still thought of myself as a journalist, and had never officially declared myself a member of any of the groups cited under the temporary restraining order. I thought it perfectly legal that I release to Mr. Morse the script, which the film company had declared so sacred that it was beginning to take on the mystique of the lesbian Pentagon Papers.

The next day, Morse published a column entitled "Basically, It Stinks." This column turned the public-relations tide for the activists, and reframed the debate. BASICALLY, IT STINKS became a favored activist sign. Morse revealed many of the plot points we were contesting and quoted extensively from the script, which, he was ashamed to say, was written by "another heterosexual man." "This is Hollywood sex," he concluded. "Audiences are being date raped."

He also revealed one of the top-secret proposed "improvements" to the script, which was to have the bisexual Catherine ice-pick a few women as well as men. My personal favorite, however, was Joe's suggestion that the image of Roxy's slashed-up little brother be replaced with a large glossy photograph of an elderly, gray-haired woman in a pool of blood. Instead of killing her little brother, Roxy could kill her mother. You had to love it. I stuck a mirror on my forehead. It seemed the only appropriate response.

The next evening, Jonathan was talking to a reporter from the *L.A. Times* in Chevy's, a Mexican restaurant across the street from the protest site, when the *L.A. Times* photographer came running in and told the reporter to come right away. "You've gotta see this!" he said. "You've gotta see this!" He charged outside, Jonathan behind him, to see a series of signs held high by the demonstrators: HONK IF YOU LOVE THE 49ERS. HONK IF YOU SUPPORT THE TROOPS. HONK IF YOU HATE *BASIC INSTINCT*. Tanya was standing in the middle of them, waving a flag, having carefully applied the bright red lipstick from Walgreen's that she always wore to demonstrations. Mark and Tanya led the chant: "We're number one! We're number one!" and closed with a rousing rendition of "The Star-Spangled Banner." The police stood extra tall, and extra confused, and the activists appeared on the front page of the *L.A. Times* "Calendar" section, proving that fifteen Queer Nationals with a photo op can beat a hundred and fifty thousand lesbians and gays marching up the street any day.

Later that night, there were only a handful of demonstrators left, Annette and Mark among them. They waited patiently at the barricades. They knew from the shooting schedule that Michael Douglas had to do a car-chase scene, the one in which the lesbian character plunges to her death in a black Ferrari when, in a fit of jealous rage, she tries to run down the Douglas character, who is now sleeping with her lover. "Salt in the wound" is a nice way to describe the feelings of the demonstrators: This scene was being filmed at the Moscone Center, named in honor of the assassinated mayor. The death of the evil lesbian who instinctively killed her little brother—or perhaps her mother—would take place under the huge black letters MOSCONE.

Michael Douglas backed up his car to the barricades. There was a camera mounted on the hood. The crew, in yellow rain slickers, was hosing down the street to get that *noir* look. Because of the drought, San Francisco streets had built up many layers of oil, which would normally have been washed away by rain. Wetting the street turned the oil-slicked road into glass. The car was only a few feet from the demonstrators.

"Michael Douglas, go home!" shouted Annette.

"Butt ugly! Butt ugly!" shouted Mark, apparently privy to some type of mysterious male thing.

Verhoeven was giving Michael instructions on how to do the take. Douglas looked nervous. His hand was up to his mouth.

"Michael Douglas, go home!"

"Butt ugly! Butt ugly!"

Douglas stepped on the gas and hit the brakes. The car skidded and hit some wooden sawhorses. The camera mounted on the hood began to wobble and the demonstrators cheered. Michael backed the car up again to the barricades. He kept fixing his hair in the rearview mirror. The crew in yellow slickers huddled, their backs to Annette and Mark, who were now leading the small group in a chant: "Hollywood bashes queers!" The crew suddenly turned, a mass of yellow plastic, and yelled in unison, smiles wide and adrenalized, "Straight-bashers!" Annette lost it. She started screaming at them, "Yeah! All those straight kids who commit suicide every year because they're oppressed because of their heterosexuality. All those straight couples who are beaten on the streets for holding hands!" They had tapped a well of rage, and she was pointing at them. They looked at the ground and shuffled around. They did not want to look at her, but she would return every single night, and on this night, as Michael Douglas fixed his hair in the rearview mirror and the Ferrari plunged the lesbian character into the Hollywood death pit, Annette's final words traveled across the brightly lit set: "You have not budgeted for my anger!"

Yet it was Jonathan whom the film company focused on. He was mediagenic. He was articulate and an extremist, but more important, he was a white male. It was easier to attack a white male. It would not do to attack Annette, a small Latina. The filmmakers could lose sympathy. But this cocky young man in leather, with a bright yellow sign saying MILITANT HOMOSEXUAL taped to his back, would be perfect. The crew began to call him by name in sing-song. "Jon-a-than. Jon-a-than." For a gay man, male voices sing-songing your name are a universal signal, a precursor to attack. Scattered in with the phone messages from the media were threats and more male voices, shouting then whispering, "Queer kike." The *Basic Instinct* lawyers appeared on his street, parked in a car at the stop sign on the corner. They smiled at him the way straight men do when they want to taunt fairies. Jonathan lived on a dead-end street, and he had made the mistake of listing his address in the telephone directory.

Jonathan was used to this. He wore Queer Nation T-shirts in tough neighborhoods, in all neighborhoods. He had taken a vow to be identifiably queer at all times, in all places, no matter what the conditions. He and his lover, Kurt Barrie, had just returned from San Diego, where they had been walking near the zoo. A group of kids on skateboards had stopped and said, "Fucking faggots." Jonathan said, "Fuck you." One of the kids pulled a hunting knife from behind his back. It looked so big, sharp, and surreal to Jonathan when the kid headed toward him, the knife flashing in the sunlight. Jonathan was scared to hell, and he and Kurt had to run. Having to run enraged and humiliated him.

I did not understand why he had to do this, to be queer everywhere and always, but he had taken his vow with absolute sincerity. I wished he would just slap a mirror on his forehead, but Jonathan had gone to war.

He believed that he was a Holocaust survivor, as was any sentient Jew of the latter half of the twentieth century. "But for thee go I," he said. Some members of his family had been incarcerated and killed, although most of the family had come to America. As a child, he had been shown the grainy newsreels of World War II Allied soldiers doing postliberation mass burials of concentration-camp victims. The most horrific image for Jonathan had been the truckloads of dead babies. He had transitioned the anger he felt at the demonization and slaughter of the Jews into an absolute refusal to be silent about his homosexuality, a refusal to accept less than fully human status. He believed that the nice moderates and liberals would do nothing to help unless their hands were forced, and if he died as a result of always being out, that was just fine. He would die with honor. He would never again be "a scared queer."

On Friday night, two days into the *Basic Instinct* demonstrations, Jonathan walked up the steps to the porch of his modest, rented Victorian. He saw that someone had ripped down the gay rainbow flag he had displayed. He went inside. It was sundown. He got out the challah, lit the candles, put on his yarmulke, and performed his customary Shabbat ritual, singing the thousand-year-old songs and prayers as a reminder of his Judaism, as a ritual to keep him solid and focused.

I went home to Cheryl and Jesse, who seemed very far away, but safe, in a world of preparations for the Black and White Ball, of reenactments of the adventures of Peter Pan. Peter Pan, says Sir James, believes that to die will be an awfully big adventure, and as I thought about Jonathan that night, I knew that he, too, was happy.

\* \* \*

I had agreed to devote Saturday afternoon to shopping with Gilbert for the Black and White Ball. It was like having a split screen in my head. On one side of the screen, I was in the midst of a media war on Hollywood homophobia, with *Basic Instinct* as the flashpoint. My own telephone rang incessantly; most of the calls were from strategizing activists, though occasionally they were from the media with outrageous invitations to, for example, be the third guest on a talk show featuring a televangelist and a member of the S & M community. No, but thank you so much for asking. One activist called with Patty Duke's home phone number. What I was supposed to do with this was a mystery to me, so I tossed it, opting to allow Patty Duke one more moment of privacy. Another activist called with the name of the caterer. Flat tires on the catering truck were suggested; this would make the coffee and food late. The actors would start to get irritable. If the food was late, the company would have to pay meal penalties. The actors would start getting picky and bitchy. They'd feel trapped in their hotel rooms. They're used to breezing into town, being big stars, greeted everywhere they go, said the activist. Now they're cooped up in hotels. They don't like the sheets, how they're folded. They have to walk by the mirrors too often, and they begin to hate their hair, which would be the beginning of the end. Finally, they become paranoid, and everyone begins to look queer to them: the desk clerk, the waiter, the hairdresser, the physician from whom they're requesting Valium.

On the other side of this split screen, beneath a crisp blue sky peppered with painted clouds, Gilbert was dragging me to every store in downtown San Francisco in search of appropriate ball attire. I had wanted to wear a white suit with trousers, something very *Grand Hotel,* or androgynously British like Sebastian's clothes in *Brideshead Revisited,* but Gilbert and Cheryl had fought against this and won. Gilbert really wanted me to wear a ball gown with a massive skirt, something Princess Di might wear to a coronation, but I soon ended that little fantasy. He took me to Hermès to look at scarves, to Chanel, to Magnin's to see the Bob Mackie gowns and one spectacular Valentino, which I loved and which cost "only" five thousand dollars. We finally went to Macy's and settled on a short, tight black dress covered with big black bangles. I would never have bought this if I had been alone. We then drove to an exotic bead store where Gilbert bought two thousand crystals. He hired a seamstress to hand-apply them to a white sweatshirt from the Gap. Casual, yet glamorous, would be his look at this year's ball.

Gilbert was making the banners at the Dream Center, where he had set up his Singer sewing machines. He sewed all day, all night with his assistants. He wondered who would fly in from New York, what Ann Getty and Charlotte Swig would wear. He just happened to mention that he had never seen a lesbian couple, and certainly not a lesbian couple in dresses, dance together at the Black and White. Great.

I brought home my dress and tossed it on the bed. Cheryl was waiting to see it, having gotten her own dress just the day before. She wanted me to model for her, but I was more interested in listening to my phone messages, in finding out if any of Joe's script changes were being accepted by the director. I heard the front door slam. Furious, Cheryl had left. I hung up the phone, appropriately guilty. Jesse was standing in the doorway with his green felt Peter Pan hat on, paper sword in hand. He wanted his favorite dinner, again, Kraft Macaroni and Cheese Wheels, so I filled a pot with water and set it to boil. Jesse waited patiently, his hands in his lap. The doorbell rang; our neighbor Terry came upstairs. Terry proudly described herself as the quintessential working-class femme: She always wore dresses when she went dancing, *and* she could fix her own car. She was very interested in the ball, and she told me I had better get interested in it quick or Cheryl would have me sleeping on the couch for the next week. While I sliced some zucchini and Jesse counted the pieces, Terry stirred the macaroni into the boiling water with great care, as if she were making one of Alice B. Toklas's French soufflés, and she told me a story. "Suzy and I were at a regional awards banquet for team excellence. The band began to play slow songs, and we waited for a fast one, so we could dance without touch-ing. But the band played only slow songs. We watched the cou-ples take the floor for almost an hour, and then we decided to slow-dance together. Everyone in the room stopped talking, and just stared. The straight people from Suzy's office got up and danced around us, to protect us."

Terry opened the grated-cheese pouch and meticulously sprinkled cheese on the cooked macaroni as Jesse looked on in anticipation.

"You must have felt very proud of yourselves," I said.

"Actually," said Terry, slowing mixing the cheese and macaroni, "my hands were sweating and my knees were shaking."

Jesse fell asleep in my arms that night as I read to him about how the Neverland with all of its moving black shadows was real now, and there were no night-lights because it was no longer make-believe. I put him in his bed and put his paper sword on the pillow beside his head. He liked to sleep with it, just in case in his dreams it was the Night of Nights, when Hook and Pan perform their final duel. I kissed him good night, dimmed the lights, and closed the door to his room.

It was dark and quiet outside, and I noticed some macaroni had fallen on the large black-and-white squares of the kitchen floor. The macaroni had hardened, so I took a butter knife, got down on my hands and knees, and scraped it off. I heard the front door open; Cheryl walked up the stairs and into the kitchen. I stood and opened my arms to embrace her. At first she had a furious expression, but she suddenly began to laugh. I didn't understand. At least she appeared to be having a really good time. Why was she laughing? I was doing everything I could to please her. I was wearing the damned short tight black bangled dress from Macy's, along with black hose, although I was barefoot.

"You've got macaroni on your bangles," she said, "no shoes, you're holding a knife, and you want me to rush into your arms?"

I put the knife on the table, took her in my arms, and kissed her. We fit perfectly together. We always had. But as deeply as I loved her at that moment, that split screen persisted in my head, and on the other side there was a beast named Joe in a shadowy paradise, thick fingers banging on typewriter keys, violent sexual fantasies distorting his face in excitement.

\* \* \*

Everyone was white. For someone from San Francisco, that in itself was disturbing. The suburban Marin town looked like a place I had visited years ago, a place where a friend had gone to have a nervous breakdown. The white clapboard restaurant where the hostess enunciated each word with care and the waiters moved slowly, addressing the clientele by name, could have easily been the dining room of a sanitarium. This world was protected, rarefied, and the people who lived and lunched in it were not afraid because violence rarely touched them. That was just Hollywood, just the movies. This was the world where Joe Eszterhas and his family lived.

In response to a letter sent to him through Supervisor Harry Britt's office, Joe Eszterhas had agreed to meet with me. I sat with my hands on the white linen tablecloth, waiting for the enemy.

Joe Eszterhas stood framed in the idyllic white doorway, a burly man whose hair and beard belonged on a Hell's Angel. He had on dark sunglasses, a short-sleeved white shirt, and plain beige Bermuda shorts. The last thing I had expected to see were Joe Eszterhas's knees. I was expecting the anti-Christ, but got a middle-aged man in white socks.

He chain-smoked for hours, and told story after story as I ordered one dish after another. He showed me how, when he was a child, one boy would come up behind him and pull his ears. The boy called him names, too, and Joe showed me how he hit his tormentor over the head from behind with a baseball bat. The boy had almost died.

"It was blind rage," said Joe. "Everything coming together. He became the symbol of a whole bunch of stuff that was happening with all the name-calling." I understood. Hadn't *Basic Instinct* become a symbol for the protesters, and for me?

"He called me names," Joe said again.

Joe is one of the best storytellers I have ever met. Having lunch with him was like having a front-row seat for a piece of performance art. Every time he wanted to illustrate something, he arranged the silverware and salt shakers. Michael Douglas was a fork, and Paul Verhoeven was the pepper shaker. Irwin Winkler, the original producer, was salt, and Guy McElwaine, his agent, was the ashtray. Soon the napkins were involved in the scenario. Alan Marshall, the producer, was a napkin with a wet stain on it. First we were in Beverly Hills, then we were in Morton's at the "A" table near the door on a Monday, the power people night. Spoons and wineglasses were commandeered to represent anonymous phone-callers and speakerphone shouting matches with Carolco's owner, Mario Kassar. Joe had documented everything. The Alan Marshall producer napkin fluttered to the ground when Joe dissected him as a gofer, an insecure man who wanted to make points with Verhoeven so that he would be hired to do other jobs.

Joe tried to explain what he meant by omnisexual, which was his way of describing Catherine, the bisexual ice-pick murderess, but at the end of his explanation, he had only described bisexuality. His monologue was elaborate; it curved into a discourse on the Catholic church and the nature of psychosexual guilt trips for both straight and gay people.

"Can you imagine the notion that you're sinning because of what you think?" he asked me.

And I asked him, "Can you imagine the notion that you're sinning because of who you love?"

He thought about that, and lit another cigarette.

Joe seemed to be afraid of no one, not studio heads or even the signatory on his three-million-dollar check. But what about the fork, Michael Douglas? Joe was very careful with the fork, because the fork was the one with the power, so I knew that I was talking to the wrong person. It was not this man in Bermuda shorts and white socks whom I should be talking to; it was Michael Douglas. Michael Douglas was the one with the power.

Joe walked me to my car.

"So what was it that the kids called you?" I asked.

"You know. Names."

"But what names, Joe?"

His arms hung out from his sides, and he looked like a little boy.

"Don't you remember?" I asked.

His arms went up a little. "Queer," he said. He cleared his throat. "They called me queer."

After all these years, there was still pain in his face, and I saw the immigrant child in Volunteers of America clothing, the Hungarian accent thick on his tongue, his mother suffering, out of her mind from lead poisoning, and I lost my anger. This was a man who probably slept with a night-light in a world where everything was make-believe, where it was a mystery why everyone was mad at him.

# CHAPTER IX

# Hooray for Hollywood

THE SAN FRANCISCO skyline was decorated with splashes of red, and there was a warm wind in the SOMA (South of Market) section of the city. I felt odd. It was Monday, April 29, 1991, and the moon was full, the perfect night for a street show. It was also the fourteenth anniversary of J.'s death, which always made me melancholy. None of the activists had arrived, and I walked around the set's heavily guarded perimeter. I felt a little disoriented as the twilight faded and the make-believe world of *Basic Instinct* asserted its power and reality. The crew moved under blazing artificial illumination. The crane lights were flung up against the skyline like huge tentacles, taller than the surrounding buildings, their cyclops eyes of light overpowering the brightening moon. I found a telephone in the Crazy 8's Billiards Bar and Grill, which was just around the corner from the set. "Crazy" was wrought in tilting neon letters of purple, green, red, blue, and orange. Above the honky-tonk lettering was a big black eight-ball. When I was a child, I had an eight-ball, the kind that you asked a question and turned over to await an answer that floated slowly in a milky fluid to the surface. My favorite question was, Is there a heaven? The answers were always the same: Yes. No. Maybe. Try again later.

I called Jonathan from the Crazy 8's, and he told me he had

just gotten word that all of Joe's suggested script changes had been rejected. If the *Basic Instinct* people had agreed to even one minor change, it would have taken the wind out of our sails, he said, but not only did they refuse, they made the statement that they would not give in to street protest. The film company had opted for escalation rather than defusion. The community leaders' meeting at the Hyatt was completely ignored. The director remarked to the press that Joe had requested the changes because his family lived in nearby Marin, and he was afraid of the dangerous, radical gays. Joe had retaliated by issuing a statement saying he was moved by the meeting with community leaders, and that he wanted to help better the lives of gay people, not hurt them. Joe's changes were rejected by the director, the producer, and the real power on the set, Michael Douglas, who on this full-moon night would become very agitated as he paced in black jeans and slicked-back hair. But this night would belong to the producer, Alan Marshall, who would achieve his fifteen minutes of fame.

There was media everywhere in response to the dueling press statements of *Basic Instinct*'s makers and Joe Eszterhas, and because the *L.A. Times* photo-op story featuring Tanya and Mark and their "49ers rally" had appeared that day. Not only were daily-newspaper reporters on the set, but so were national and international radio and television reporters and writers from New York–based slick magazines. If I had had an eight-ball, and had asked it what Alan Marshall's thoughts were that evening, the words of Bay Area performance artist Dee Russell might well have floated to the surface: "Justify my publicity stunt."

I hung up the phone in the Crazy 8's and went outside. It was getting close to nine o'clock, and the demonstration would be starting. I was all in black, no stickers, my videocamera slung over my shoulder. I had to be very careful. If I were arrested, my fight to adopt Jesse could be jeopardized, yet I could not stay away from the protest this night. There was something personal about it, but I could not yet quite put my finger on what. I was standing in the darkening twilight, under the neon sign of the Crazy 8's, when Officer Lea Militello and her partner drove up in an unmarked brown police car.

"What's it gonna be like tonight, Phyllis?" she asked with a little smile similar to the one she had during LABIA's discourse on mirrors and the queer third eye.

"I'd like Jesse and your boy Ryan to grow up with some other images," I said. "How about a heroic lesbian cop? What's wrong with that?"

Lea and her partner laughed and drove around the corner. I walked to my car, which was across from the favored demonstration site at the mouth of an alley called Clementina. As I sat in my incredibly obvious red Ford Escort, I watched in my rearview mirror as cars pulled up and neared me slowly, eyes searching, letting me know they saw me. It was not as if I were hiding. I was not sure who was the police and who was security for the movie. Suddenly, there was a rush of police cars, at least half a dozen. They circled the block. Then another unmarked car came up on me very slowly, lights dimmed. Perhaps they were interested in me because I had been walking around with a videocamera slung over my shoulder. Not only did I want a visual record of the protest, but the videocamera would help to prevent me from being accidentally arrested. Yet another cop car did a drive-by of me in my car. I regretted not having an ice pick to dangle coyly from the open window. The police cars and vans came around the corner again, and took a sudden turn down an alley behind my car.

I had been talking into my hand-held tape recorder, and I realized that at a distance it might appear to be a walkie-talkie. Maybe they thought I was the point person for the lavender revolution, and I was somehow communicating from my red Ford Escort with the masses of Queer Nationals, the raging hordes of hairdressers and plumbers who were getting ready to storm the set. I was actually hoping that at least ten people would show up.

It was ten minutes before nine, and there was not a radical in sight. Finally, three protesters came around the corner. I watched them shake hands at the barricades. All these cops, and there's three guys and me. Another cop came by on a little red motorcycle. He stopped and looked up to the roof across the street from me. Yeah, I thought, we're going to have people on the rooftops, queer Tarzans and Janes swinging down in guerrilla drag.

Another paddy wagon went down the alley behind me as a young woman sauntered down the street to join the protesters. I got out of my car and walked down the alley that the paddy wagons had entered. At the end of the alley, inside a chain-link fence, there was a massive police presence, including what I now could recognize as an arrest team. As I walked up the alleyway, a man on the rooftop across the street aimed at me with a high-powered camera and clicked away. I waved. There were now about twenty-five protesters at the barricades, chatting to each other and the press. There was a press person for every demonstrator. A cab pulled up and three protesters got out. I had never seen demonstrators arrive by taxi.

Pam Bates was wearing a black trench coat with deep pockets. She had been on a shopping expedition to a nautical supply store at Fisherman's Wharf, one of those places that has a gigantic anchor outside. Every once in a while, she would reach through her coat from the pockets and trigger a compressed-air horn, which is used by speedboat operators and is, conveniently, the size of a can of hairspray. The sound poured out from underneath her feet and vibrated off the buildings. It was difficult to tell where it was coming from, especially with Pam posing so nonchalantly.

Mark Pritchard had made a huge sign that said HOLLYWOOD EQUALS HOMOPHOBIA. He stood right at the barricades, holding the sign high above his head, the words facing the protesters and the reporters. He realized that his sign was blank on the side facing the movie company, so he decided to write a message for them, too: BUTT UGLY DOUGLAS GO HOME. This had definitely become Mark's theme. He didn't think that Douglas would actually see his sign, but he knew that some of the crew would, and that it might get back to him. Mark would get his wish. When *Basic Instinct* was finally released, Maria Shriver did an up-close-and-personal interview with Michael Douglas, in which she teased him with, "But Michael! You're naked!" One of the images of the protest that her show transmitted across the country was of an impish Mark Pritchard, his chin resting on the BUTT UGLY DOUGLAS GO HOME sign.

Jonathan moved to the barricades, and the show was on.

"Hollywood, you stink."

The television news camera lights came up as whistles blew, air horns wailed, and the chants accelerated. The location of the nautical compressed-air horn baffled the police as Pam Bates stood by, apparently in a condition of Zen-like calm.

"Ice picks for peace! Ice picks for peace!"

The *Basic Instinct* lawyer, primly dressed in his Brooks Brothers suit, came to the barricades with a pristine white megaphone and read from the temporary restraining order: "By Order of the Honorable John Dearman . . ." as one young man mercilessly blew bubbles all over him, and a very uptight curly-haired assistant to the attorney literally threw copies of the TRO at the demonstrators, hitting some of them in the face. In retaliation, copies of the TRO were picked up from the ground and thrown back over the barricades at the *Basic Instinct* lawyer, who continued to drone on about glitter as his terrified surrogate tried to retrieve the TROs from the ground. Bells began to ring, air horns wailed, and a police officer's stern voice over a megaphone warned, "Do not touch the barricades."

"Murderers! Murderers!" shouted Jonathan and the demonstrators, pointing their fingers at the crew and the producer.

"Love your shoes. Hate your script!"

"Butt ugly! Butt ugly!"

"Shame! Shame!"

"Hollywood bashes queers!"

Annette was relentlessly blowing her gay-bashing whistle. Just on the other side of the barricades was a crew member wearing a fleece-collared leather bomber jacket, his long greasy hair in a ponytail. He laughed and pointed at her as the TRO was being read.

"Isn't she cute?" the guy said. "Check her out. Check out the little one."

I was standing in the midst of the demonstration, my video-camera up on my shoulder. I was getting nice close-ups of leather jackets with neon stickers, and Brooks Brothers suits. I was standing beside Jonathan, whose rage was extraordinary. My eye suddenly came away from the lens as the crew member again taunted Annette, and in the burst of a well-lit, colorful world, I pointed at the producer with my free hand and shouted, "Shame!" I put the camera back against my eye, but again I could not resist the desire to shout, yet I still kept filming. Clearly, I had crossed the line. I stepped back, realizing that I had to be careful, keep myself under control. I was risking arrest.

I moved down the alley to the street, and saw that a team of police on red motorcycles was surrounding the area and an arrest squad of about thirty officers in full riot gear was approaching, batons in hand, plastic visors snapped up, guns and Mace on their hips. They were a full block away but approaching rapidly, their feet hitting the pavement in unison like a marching band gone crazy. I ran back down the alley and told Jonathan what was happening, and he led the protesters away from the barricades, singing a rousing rendition of "Hooray for Hollywood." The band of protesters, now about thirty strong, danced up the block, away from the marching arrest team. Straggling protesters sang the marching chant of the Wicked Witch's guards in *The Wizard of Oz* as the arrest team took up a position on the now abandoned barricade. I followed the band of protesters around the corner. They were delighted with the fact that the second barricade was positioned directly under a low overpass that acted as an echo chamber. This echo chamber also made it quite certain that everyone on the set, including the director and Michael Douglas, could hear Queer Nation's terrific rendition of "The Star-Spangled Banner."

Again the lawyer read the TRO, bubbles popped on his nose, and the shouts of "Shame!" echoed under the bridge, all of this under a spectacular San Francisco skyline. I approached Lea Militello and told her that most of these demonstrators had never been arrested and did not want to be arrested. What were the rules? She consulted with the lawyers and with the producer, Alan Marshall, and when she had finished, she called Jonathan and me over to her. Apparently, there were three major sets of barricades, and once the TRO had been read at each location, anyone remaining there was subject to arrest. Jonathan explained the rules to the demonstrators, who moved away from the site and turned the corner, the red police motorcycles escorting them every inch of the way. I was lagging behind, believing all was over. The demonstrators walked down the block and were straggling along, en route to their cars to go home. They had not quite reached the corner. I saw Alan Marshall and stopped to film him. He had pasty, hanging cheeks, and a large belly. He was middle-aged, and his hair was short and white. He cultivated a stereotypical British reserve of expressionless, superior self-control, similar to that of the Buckingham Palace guard when they have the queen's Welsh Corgis nipping at their heels. He hated being filmed by me. He was talking with the officer in charge of the demonstrations, and he asked if there was anything the police could do to stop me from filming. The officer shook his head sadly. Sorry. They could not stop me from filming him. That was not covered by the TRO. Marshall looked down the block and studied the backs of the demonstrators.

"Send in the cops," he said to the officer in charge. I couldn't believe it. The demonstrators had just been told that there would be no arrests if they stayed within the defined parameters.

"Yes, sir," said a clearly animated cop, snapping to attention. Marshall and this police officer were definitely in their own movie.

Most of the demonstrators had turned the corner when the police brigade lined up and someone in charge shouted, "Move!" They snapped their clubs into their hands in unison, then froze in their tracks.

"Move up!" shouted the commander, and the police formed a tight line.

"We're gonna move down the street. Then get 'em and encircle them." It was like a bad dream, the intensity of this display of force. None of the demonstrators had any weapons, unless you counted glitter and whistles, and most of them had never been arrested. I hoped they would not panic.

I ran alongside the trotting police to the end of the block and turned the corner only to see that the activists had already been surrounded by the motorcycle police in front of the Shanti Project, an AIDS hospice network group. John Woods and I were filming everything, but I got too close to the arrest circle.

I heard a mechanically amplified voice: "The woman with the videocamera. Get back." I got up on the sidewalk, not sure where

I was supposed to go. My heart was beating so fast, I thought I might lose consciousness. The voice persisted: "Get off the sidewalk." I obliged and stepped into the street. A cop charged me. "Get on the sidewalk," he ordered. "They just ordered me off. Where do you want me to go?" I asked in my most polite tone of voice. My mouth was absolutely dry and I could not swallow. I could only hope that I would escape arrest, not only because an arrest might jeopardize Jesse's adoption, but because Cheryl would kill me. The demonstrators were absolutely silent beneath the massive cyclops eye of a light crane that ironically shone down squarely upon them.

"Over there! Over there!" the cop shouted at me, his baton squared across his chest as he herded me backward toward the sidewalk and the arrest circle. I saw Lea Militello, and I shouted to her. She called the cop off and he let me stand far to the side, near the backup arrest team. He was awfully disappointed.

The silence was strange as a young man who had been trailing the group was escorted toward the arrest circle. He had chronic arthritis and he walked very slowly. For some reason, although the police officer had been alerted, he insisted on holding the young man's arm up high and at an uncomfortable angle. At the arrest circle, the wall of blue uniforms opened and deposited him. Jonathan kissed his cheek, and then Annette and Jonathan began to shout: "Hollywood greed victimizes us," but after a moment, there again was silence. One small hand lettered sign was visible: STOP HATE. Then Jonathan saw Alan Marshall, and began to challenge him. "Doesn't it bother you that these people—I'm talking to you"—Jonathan made eye contact with Marshall—"that you, the producer of this film . . . doesn't it bother you that you're willing to do this, for entertainment?"

The sky was black, but the scene was illuminated like a movie set. It was clear that most of the demonstrators were very frightened that the police would suddenly charge. There had been a terrible police charge in the Castro during an ACT UP demonstration on October 6, 1989, when the heads of bystanders had been broken open as the cops shouted, "Faggot!" John Woods was now filming from the other side of the street, having camouflaged himself with the news media. Annette could not see either of us, and she became frightened because our videocameras were the best form of protection for the activists. She was too small to see over the tightly packed blue uniforms of the police, and she began to feel a horrible anger. She snapped into a role, the role of the "angry lesbian," and it was as if she were watching herself perform. This role stopped her from hitting anyone or getting violent and losing control out of panic. It also stopped her from being visibly frightened. She looked at Jonathan's face, and he seemed frightened to her, and that was not helping matters. He was marching up and down inside the circle, shouting, "Does everybody realize what's happening here? The producer is going to make citizen's arrests of us in our own city. Does everyone have an analysis of this?" It was indeed quite strange. Alan Marshall had been given the power to use the police as his private force.

The encircled demonstrators were getting more tense, their faces more frightened, but Mark Pritchard had a sudden upward rush of adrenaline, an inspiration close to divine intervention. Yes. He had an analysis of this. This is theater! he realized, and Mark did love theater. He spotted Alan Marshall and turned on his best high school teacher's voice. "Marshall. What are you doing in our town, Marshall? Marshall. I'm calling Donald Wildmon of the American Family Association. I'm gonna tell him this movie's about drugs and sex. I'm telling him that drugs and sex take place in a church. I'm telling him the movie glorifies lesbians."

The fearful tension was broken, yet another wall of police arrived. There were at least five police officers on the movie set for every demonstrator. Mark, of course, was the first one selected for arrest by Mr. Marshall, who had to walk up to the police line and identify the protesters one by one.

"Arrest him," said Marshall, his hands in his pockets.

"Which one? Who? Who?" asked the cop. "You have to point at him."

Marshall pointed at Mark and said, "This guy. Arrest him."

The police line opened and two cops reached in for Mark, tied his hands behind his back, and walked him forward about ten feet into the bright Hollywood light. It was very quiet, and Mark was quiet, too. He didn't want anyone to freak out. He wanted to demonstrate how to be arrested by giving no provocation to the police. They took Mark's picture, and brought him to the paddy wagon. The stink of old urine made the accommodations less than desirable.

The next one arrested was Annette. She was so small that the cops practically had to kneel to cuff her. They brought her forward and stood her in front of Alan Marshall.

"That's a real lesbian you're arresting," I shouted. "She's not a psychotic, homicidal pervert! She's a real person!" I couldn't believe my mouth was working like this, but I just didn't care anymore. Marshall looked over to me, but could do nothing. We were over a block from the movie set, an absurd distance beyond the one hundred feet required by the temporary restraining order, and Lea Militello had spoken for me. In the end, none of these arrests would hold up in court, but the arrestees would never forget their humiliation and fear.

Jonathan was brought forward; when he stood in front of Marshall, they pulled the cuffs especially tight on his wrists because, after all, Jonathan was the very dangerous Lavender Menace. Jonathan said to Marshall, "You slimeball." And he made a vow that before this was over, Marshall would experience what Jonathan and the other demonstrators had experienced this night. "This is not the end of it," said Jonathan, and Marshall smirked.

The police finished loading the first van, slammed the back doors, and locked them. Slowly, the van began to rock back and forth from the weight of the demonstrators pushing it from the inside. There were vague shouts of "I haven't got my seat belt on!" That sounded like Jonathan. Then I heard something most peculiar. They were singing "Happy Birthday to You" to Mark. The first van pulled away, and the next van pulled up in its place.

Lea Militello walked away from the scene, enraged. She had consulted with the *Basic Instinct* lawyers and had then told the activists that they would not be allowed to return to any particular set of barricades or they would be in violation of the TRO. Other than that, they could just go home. Yet Marshall could not resist having the demonstrators arrested, and he had given the order anyway. The filmmakers had made a fool of her, and some of the activists who hated the police were sure she had known what she was doing.

There were thirty arrests; I filmed each one. As the last arrest was completed, and the vans pulled away, and the police marched back to their clubhouse, Alan Marshall walked tall back to the set, and the movie light that had illuminated the scene went out. The arrests had all happened under the sign for the Shanti Project, the place that provides compassionate companions to those dying of AIDS. *Shanti* is the Sanskrit word for "the peace that passeth understanding." It is the word, three times repeated, that closes T. S. Eliot's "The Waste Land."

It was late, I was alone, and the street was deserted. It was not a part of town safe for women, lesbians, or gays. I walked up the street, past the Crazy 8's. The neon sign evoked a terrible sadness. I knew that this was the anniversary of J.'s death, but that was not really the cause of my feelings. It was then that I saw the image that I had been carrying with me since my adolescence.

When I was watching the arrests, especially Annette's, I had felt it, but I did not know what it was. I saw it clearly now in my mind. It was from the movie *The Fox,* which was the first image of lesbianism that I had ever seen. It was 1968. I was seventeen years old. I was so excited. There had been a lot of advertising for the movie, and I had read the word "lesbian" for the first time. I had looked it up in the dictionary and discovered the word for what I was. Sandy Dennis played the lesbian, Jill. She is in love with a bi-woman, who lives with her on a farm. A straight man arrives; the bi-woman is "cured," and so becomes straight. This was not enough, though. The closing image, the image that I saw hundreds of times in my mind's eye, the one my adolescent mind watched over and over in explicit detail, was of the lesbian lying crushed to death beneath a huge tree that the man has just cut down. She is dead as poetic justice for her crime against nature, her perversion, the huge tree between her legs, her pelvis snapped, her dead eyes open, blood trickling from the corner of her mouth. More than twenty years later, and Hollywood is still churning it out about lesbians and bi-women, this and nothing much else. The sex is more explicit, but the sin and punishment are the same.

I could see the lights of the *Basic Instinct* set, which dominated the skyline, and although I felt angry, I also felt a tremendous release. The movie industry had been confronted. The filmmakers had not acted with impunity, and there had been enough press coverage so that adolescent lesbian and gay teens could hear the message the Queer Nationals were desperately trying to send to them: This is a lie. This is not you. They are censoring our true lives.

I drove to the Hall of Justice and stood outside with a handful of others, waiting for the release of the arrested. I was pacing nervously, imagining the worst. What was happening was this:

The temperature inside the arrest vans was very high, and it had been hard to breathe. Annette got out of the van, holding her hands above her head; she faced the processing police, who were enthroned in their elevated glass booth. "It's my first time," said Annette. "You should be gentle with me." The police were visibly annoyed as they herded the protesters into gender-segregated, side-by-side holding pens in the underground police garage for what would come to be known as the Hooray for Hollywood arrests.

Jonathan and Kurt argued with the police that, legally, they should be cited and immediately released, but the officer in charge called the film set and asked what time filming would be concluded. This was against the law, and Jonathan and Kurt did not let up until everyone had been processed out.

As Jonathan and Kurt took their macho stand, Mark saw that there were small wooden steps of varying heights and plastic orange traffic cones in the men's holding pen. He set them up and led some of the men in a series of show tunes. *West Side Story* was one of Mark's favorite shows; its famous line "She's queer for Uncle Sam" took on new meaning. Mark led performances of "Tonight" and the dance of the Jets.

"The queers are gonna have their way to-night!"

Flawlessly, Mark segued into *The Sound of Music*'s "You are Sixteen." Mark was the ringleader; the young men with him were positively adrenalized as Mark tried to lead them in "The Lonely Goatherd," but no one could remember the words. They had better luck with "Do Re Mi," as the middle-aged cop who was guarding them just chewed on his pipestem and Jonathan continued his argument about how long they could legally be held. The women, Annette and Tanya among them, were laid-back and smiling. They lounged in their holding pen, smoking their cigarettes and watching this very off-Broadway show, teasing the men as they climbed the little wooden staircases while demonstrating an amazing range of uses for orange traffic cones. In a final closing nod to Madonna, "Like a Prayer" was performed, and I am absolutely certain that Harvey Milk would have loved it.

Outside, we were worried to death about the poor dears. Sodas and chips were purchased to feed to them upon their release. Slowly, in twos, like an inverted Noah's Ark, they began to emerge from the wide, brightly lit underground garage. They looked as if they were returning to earth from some Spielberg-like adventure in outer space. It became clear what was going on inside, and a party atmosphere developed in the street. By one-thirty in the morning, everyone had been released. Suddenly, a pack of meter maids rounded the corner and charged the Hall of Justice, their Cushmans (three-wheeled enclosed motorcycles) at full throttle, and the Queer Nationals leaped to the sidewalk in fear for their lives. ACTIVISTS KILLED BY METER MAIDS. It would have been a truly San Francisco headline. Apparently, this was the meter maids' nightly ritual, their "Born to Be Wild" return to the underground police garage. Everyone needs a release, even meter maids.

❖

Tanya Tandoc called to say that the *Daily Globe,* an *Enquirer* wannabe, had contacted her persistently. They wanted to get a picture of lesbians holding signs and, if possible, ice picks. We imagined the headline: LESBIANS GO PSYCHO OVER FILM. Tanya told them they would have to call AP or UPI, or come to a demo, that we would not stage something for them, especially not since they kept interrupting her while she was trying to watch *Star Trek.* When the *Daily Globe* story did appear, the headline was: FURIOUS GAYS BASH DOUGLAS ON SET OF SEX-MURDER FILM. The article reported that "Michael has received several death threats, an insider reveals, and he's hired round-the-clock bodyguards.

. . . Michael's wife, Diandra, is very worried. Michael is worried for his family and the crew, more than for himself."

What a guy. Michael Douglas. Hollywood heir. Creature of the movies. The turtlenecked one. The real power on the set, the real lure for the press. It was Michael Douglas I wanted to visit, and I got my wish when his publicist arranged the meeting. *Basic Instinct*'s writer, director, and producer might well be the focus right now, but when the movie came out, it would be Michael Douglas's movie. It would be Michael Douglas's name that would forever be attached to *Basic Instinct*. When I told Joe Eszterhas about the arranged interview, I think he was shocked that I had penetrated so deeply into his world. Joe warned me that publicists were lying amoral slime that bred in cesspools, that that was their job description, and that I should never believe anything any publicist ever tells me. Yet for Michael Douglas, he had only awe that bordered on reverence. It must have been painful for Joe when Michael called him a "lying opportunistic crock of shit" and a "pretentious preposterous media whore." Joe warned me to be careful with Michael, because I would have no way of knowing who he really was. Michael, said Joe, was one of the greatest actors in the world, and one of the most powerful men in Hollywood. I was to remember that at every moment.

I must admit to being a little nervous. Douglas had played Gekko, the evil Wall Street financier, very convincingly, not to mention the furious husband in *The War of the Roses,* and we *had* been calling him Butt Ugly, which he probably didn't like.

❖

"What makes you think I don't have an ice pick in my bag?" I asked.

Michael Douglas and his publicist stood expressionless in the open doorway, and I do believe that for one perfect moment they considered this a possibility. The publicist was wearing an outfit identical to the one I had put on Jesse that morning: a short-sleeve blue pullover shirt with three buttons, and a pair of loose-fitting blue-and-black designer pants. Jesse called them his happy pants. The publicist, satisfied that I was not armed, left Michael and me alone. But he remained outside the closed door for almost two hours.

Michael's hair was short and he wore glasses. He looked older than I had thought he was, not realizing he was almost fifty. He wore jeans and a tailored shirt. In fact, we had on the same outfit. We sat on separate couches at an angle to each other, and he put his legs up on the coffee table and began to jiggle one foot. I was not sure if he was nervous or angry.

Whereas Joe used the silverware, napkins, and ashtray to tell his stories, Michael used his voice, his gestures, his imitations, and reenactment of dialogue. As Joe's targets were the producer and director, Michael's target was Joe. When he recounted the conversations at the "A" table at Morton's, he showed me the expression he had had on his face as Joe or Verhoeven spoke, the gestures he had made, the tone of voice he had used. Whenever I said something sympathetic about Joe, Michael became angry, clenched his teeth, and reminded me that Joe *had written the damn script.*

I asked him about his character, Nick, also known as Shooter, a cocaine-snorting San Francisco police officer who, in a jacked-up state, shoots tourists.

"Joe said that your character was motivated by the same homicidal impulses as Catherine," I said.

Michael thought about that. "Everybody has their own choices," he said. "I felt that this was a guy who had definitely sinned, had made some crucial mistakes, and that the movie was a question of whether he was redeemable or not. It was about redemption. Whether he should be redeemed."

He did not agree with Joe's vision of Nick, matching homicidal impulses with Catherine, which was supposed to be the basis of their attraction to each other.

"And how could he be redeemed?" I asked.

"He could solve the crime and find the murderer, right?"

He drew an analogy to *Fatal Attraction*, another controversial vehicle in which he had starred. It had been difficult to get *Fatal Attraction* made because, as Michael explained, how could one have sympathy for an adulterer? Michael seemed very attached to that character. "How do you feel sympathy for a guy who commits adultery and has a wonderful wife in the first act? And one of the surprises of *Fatal Attraction* was that people cared for this guy at a certain point. They forgave him."

Michael put his feet on the floor. He leaned toward me and repeated, "He's forgiven." He paused. He looked as if every antenna in his being were up, as if he were trying to read me.

"Under Joe's scenario," he said, "which is dark, my character doesn't deserve redemption. He's a total motherfucker. He's evil. My concern was, in a large Hollywood production, and as a producer as well as an actor, can we make a picture where there are no redeemable characters? Do you really want to look at a picture where you don't care about anybody? Okay? That's a dramatic decision. That was at the same time that we heard that there was some concern from GLAAD."

I'd say there was "some concern from" the Gay and Lesbian Alliance Against Defamation. GLAAD had, in fact, taken out an ad in the trade papers, blasting *Basic Instinct*.

"Quite honestly and ignorantly, it had never even passed my mind," he said with respect to GLAAD's concern.

"Why do you think that it didn't?" I asked the question as if I were talking to a confused child, and he seemed to relax.

"Well, because the aspect of someone's sexuality was not really addressed."

"How about the thing when Roxy—" He cut me off.

" 'Man to man'?" he asked. He pulled himself up tight in his seat. He seemed anxious to defend that line.

"No," I said. "The scene where your character goes into Roxy's past, and there's a close-up on the little boy, her little brother, whom she's slashed to death." As I spoke, he was shaking his head and interrupting me constantly, but I decided to complete the thought. "And your character says to Gus, Why would anybody do that? And the answer is because she was on the farm, and she was tired of all them boys getting all that attention." Michael was getting furious. Was it that people were not allowed to complete their thoughts in his presence if those thoughts were not the same thoughts as his? I was undaunted. "Because the character is lesbian, this connects the murder impulse with hatred of males, which then gets manifested in her as a lesbian." Michael seemed very angry, and he made a show of controlling himself, but letting me know he was controlling himself. This didn't really bother me. It was one of my techniques, too.

"I understand what you're saying," he said, his voice slow and deliberate, "and I just want to share with you, I know now. I've been confronted, and reviewed, and everything else. What I'm saying to you in the same way as I always have about *Fatal Attraction* when single women said to me, You cannot make, how dare you make a movie that shows a single woman—"

"Well, you know what?" I said.

"—and show," he continued, his voice rising above mine, "that this is the way a typical—"

"You know what?" I said. I was getting louder, along with him. "I don't care about *Fatal Attraction*." That got his attention. "Frankly, there are several movies that have single women as the hero." He launched again into his prepared argument, and again I tried to stop him.

"So, you know? I could care."

He remained steadfastly on course with *Fatal Attraction*.

"She wasn't the hero," he said. "She was the villain."

"I don't care."

"Okay," he said. "You don't care. But I'm trying to say that other people—a black person has very strong feelings in how he's portrayed. Italian-Americans. I totally accept your point. I'm saying to you I understand from your point of view, and your politics—"

"Well—" I said, but he could not be stopped.

"I don't really want to have an argument, or debate, about how I could have been so insensitive." My radar went up with that remark. It seemed to be a phrase he had heard before, perhaps with some frequency. I could just imagine people saying to him, "How can you be so insensitive?"

"No no no," I said. This was getting out of hand. "That's not what I'm—"

"What I'm simply saying to you—"

"Well—"

"Wait a minute!" He was intense, and so was I. I couldn't

believe how angry I was at the man as he continued, "What I simply said to you, is that I didn't see it."

"Right," I said.

"You can tell me now, and point out to me all the things I should have seen, but that's a little unfair as a Monday morning quarterback when everything's going down. I'm just being honest to you, saying I was taken by surprise. Particularly someone who has never thought of himself as being homophobic, and has been quite supportive of all aspects of gay rights."

"Mm-hmm," I said.

"I didn't see it. I understand that as a minority group, you don't want that portrayed as an image—"

I interrupted him. "That's not my position. My position is that those are the *only* images Hollywood studios produce. You see, I want there to come a time when there are enough images that this is just a campy movie. In ten years, lesbians could watch this on video and say, 'Oh God. Here comes the ice pick.' But at this point—"

"I would say to you, quite honestly," he said, "as a woman's activist, you ought to take offense—"

"I'm a lesbian."

"I understand."

"I'm a lesbian activist."

"I know you're a lesbian." He was getting very irritable. He was trying to emphasize that all women should be angry about the movie, not just lesbians. We simply were not each other's dream date. He tried a new angle. "A lot of women are totally up-front in this picture as far as murders and everything else," he said. Now he was trying to tell me that the fact that the female characters were committing the murders was a step forward for feminism. I smiled, but he was undaunted. "The truth is," he said, "it's a good part." He tossed his head as if he were a stallion. "I've got time with you," he said, looking at his watch, "but I've got other stuff to do." I supposed the interview was about to end. It wasn't really an interview, but more of a dialogue. I hadn't intended it this way, but there was no other honest way to proceed. Because he was so powerful, I wanted to influence him, even at the risk of angering him. His publicist had suggested to me that if the interview went well, rather than wait for it to appear as part of my book, he might even call me and ask me to write it up for, oh, *Good Housekeeping*. Apparently, that would not be happening.

I asked Douglas why he did not support any of Joe's suggested script changes. "After Joe met with the community representatives, he changed his mind because he got it."

"Fine!" said Michael, very irritated. "We're in the middle—I'm glad that he got it. We're in the middle of shooting a fucking movie. All I'm doing, I'm acting. I'm making a movie. I mean, we had a number of gay and lesbian people employed in movies. I deplore any kind of gay-bashing. I don't see, in the world that I live in, or in San Francisco, the kind of abuse or the kind of stereotypical things that some of the people feel so strongly about. I mean, I'm sure it exists, but—" He was winding all around something, and when it became clear where he was going, I was stunned. Remarkably, because he had not personally witnessed gay-bashing, he doubted that it was a serious problem.

I took out a photograph of a man named Lesle Kovacs, a forty-eight-year-old assistant to Alan Marshall. Kovacs was wearing a black jacket that bore the inscription I LOVE YOU TO DEATH.

"This man called the demonstrators faggots on the very first night," I explained, "and later, he saw a photographer, Jane Cleland, taking his picture, and he walked off the set, over to the sidewalk where she was legally standing, and flipped his elbow up against her camera, pushing it into her face. He then called her a sick fuck."

"Ohhhhhh," Michael was skeptical.

"He was arrested," I said. "And so was Alan Marshall, for false imprisonment."

"We-e-e-ll," said Michael. "I'm just telling you I think it was brilliantly orchestrated."

"What?" I asked.

Michael thought that we had manipulated the press and that Jonathan was the mastermind. He knew Jonathan's name. He even called him Jon. Jonathan would be pleased.

"Did you receive death threats?" I asked. My voice was quiet.

"No," he said. He relaxed against the couch, smiled, and shrugged his shoulders. I showed him a copy of the news article, FURIOUS GAYS BASH DOUGLAS ON SET OF SEX-MURDER FILM.

"Not true?" I asked.

"Not true."

I wanted him to understand that just because something does not happen under his nose does not mean that it does not exist.

"Roberta Achtenberg," I said, "our lesbian supervisor, and her partner, Mary, and their five-year-old child have received real death threats."

When I mentioned their child, it caught his attention. "Yes," he said. I realized that his love for his own son was a common ground, and he listened carefully as I told him the details of the last three weeks of Roberta's campaign.

"As liberal as I am perceived," he said, "and as supportive as I have been on a number of issues—I've raised more money in a single night for the Gay Men's Health Crisis at Radio City Music Hall. I've got plaques in my name."

"I've got plaques." He seemed to be pleading to be heard. His face was a mass of amazement, but I could not tell if it was sincere. He said he felt as if he were in the movie *Gaslight,* where the evil husband tries to drive mad the good and very rich wife so that she can be locked in an asylum, and he can get all of her money.

I was certain for the first time that he was being genuine, but his voice suddenly became patronizing, as if the moment of true vulnerability had frightened him, and he returned to his defense of *Basic Instinct.*

"The movie is a detective psycho thriller," he said.

"I understand that," I said.

"The changes that were requested were absurd. So, a woman, 'man to man'—"

I could not quite understand his fixation on this line. The context, as I've mentioned, is that his character has just slept with Catherine, Roxy's bisexual lover, and he says to Roxy, "Hey, Rocky. Man to man. She's the fuck of the century, isn't she?" Why he wanted to keep bringing up that line, I do not know. For someone denying lesbian-baiting, it really was not a terrific defense.

"It's a funny line," he said. "I mean, I don't see necessarily the worst thing in the world if a guy was talking to a lesbian, and he said, Man to man. You can take a strong offense with it, but—"

I started to get hot. "But what about the connection of violence with my sexuality?"

I was extremely angry, and I didn't care if what I was about to say would end the interview. "One of the reasons lesbians don't get custody of their children," but I stopped. He was looking at me through tinted glass, a curious child peering into another world.

"I know it seems so far removed from your world," I said. "I know you didn't start out on this project with any intention of hurting anyone."

"Homosexuality and lesbianism has never been accepted through the history of time!" he said.

"Right." No kidding, Michael.

"Okay?" he said. He decided to challenge my intensity.

"Got it."

"I mean," He smiled and gave me a sort of "man to man" look.

"I do understand that," I said.

"All right," he said. He seemed to be preparing to give me some earth-shattering historical perspective. I could tell he'd been digging around in his mind for every possible point in his favor, and who could blame him? He seemed to think he would have me with this one.

"I mean," he repeated, "it's never been—"

"I understand that."

"So," he said, flipping his head back, "I would appreciate you in 1990—and everything else—we all try to understand. But also, just say, that this has always been an uphill battle."

What the hell was he talking about? I let him continue. It was fascinating.

"As far as the combination of sex and violence, certainly I am making—I have made some socially responsible movies in my time. *Basic Instinct* is a high-priced detective pulp movie which involves sex and violence, and through this whole experience, nobody's more guilt-ridden with all the problems we have in this world to spend millions of dollars to make two hours of enter-tainment and escapism involving sex and violence." He was completely shut down, giving a speech. "You can accuse me of flippancy, or lack of sensitivity. It is difficult to constantly try to make pictures that have a social message. I swear to God. For a secondary character who's a lesbian."

"Roxy, you mean?"

"Roxy," he said. "Eleven pages."

"Then there's the bi-woman, Catherine," I said.

"There's this bi-woman," he acknowledged with exaggerated patience. "I understand to a lesbian or gay person, it does not create the image that they want for them and the problems they have, just as I understand the same thing happens for black males, or for Italians."

That was it. I couldn't take the Italian argument, not twice around. I controlled myself as well as I could, but I kept seeing my son's face. I kept seeing Jesse, looking at me, and he seemed so vulnerable. I felt enraged, tears slightly stinging my eyes. I was mortified on one hand, and yet I could not let Michael continue.

"Can I stop you for one second?" I asked.

"Sure," he said. He saw what was happening on my face, and he relaxed himself even more on the couch, but his shoulders had lifted up a little. He was not prepared for this—nor was I. My emotions had caught me off guard. Michael folded his hands in his lap, his mouth slightly open.

I gathered myself as well as I could. "Black people do have some films now that show their heroism. I feel really emotional right now, because you're sitting here—" I wanted to stop the tears, so I chose anger, and slapped my open hand forcefully on the glass coffee table that was between us. "And you're giving me your nice, clean answers to everything, and telling me why you're right." I again slammed my hand on the table. "I have a child who's three years old, whom I have to bring up in this society. And I'm sorry that you're so offended by my feelings, but this is one more thing that we have to deal with when it comes out. You know? I'm sorry I'm so emotional. I didn't even realize—It's a little bit embarrassing."

"I'm sorry," he said. "I—"

"I have this little boy." My voice was soft now, the anger was gone, and I knew I could hold back any tears. I did not want to frighten Michael. I wanted him to experience the world from another point of view, even for just a moment. "I would like, by the time he is old enough to go into the theater, for him to be able to see an image of lesbians that's not psychotic, homicidal, or suicidal." Again I saw Jesse's image, his sweet face, and the emotion came up in me again, but this time I did not bother to hide it with anger. "I'm sorry about this," I said. "It's really hard, and I'm trying not to do this." I knew that the level of my emotion wasn't caused only by Michael Douglas and *Basic Instinct,* but I also knew that Michael was in a position of power, and that if my vulnerability could genuinely touch him, perhaps someday he would use that power to help us.

"I don't believe you ever intended to hurt anyone," I said, and I was sincere. "This is just a movie. In ten years, I hope we watch it the way we watch Bette Davis smoke through her veil, and that we laugh."

"Right," he said. He really wasn't a bad guy, but he had, as he explained, lived a "cloistered" existence.

"I know this sounds very insensitive," he said. He must hear that quite often. "I'm going to defend my position."

"You're just not in my world," I answered. "How would you know?"

"I'm not in your world, nor you in mine."

We looked at each other and it was a strange moment: We might as well have been from different planets. But there had been a connection when I told him about Jesse.

"I'm reevaluating," he said, "and certainly this is the price you pay, I guess, for doing pulp. And I wish I'd found something that had more socially redeeming value."

"I'm sure you will," I said. I felt like Ingrid Bergman as the sister superior opposite Bing Crosby's Father O'Malley in *The Bells of St. Mary's,* when she goes to work on opening up the heart of Mr. Bogardis, the bitter elderly man whose building she wants contributed to the convent for a grammar school.

In all sincerity, Michael said, "I understand the image of a lesbian being a murderer is not one that is a positive portrayal."

Michael then decided to help me and the revolution by giving me some public-relations tips, and I listened with great care.

"I understand the dilemmas and the difficulties," he said, "but I don't think that the overt demonstration of sexuality—"

"What do you mean? Like the kiss-ins?"

"The kiss-ins," he said.

I tried to console him. "The New York kiss-ins are very light pecks, but San Francisco has the traditional deep French kiss." They don't call it the Barbary Coast for nothing.

"Right," he said. I guess we were communicating.

"And it really offends people," I said.

"Only only only for the fact—Actually, anybody can do whatever they want behind closed doors," he said.

"Well," I said, "not in twenty-four states in this country."

"I understand," he said. "I understand." He was irritable again. He seemed to hate this kind of fact, seemed to believe he could will it away.

He was still so terribly focused on the kiss-ins, and I started to laugh. Here was Michael committing theatrical sodomy on one woman, and cunnilingus on another, who also chose to reveal that they shot the scene without a crotch patch, but he thought the Queer Nationals were going too far with a deep French kiss in public. Maybe I should just dial "O" for O'Malley.

Michael paused, and I saw a shift. Something was bothering him. I was certain his concern was genuine. He hesitated, but then he confided that he was upset when he was told that at the community meeting at the Hyatt with the producer and director, the activists had suggested that he be replaced by Kathleen Turner. Michael sat back on the couch, his hands folded, his thumbs twirling, and he drew into himself.

"That was a joke, Michael. That was not—"

He was serious, and became adamant. "Oh no no," he said, looking at me. "At the meeting. One of the requests in the story script meeting was absolutely—"

"It was a joke," I said, amazed at the depth of his feeling.

"It was one of the requests," he insisted. "I'll show you Eszterhas's notes. . . ." This had disturbed him deeply. I was quite surprised.

"That was not real, Michael. It was not real."

"My character was listed as: 'Change the character to a female,' " he insisted.

"That wasn't real."

"It wasn't real," Michael repeated.

The truth is, the activists had not wanted to replace Michael Douglas with Kathleen Turner. Their choice had been Susan Sarandon. But I didn't have the heart to tell him.

❖

Although I knew the producer, Alan Marshall, to be merely a napkin with a wet stain on it, he was Jonathan's focus. As the story line of *Basic Instinct* had been personal for me, so Alan Marshall was personal for Jonathan. It was also becoming clear that Marshall was just as focused on Jonathan. During the meeting at the Hyatt, it had been upon Jonathan that Marshall had fixed his stare. Jonathan had written this off to Marshall's sexism, to the belief that Marshall saw only other men as having power.

On one drizzly night of protest, Marshall was close to the barricades. He was taunting Jonathan, barely moving his lips, his impassive expression of superiority ever present. His tactic was to attempt to infantilize those he was fighting. "You silly little boy," he said. "You think you can stop me."

A gay man lived on the North Beach hill where a car chase was being filmed. Jonathan convinced him to have a birthday party on the night of the shoot, and to invite Queer Nation. The police had to open the set; five by five, the activists walked up the hill and into the house, which was right in the middle of the shoot.

Although Marshall seemed slightly surprised by the birthday party tactic and by the fact that it would be illegal to prevent anyone from going to a private home even if it was in a filming location, the episode still did not crack him open enough for Jonathan. That happened on the last night of the shoot.

*Basic Instinct* had run out of permits for San Francisco, and it was impossible to get more permits in a timely fashion. They would have to finish up in Oakland. At the end of the last San Francisco work night, the police were still holding the Queer

Nationals on the sidewalk, but Jonathan decided to cross the street. A cop grabbed him, and Jonathan said, "The shooting is over. There is no restraining order in effect. This is a public street. Get out of my way." And the cop did.

Seeing that Marshall was standing by himself, Jonathan walked quickly to him and stood close to his face. "This is not the end of this," he said. "You think you got off." Jonathan was inches from Marshall; he turned and said, "People! Let's come!" and *boom*, Marshall was surrounded by the Queer Nationals. No one touched him, no one spoke except Jonathan, but the Lavender Menace was finally real to Mr. Marshall, and Jonathan saw a hairline fracture of fear in his face. Immediately, Marshall's lawyer tried to force his way between them and said, "You can't touch him."

"I'm not touching him," said Jonathan.

A pack of Hell's Angels, who had been hired by *Basic Instinct* as security, muscled their way in, pushing Jonathan and the Queer Nationals out of the way, but that didn't matter. Marshall had experienced a few seconds of physical threat, the kind of threat Jonathan felt almost constantly as a visible gay man, and Jonathan was satisfied.

❖

The day was windy, Jonathan and I were drinking tea. I confided in him that during the *Basic Instinct* protest I had found within me places that still hated what I was. But after I had shouted "Shame!" at the moviemakers, those places had vanished. He nodded, respectful and intense, sensing my discomfort at admitting that I had found homophobia within myself.

"Did you feel that?" I asked him.

His voice was very quiet, as if we were sharing a secret. "Yes," he said. "And I grow in power through every protest. I grow stronger. The more I assert and take pride in my queerness, the bigger I get. And one of these days, I'm gonna get so big that they won't be able to hurt me anymore. And I kind of think that Harvey got so big that even killing him didn't hurt him."

*Basic Instinct* left town on May 7, 1991. At noon on May 9, across town at the Asian Art Museum, a disturbed woman in red sneakers leaped onto the six-foot-wide pedestal that was the palette for the Tibetan monks' Kalachakra mandala. She kicked at the delicate sand painting and shouted about Tibetan death cults and the CIA. In one breath, the sacred representation of an ideal world, where every sound is prayer and every being God, was destroyed as two hundred horrified people watched. But the monks simply smiled, crossed their arms against their orange silk robes, and stepped back respectfully to give her room.

In my heart, I hoped that to step back would be my solution someday, or that I could at least truly feel the peace that Jonathan described feeling, that I could see the word *shanti* and not find it to be a mystery. I had experienced that peace briefly when I stood beside Tom Ammiano at a press conference on the perimeter of the *Basic Instinct* set, where he explained that we were not asking to censor Hollywood, but we were asking for parity, and I explained that I spent more time scraping SpaghettiOs off the floor than I did wielding ice picks. But that split second of peace was soon gone, and the best I could do was find the humor, which has always been our lifeline. *Basic Instinct* had left our city, but the chant "Ice picks for peace" would stay with us forever.

# CHAPTER X

# Just Always Be Waiting for Me

BY THE THOUSANDS they came, by bus and private jet, by taxi and romantic ferry across the chilly bay, and they were all wondering, What will the midnight surprise be? They wrapped themselves in white sheets that they had fashioned into togas. They stepped carefully into the street in Yves Saint Laurent chiffon, in armored tunics of riveted metal with mink trim, in Valentino gowns and Armani evening suits. There was the smell of hair spray, Dippity-Do, and Elizabeth Taylor's Passion perfume. There was poached salmon, rare lamb, black-and-white truffles, and oysters on the half shell. A uniformed chauffeur opened the door of a white Rolls-Royce, bowing slightly at the waist as a couple stepped to the sidewalk: first, a black man in a white dinner jacket, who then turned and offered his hand to a white woman in black silk. Arm in arm, they walked into the Opera House. This was definitely not a Queer Nation demonstration. It was the Black and White Ball, the most elaborate fund-raiser, the biggest block party, in the country, and for the first time in a long time people were in the San Francisco streets for some purpose besides a protest.

I held Cheryl's hand as we passed beneath a gigantic mirrored glass ball that hung from a crane as high as a Hollywood movie-set light. I was nervous, but we were with Cleve and Gilbert. I had forgotten how beautiful Cheryl was. I had been so far away from her and Jesse. I was out fighting for the right to love them, and in the process, a wall had been thrown up between us.

The swiftly roving high-powered lights of sky trackers criss-crossed in the sky above the Civic Center. We went to the Green Room in the War Memorial Building, where Judge Donna Hitchens's reception had been held as a massive war protest had wound its way through the city, helicopters waltzing above. Now, from the balcony, Cheryl and I stood with Cleve and Gilbert to view Gilbert's handiwork on City Hall. The black-and-white banners, with their waltzing man and woman, fluttered in the brisk wind. Gilbert was splendid in his white Gap sweatshirt with its two thousand hand-applied crystals, and he was ecstatic. He had sewn on his Singer at the Dream Center for hundreds of hours, and the banners were perfect. This was the first year that he did not come in drag; he discovered that he could get just as much attention without having to impersonate or parody a society lady. This was also the first year Gilbert was able to wear comfortable shoes rather than high heels, although he insisted that he loved heels.

Cleve was not at all into fashion, and he felt like a penguin. He took off in search of the oyster bar, where he knew he would feel happy, his diamond stud earrings flashing as he walked. Cleve did not seem quite comfortable at this very straight event and in these very straight clothes. And I noticed that his movements were followed by young girls who did not recognize him.

Any illusion that we were a straight foursome disappeared when I was alone with Cheryl; we wandered, hand in hand, through the decolorized reality of the ball. It was crowded, and it was early, so no one paid much attention to anyone else. The prevalent atmosphere was one of an exotic scavenger hunt for the best delicacies.

I felt a certain discomfort at taking Cheryl's hand in this world, but I would not deny her that. Cheryl was striking in her off-the-shoulder dress from Saks, her dangling earrings, her long black gloves. I had not seen such radiance since she first discovered she was pregnant with Jesse. Yet she still seemed a distant picture. Perhaps it was all that black and white, as if the inside of my video camera had come to life. The street protests, the shouting, the confrontations, the endless discussions with straight people about whether or not I had made a "life-style choice" and so had to take the consequences—these had taken their toll on me. I could only explain so many times that I had a lovely mother and father who adored and pampered each other, and that nevertheless I had been lesbian since puberty.

I had decided to deal with the ball as a visibility action, to confront its heterosexual privilege. It certainly was true that there were no other identifiable lesbian couples in evening dresses, but that was not at all why Cheryl was there. She was there because she loved me, and she had always wanted to go to the Black and White. She was there to enjoy herself, to dance, to make up for proms lost. In so many ways, although she was not a militant on the street, Cheryl was more liberated than most activists. As we wandered outside from venue to venue, everything connected visually by Gilbert's flags and thousands of black and white balloons, I defiantly held Cheryl's hand, but her delight soon gently pushed aside my fear and judgments, and I began to enjoy the extraordinary decor and the playfulness of the city.

Davies Symphony Hall looked like it had been designed by someone with a dalmatian fetish, large black spots marking the stairs that led to the stage where fabulous couples did the samba and tastefully downplayed lambadas to tunes by the Xavier Cugat Orchestra. Outside, a white double-peaked tent had been erected over the drained reflecting pool, its sunken dance floor covered in black Astroturf. A younger crowd contorted there to Boz Scaggs and the Solid Senders, to Lady Bianca and Her Band. Inside the Civic Center Auditorium, the images of the musicians—the Dynatones and the Limbomaniacs—and random dancers were projected from the stage onto a suspended twenty-five-foot reflective ball.

Cheryl and I danced in all these venues. I felt relaxed and in love in the crowd of a thousand waiters and thirteen thousand guests, scooping handfuls of the one hundred and sixty thousand black-and-white jelly beans, tasting crab cakes with jalapeño sauce, and seviche with mango and roasted-orange relish.

When we made our way to the street, we saw a very excited, very drunken young lady delighting in the San Francisco version of a rickshaw, which is propelled like a bicycle. "Look at the ricochet! Look at the ricochet!" she shouted rapturously to her boyfriend, who looked at us in tremendous embarrassment. A stiltwalker in a tuxedo with the longest black trousers in the world walked by slowly, tipping his top hat as Cheryl and I entered the Opera House to meet Gilbert. The spacious marble halls were decorated with avant-garde black-and-white faux pillars. We nibbled on chocolate-dipped strawberries before we entered the Opera House's theater. The atmosphere inside was unlike that of any other venue at the ball. The theater is a world-class room, seating over three thousand, with a stage that has seen everything from Wagner's *Ring* cycle to the great performances of Leontyne Price and Pavarotti. Gilbert was waiting for us with his friend, Adrienne. Adrienne was in her fifties, a former New York beatnik whom he had transformed for the evening into a very convincing society matron in yards of black sequins.

At center stage was the San Francisco Symphony orchestra, playing exquisite waltzes as women in gowns and evening dresses and men in tuxedos floated around the musicians, whose strings resonated, each note pristine in the nearly perfect acoustics of the house. It was perhaps the most elegant of San Francisco moments, and I had never felt so vulnerable. It was one thing to rock and roll, it was another to take Cheryl in my arms in such a romantic setting. Gilbert and Adrienne led the way to the banistered ramp that had been built so that the dancers could easily get to the stage. My hands felt hot, and I was uncomfortable, but Cheryl looked as if she could not wait to waltz. As we stepped onto the stage, I took her hand. We stood to the side for a moment, and Cheryl looked at me. On her wrist was the gardenia corsage I had given her. She was waiting for me to say the word, but I hesitated.

"What is it?" she asked, and I could see that she was afraid I would not join these dancers.

"Shall I lead?" I asked, and she proudly lifted her chin as we joined the straight couples on the Opera House stage, Gilbert and

Adrienne twirling past us, Gilbert looking every bit the Cheshire
Cat. Cheryl and I waltzed around the orchestra as they played
Strauss's "Voices of Spring." We were just feet from the musicians, and many of them began to watch us, little smiles playing
across their lips as they rocked gently to the sound of their music.
It was the oddest sensation of my life. Every moment or two, one
of the society couples, the Gettys or the Schwabs, the Swigs or the
Pelosis, would seem to float by, smile and nod, then waltz away
as if it were the most natural thing in the world that two women
in evening dresses should be dancing alongside them. A cluster of
photographers soon discovered us, and one stumbled in front of
another to get a better shot, but by then, I felt at ease. Cheryl
looked only at my eyes, and after a few minutes, I put down my
radar. There was absolutely no danger. I was simply dancing
with my lover at the ball.

"You've seemed very far away," Cheryl whispered, "but I
want you to know how proud I am of you."

One two three. One two three. Spin two three. Spin two three.

"You're not pulling away from me, are you?" she asked.

I stopped on the Opera House stage, and as the symphony
played, I kissed her lightly on the lips. We walked off the stage,
hand in hand, and in the foyer we laughed when we saw the
society ladies, in their ten-thousand-dollar gowns, playing with
black-and-white yo-yos. Outside on the street, we giggled at the
animal-rights protesters who tormented the society ladies about
their furs, following them from venue to venue with antifur
protest signs. At midnight, marching bands, dancers, and roller
skaters were framed by red, white, and blue fireworks bursting
above City Hall as the Cal Band played "Born in the U.S.A."
That was the Midnight Surprise, and I felt so happy that I lived
in San Francisco, and I made certain to get a black-and-white
yo-yo to take home to Jesse, who a few days before had solemnly
informed me, "You can't fly, Mama Phyllis, but you can dance."

❖

The next Tuesday, I received the long-awaited phone call from
Priscilla Judkins, the adoption worker. She informed me that the
first home visit would be in two days, at two o'clock. Only Jesse

and I should be there, so she could observe us interact. I had been waiting for so long that I had forgotten that the process was real. The anxiety that I had been masking with activism intensified, and I was almost overcome with dread. I couldn't eat, and it was difficult to sleep.

I was methodical as I prepared for the home visit, each house-keeping chore bringing memories of Jesse's birth, his arrival home, my insistence that he was not going to have any kind of religious baptism, especially one that mentioned casting out Satan. I remembered filling the house with white carnations. I remembered how, when he was four days old, Cheryl had held him for the private candlelight ceremony to welcome him into the world, and to especially thank him for coming to our house. I remembered how he had looked at me and smiled and grasped the white flower.

The doorbell rang as I was scrubbing the bathroom sink with Comet. I went to the front of the house and pulled aside the drapes. Looking down to the sidewalk from our second-story window, I saw that they were back again, this little pack of Jehovah's Witnesses who just could not seem to stay away from our house. There were three of them this time, purses on their arms, *Watchtower* magazines at the ready. They had been by to save me on several occasions, and I had explained to them that WE'RE LESBIANS AND WE WANT YOU TO GO AWAY AND LEAVE OUR FAMILY ALONE. This did not work. They made Dana Carvey's Church Lady seem moderate. This time, Jesse and Cheryl were not home, and I would be able to do as I liked. I slid open the window and looked down on the familiar faces of the ladies, who were primed—again—to convert me. Before they could speak, I lifted my arms in a gesture similar to one I had seen perfected by Jimmy Swaggart. I shouted down the heavens, and called to Almighty God to purge these poor living creatures of the evil Satan that had infested their very beings. And then, sufficiently swelled by the Spirit, I pointed down at them in my best Jehovah voice and shouted, "I command thee, Satan, to leave these women's bodies. I cast thee out. Out, you cursed monster that would call one evil and another good, that would call one demon and another angel, that would attack, divide, and destroy families. Out, devil! Out, Satan!" I paused. The Witnesses were furious but, at long last, speechless. "Thank you, Jesus," I concluded as I slammed shut the window and returned to my bathroom to scrub my sink.

I was trembling—and thankful that Cheryl was not there, because she absolutely hated scenes—but I just did not know what to do with these women. Casting Satan out of the church ladies, however, was probably not a good way to prepare emotionally for examination by the State of California.

That evening, I was too nervous to stay in the house, and I took Jesse with me for a drive. As we drove across the city, I played the audiotape of Disney's *Peter Pan*. We sang along about the crocodile, Jock the Croc, who ate Hook's hand after Peter cut it off and tossed it to him. Jesse liked to follow up the song by making a clicking sound with his tongue in imitation of the tick-tocking clock that the crocodile has swallowed, the ticking sound that terrifies Captain Hook.

While Jesse was ticking, I could feel the plotting elements of my mind snapping into place for the next day's home visit. I was calm and methodical, but I knew that just below the surface there was a tremendous surge of energy that had to be kept under control. I had to be very, very nice. Polite. Nonconfrontational. In other words, not quite what I had become. I most certainly had to make a point of not casting out demons.

San Francisco was spectacular and dreamlike that night. The fog had lifted and there was a dark blue sky, with a band of pink coming up over the Golden Gate. The Transamerica Pyramid building was an angular, elongated Egyptian eye spiking into the sky, the shades of blue progressing to the color of ink at the building's tip. I drove down Nob Hill, behind Grace Cathedral, and Jesse and I could see the fog slowly, mistily rolling in, but it was thin and broken, trailing like a woman's torn sheer dress, then finally merging to form a gauzy blanket that obscured the cable car as it climbed up the hill.

Jesse was at school. I was to pick him up and bring him home before Priscilla Judkins arrived. Cheryl and I walked through the rooms, moving things around. We put the bright green identification wrist bands for the Black and White Ball in a drawer in case Ms. Judkins thought they were some sort of sex toy. Into the closet in my studio went everything questionable. I had read a study comparing lesbian and heterosexual mothers' purchases of sex-typed children's toys. Baby Mary, Jesse's baby doll, went into the closet. I phoned my mother in Massachusetts and told her that I hoped I wasn't overreacting with Baby Mary. She ordered, "In the closet!" My parents were extremely excited about the fact that if the adoption went through, they would become Jesse's legal grandparents, and my mother did not want me to take any chances.

We decided that Jesse's boy doll, Buddy, could stay out, but Baby Mary was not lonely for long. She was joined by a humorous print I had of a mother feeding her little boy spaghetti from a frying pan. Some of the spaghetti is falling on the floor, and a little mutt dog is eating it up. The mother is wearing a white apron that is splattered with spaghetti sauce. The title of the print is "Jackson Pollock's Mother." I think its subtext is the triumph of the artist over even his mother, but if you didn't get the joke, it could look like child abuse. Into the closet with it. I studied the portrait of Marilyn Monroe on the kitchen wall. It was just her face and hands, but I decided not to take the chance. Marilyn came down. As I was locking her away, Cheryl objected.

"She looks wholesome," she said.

"She looks wholesome to us, but it is indeed Marilyn Monroe, and my mother told me, 'Where there's a doubt, into the closet with it.' "

There was a problem: When Priscilla Judkins arrived, she would see all these hooks on the walls, and vague outlines where pictures had been hanging for years. I started to take the hooks off the walls, but Cheryl insisted that taking the hooks out would leave little holes, and that would look worse.

There were newspaper articles about *Basic Instinct* all over my writing studio. On top was the *Daily Globe* tabloid article headlined, FURIOUS GAYS BASH DOUGLAS ON SET OF SEX-MURDER MOVIE. Into the closet with it.

Cheryl decided to take down some of Jesse's finger-paintings from the refrigerator because he used a lot of black. Ms. Judkins might think he was depressed. We knew he just liked black, but why take a chance?

"That one's just dark blue. Leave it up," I said.

"I'm telling you, there's a lot of dark colors," said Cheryl.

"You're right. Take it down. When in doubt, take it out."

This certainly was not very radical-activist-in-your-face of me. The advice from my mother and everyone I knew was: Volunteer nothing.

"Telling you not to volunteer anything," said Cheryl, "is like trying to hold back the tide." She suddenly became serious and said, "You love to shock, and you're going to have to overcome that character flaw right this minute. You have to learn to love to bore, so she'll leave in an hour, and not stay on for the second show."

Others preferred to torment me with humor. My friend Michael LeBoff called to let me know he would be dropping by during the home visit, and he would be wearing a brassiere over his motorcycle jacket. Pam Bates called to ask if I wanted any Queer Nation stickers for the refrigerator.

There was a hole in the living room wall where we had removed an old gas heater. Cheryl taped the hole.

"What if Jesse got stuck in it during her visit?" she said.

"He'll probably be incredibly attracted to the tape and spend the entire visit trying to pick it off," I answered.

I found myself looking at my heating pad and wondering if it could have some negative implication. I couldn't decide, so, when in doubt . . .

*Rolling Stone* magazine. In the closet! I removed the incense sticks. She could think I belonged to a cult. Oh, God! The book I bought for Gilbert's birthday, *Jesse's Dream Skirt*, which is about a little boy who wants to wear and dance in a rainbow skirt.

"That's gotta go," I said.

"You bet that's gotta go," said Cheryl. She looked around. "Do we have any pictures of men?"

I scanned the house, and pointed out that the picture on her calendar was of Serge Diaghilev, the great Russian ballet impresario who discovered Nijinsky and who happened to be homosexual.

We cracked up.

"We had a picture of Mother Teresa once," I said, regaining my composure. "I could dig it out and pin it up."

"Too much," said Cheryl thoughtfully. Then her eye was caught by a particularly problematic object.

"The Ouija board!" she said with alarm.

"I use it as a tea tray," I said defensively, but Cheryl didn't care. Into the closet it went.

Cheryl was picking up papers from the kitchen table.

"No. Leave that," I said, referring to the newsletter from the Unitarian church where Cheryl taught Sunday school classes for eleven- and twelve-year-olds.

The goldfish were all right, we decided, even though there was a little underwater Buddha in the bowl.

Cheryl went through Jesse's desk and found what to her was a smoking gun: "Playing cards?" she questioned, something judgmental and fundamentalist in her face.

"Playing cards! No!" I shouted, half mocking her. I concentrated on removing the toy coffeepot and coffee set. Too femme. But the little medical bag was good.

"Do we have any guns?" asked Cheryl wistfully.

"Damn. No guns," I said. "But you know that little . . . what do they call them . . . action toy? That blue thing? Let's prominently display the action toy. The blue guy."

"What blue guy?"

"Torso Man."

"Torso Man," she said. "Of course." (Jesse had somehow permanently disconnected the arms of the figure.)

I noticed that Cheryl was stashing the playing cards in a Chivas Regal Scotch bag.

"Where did you get that?" I asked. "We don't even drink!"

There was a small sign on Jesse's door: A CHILD IS NOT GOING TO BE SOMEBODY. A CHILD IS SOMEBODY. That was good. The star baby picture. Cheryl's childhood beagle puppy picture. I went through Jesse's books. Anything could be in there. *Pet Parade.* That was okay. *The Very Hungry Caterpillar.* That was probably in half the homes in America. *Uncle Nacho's Hat,* in English and Spanish. That was good. I prominently displayed *Uncle Nacho's Hat. Peter Rabbit* was okay. *Little Bear* wasn't bad.

Then I got to *Madeline*. Hmmm. I just didn't know about *Madeline*. *Madeline* went into the closet. You never know. *Good Night, Moon*. That was always good. Dr. Seuss. *Tootle the Train*. *Rosie and the Rustlers*. I didn't know. I buried Rosie with *Madeline*.

Jesse had a little rainbow flag on his bureau that he liked to wrap his stuffed animals in when he was putting them to sleep.

"What do you think, Cheryl?"

"When in doubt, take it out," she said. I would have to keep this a secret from Gilbert.

There was a permanently displayed Valentine's Day greeting-card from my parents that pictured Shirley Temple. Jesse especially admired her tap-dancing, which he emulated. Sorry, Shirley. Into the drawer. I hated to do it, but his red-and-white leather "fancy shoes," as he called them, the ones he loved best, had to go. Even our friend Jenny Curley, who was a child welfare worker, and lesbian, referred to them as his "girlie shoes."

There was one more book on top: *Heather Has Two Mommies*. This is the story of a lesbian couple who decide to have a child through insemination. It is written with great care and love. I would not hide that book. The first time I read it to Jesse, he was absolutely silent and riveted to the words and pictures, following the story of Heather, Mama Kate, and Mama Jane, whose lesson is that each family is special, and that the most important thing about a family is that all the people in it love each other.

I took a last look at his room. It was too late to do anything about the little gold birds on the wallpaper.

I moved through the house once more. Anything that hinted of activist political involvement had to go, of course. Certainly, even though Mayor Agnos had thought they were wonderful, the WHAT CAUSES HETEROSEXUALITY? bumper stickers needed to be put in a drawer.

I decided that the portrait of Rimbaud that J. had willed me would stay where it was, but our sleep masks had to go. A visitor had once actually thought they were sex toys. All the little New Age trinkets went into the closet—the rocks, the crystals, the affirmation tapes, and especially the dusty feminist tarot cards.

Antifungal cream. Had to get rid of the antifungal cream. A bolo tie. Too male. Got rid of the bolo. Earrings in the shape of a cross. Hmmm. Could be thought of as anti-Christian, pro-Madonna. Got rid of them, too. *Nocturnes for the King of Naples,* by Edmund White. Definitely into the closet.

The hand-knit blanket of lavender wool. I held it in my hands. The knitting was very flawed, but this was what Cheryl made for Jesse while she was on bed rest, trying to keep him growing inside of her. She had wrapped him in it as soon as she got him safely home. The lavender blanket stayed. I didn't care if it was not a "boy" color.

"Cheryl, she's just not going to go through this pile of papers, is she?"

"I think she'd need a search warrant, Phyllis." Cheryl was deadpan, but then she smiled. I took a deep breath and told myself, "Dull, Phyllis. Be dull. Be one with dullness."

I looked around and realized I'd never been so happy to see a Bart Simpson doll in my life. I tossed it onto the living room rug, to give it that just-played-with look.

I began to vacuum and dust again. I couldn't get out of my mind that I was Wendy Darling doing Peter Pan's spring cleaning. Cheryl found a fairy wand with pink and silver magic glitter strips from his aunt Nivedita. Into the closet, along with a copy of the *Tibetan Book of the Great Liberation,* which had somehow made its way between the sofa pillows. You could now barely close the closet door, and there was absolutely nothing left to clean.

Cheryl was finishing a careful display of femininity on the bureau. Laid out carefully were our accoutrements for the Black and White Ball: black-and-white fake pearl bracelets, patent-leather handbag, earrings, lipstick, perfume samples. It seemed as good a time as any to ask her. I had to get the words out quickly before I lost my courage.

"Cheryl. Are you sure you want me to be Jesse's legal parent?"

"Yes," she said, without a second's hesitation, her voice strong and clear. It meant so much to me. "Absolutely." She hugged me, and left the house for work.

I went to get Jesse from school, but I was early, so I went to

Café Commons for a bagel and cream cheese. There was a parking space in front of the copy shop I had used to get the adoption form copied, where the woman had fed the form through and I had looked up to see her ripping it slowly in strips out of the machine. I looked through the glass storefront and saw her. She was still there. "It is hard when you are fighting for a child," she had said.

Jesse decided he was very tired and would take a nap. He would probably wake up at the end of Priscilla Judkins's visit, and I would offer him a Popsicle, which always put him in a good mood. I had checked and rechecked everything. I looked at myself carefully in the mirror, to be sure that each hair was in place. Satisfied, my eye traveled down, and I saw that I had accidentally zipped a blue sock up into my tasteful ladies' slacks. I was horrified. I couldn't believe it. I had thought that everything was just perfect, and here was this long blue sock hanging out of my zipper, the toe pointing downward. If I had missed this enormous sock in this most ridiculous of places, what else had I not noticed?

I heard the sound of a motor near the house, but no car stopped. I decided to take a random reading of the *Beginner's Book of Zen,* and I read it aloud. "When you become you, you then become zen. When you are you, you see things as they are. You become one with your surroundings." I laughed. "Dear God," I prayed out loud, "don't let me say anything like that." I then realized I was talking to myself.

I looked out to the street and saw a middle-aged woman in a small, white, boxy car. She went to the top of the hill, then turned the car around. She then pulled up in front of my house. I had to let her in, this stranger who knew nothing about our world, and I had to tell her my life story. I had to prove I was Jesse's mother.

She rang the bell, and I tried to become a Stepford version of myself. I descended the stairs perfectly, opened the door, and invited her in. When she was halfway up the stairs, I thought to ask, "You are Priscilla Judkins, are you not?"

She stopped on the steps and studied me without expression.

She was about my height, a very ordinary-looking woman, perhaps in her late forties, early fifties.

"Who would I be?" she said. She seemed to be particularly curious about what I looked like. I checked my zipper as discreetly as possible. The sock was definitely gone.

She continued up the stairs to the living room, and she took a seat on the couch. I was nervous, and I offered her tea. She looked at me without expression for a few minutes as the water boiled, and then the questions began. When did I know I was a lesbian? I did not know if she meant when did I first feel special love for another woman, or when did I first have sex. I had always known I was lesbian, since my early adolescence, but it had been years before I had had sex with anyone. In fact, my first sexual experiences had been with men, but this did not seem to interest her. She then fixated on questions about Jesse's donor and male role models. Father's Day would be coming the next month, she said, and then she was silent. I told her about the special relationship Jesse had with my father.

"He sends a card to his grandfather," I said.

"But that's *your* father, not his," she said. "I think you should have Jesse send a Father's Day card to the lawyer who has the donor's name and address, and ask him to send it on to him."

I got a terrible headache. Jesse had no abandonment trauma. He had two parents, and he had always had two parents. His donor had been just that, a donor. I could not remain silent. What if she was going to other couples and telling them this? It was so foolish, and so potentially destructive.

"My father will call Jesse. My father loves Jesse," I explained. "Sending a card out to the unknown would mythologize the donor, and create a sense of expectation and disappointment, perhaps even rejection. Jesse has never been rejected. No one has abandoned him. My father will call him. He loves him."

Priscilla paused and thought. "I have an idea," she said.

I couldn't wait.

"You should contact the lawyer, and get a picture of the father, and give it to Jesse."

I couldn't believe it. "When Jesse is eighteen, he has the right to contact his donor," I said. If Jesse should exhibit any serious psychological problems around the identity of his donor before that time, I will contact the lawyer, and ask the donor to meet with him."

"But you should get the picture. It's very important," she insisted.

"That's very interesting. We'll have to think about that," I said. A headache was now spreading and compressing like a tight metal ring around my forehead.

"How did your family react to you being a lesbian?"

"They loved it," I said, the portrait of sincerity. "Especially my father."

"How unusual!" she said. I was certainly stretching it, but so was she.

"Yes. How about that? They're also very excited about this adoption, about becoming his legal grandparents."

"Well," she said, "there's precedence to this, but it's not really legal. In San Francisco, there's precedence."

"That's very interesting. We'll have to think about that."

"What makes you think your . . . your . . ."

She was searching for a word.

"I don't know what word to use," she said, looking at me with frustration on her face.

I was very nice, calm, pleasant, zen. I couldn't imagine what question she was trying to ask. I tried to help her.

"If you were going to ask a heterosexual the question, what word would you use?"

She perked up. "Marriage."

I said, "Relationship."

"Oh!" she said. "What makes you think your *relationship* will last?"

"Do you ask heterosexuals that question?" I could not reel the words back in.

"I hope I didn't sound obnoxious," she said.

"Flexibility. That's what keeps us together," I said, regaining my composure. "Flexibility. The ability to go through profound changes together, like having a child."

"You shouldn't be in denial about Jesse's need to know immediately and have all his questions answered about his father. You should not create taboos."

"That's very interesting. We'll have to think about that."

"What first attracted you to Cheryl?"

I wanted to say, Her harem-girl Halloween costume, especially the way she held it together with strips of bicycle inner tubes. "Her joyfulness, and her bravery," I said.

"Are you in an exclusive relationship?"

"What do you mean?"

"You know."

"Yes, I am." Would she possibly ask this of a straight person?

"Did you have any trauma coming out?"

"No." Unbelievable that I could get that out of my mouth with an absolutely straight face.

"Why did you have an anonymous donor?"

"I didn't want to chance going up against a straight white man in a courtroom."

"How interesting! I never thought of that! Usually it's because the woman who didn't give birth feels threatened by men. I never thought of a legal courtroom situation."

She looked around the walls at the picture hooks.

"Does he know whose tummy he came out of?"

"We told him, but he's not terribly interested," I said. "He's not even three years old."

"You can't shelter him forever," Ms. Judkins insisted.

"Well, we have him in a good nursery school. When they sing 'Farmer in the Dell,' they sing 'And the farmer takes a partner.' "

"He won't be in a school that says 'partner' forever," she snapped.

"Yes he will," I said.

"Well, we'll see."

"Yes, we will."

"What are you going to do for Father's Day?"

Did her father abandon her? Her husband? What was this?

"I'm going to have Men's Day," I said. "A day to honor the men in our lives. We like men. We really do."

I could see that she believed the *Basic Instinct* stereotype of lesbians hating and fearing males.

"Have you told Jesse why I'm here?" she said.

"I told him a lady was coming to meet him, to see if he liked living with Mama Phyllis."

"But did you tell him it was an adoption? Did you prepare him?"

"He doesn't understand the word," I said. She did not understand that there would be no tangible difference in his life, except that he could be covered by my health insurance.

"It's very traumatic," she insisted. "They have to go into a courtroom. To City Hall. It's a big building."

"He's been to big buildings," I said.

"Wake him up, please. I need to see how you two relate."

I woke Jesse up, and got him a Popsicle from the refrigerator.

"Hello, Jesse! How are you?" Priscilla's voice was loud, and she leaned too closely into his face. He rearranged himself on my lap and turned his back to her, sucking his Popsicle and looking out the window. He refused to perform. This was a child who talked and danced and jumped through his entire waking life. He rested his head against my chest and ate his Popsicle. He answered not a single question. He would not even acknowledge Judkins's presence.

"Well," she said after fifteen dull, dull minutes, "he's shy. I'll go now. I'll be meeting separately with Cheryl, and then I'll come back and meet with all three of you together. Make sure he has been up before I get here."

"Thank you for coming," I said.

She stood and said, "Before I go, may I look around?"

"Certainly!" Just stay away from that closet door, the one that's slightly bulging, I thought. As she toured each room, examining the tables, the telephones, the walls remarkably empty of artwork, Jesse did not move, but he clicked his tongue, just twice, sounding remarkably like a clock in a crocodile's belly as I followed Priscilla with my eyes.

"What was that noise?" she asked.

"I didn't hear anything," I said, and Jesse buried his face in my chest, hiding a little smile.

"Well," said Priscilla Judkins, having taken the tour, "I'll be in touch."

"Thanks again for coming. We really appreciate it," I said.

Jesse and I sat on the couch as Priscilla let herself out. We listened to her turn on her car engine and drive away. She had not asked me one single question about how I mothered Jesse. Jesse sat up in my lap and smiled. He went to Cheryl's and my bedroom and began to jump on the bed as high as possible.

"I love you, Mama Phyllis! I love you!" he shouted. I got onto the bed, held his two little hands, and we jumped together.

"I love you, too, Jesse. I love you, too."

The caw of a large crow sounded outside the bedroom window, and Jesse and I immediately stopped jumping. We went to the window to get a better look. From the sound of his caw, he had to be enormous, and there he was, the size of a raven, full of complex commands, with many variations in his caw. He spread his wings and raised himself up off the telephone wire for a moment. All the other birds moved away from him. He clearly controlled the territory. His caw broke and echoed against the darkening gray sky. He really did seem to be giving orders, and I wondered what they were. I opened the window so that Jesse and I could get a closer look at him. He became quiet, and let us admire him. All the other birds had moved backward, away from the telephone wire where he was perched.

"It's Peter," said Jesse in a reverent whisper.

"What do you mean, darling?"

"You know. It's Peter. We were waiting, Wendy."

Jesse took the presence of the crow as a special sign for us. He smiled from deep within his heart, and I remembered the line from Sir James's *Peter Pan*: "Just always be waiting for me, and then some night you will hear me crowing." I put my arms around Jesse. I had never loved as I loved that child, yet there was this shadow between us.

That day was May 15, and at San Francisco's Asian Art Museum, the Tibetan Buddhist monks began the second Mandala of Wisdom and Compassion, placing each grain of colored sand by hand. But in Sacramento, it was a different story. Reverend Lou Sheldon of the Traditional Values Coalition, in concert with Congressman William Dannemeyer, launched a drive to change the state constitution so that no law in support of lesbian and gay rights would be legal. They wanted a specific amendment written forbidding same-sex parents; they cited as their reasons moral deprivation, child molestation, and bestiality. The proposal would be known as the Family Protection Act.

On May 29, Priscilla Judkins sat at the kitchen table with Cheryl and me. It was our second home visit, and Jesse busied himself with his toys in the living room. He was hammering with great purpose on his plastic construction set. He simply would not talk to Priscilla.

"So," said Priscilla. "What are you going to do when you suddenly have this big man in the house?"

"Get a bigger house," I said.

Priscilla was silent.

"What are you going to do when he starts to date?"

"He's three!" I was getting angry.

"You have to start thinking about this," she insisted.

"He can date whomever he wants," I said, an edge in my voice.

"Let me answer this one," said Cheryl in her calmest voice. I got up and leaned against the sink, my arms crossed against my chest.

"When it's time for Jesse to date," said Cheryl, "I hope AIDS is not around. We will teach him about safe sex, and that he is to treat with respect whomever he is dating."

Priscilla Judkins's attention came back to me. "Call Jesse into the kitchen," she said, and I did. She leaned over in her chair toward Jesse. She was overwhelming him, I could tell. For some reason, she spoke louder when she talked to him.

"Jesse!" she said. "Jesse!" He walked toward her, tentatively, and stood in between her and me. "Who's that?" she said, pointing in an exaggerated way at me. "Who's that?"

He leaned a little toward her, his blond head tilting to the side, curious as to what in the world she wanted. He followed her pointing finger and looked at me, then back at her.

"Who's that? Who's that?" she said.

He went closer to her than he had ever been. She was leaning forward, and he leaned forward. They were about a foot apart, his little face right up in hers. He shouted, "Mama Phyllis!" He waited, to see if it had sunk in, then he straightened up and walked back into the living room, making it clear that he had concluded his interaction with her. Cheryl bowed her head to squelch her laughter.

Jesse's shout had been loud and sudden, and Priscilla was all a-dither. "What did he say?" she demanded. 'What did he say?'

I smiled, and in a calm voice said, " 'Mama Phyllis.' He said, 'Mama Phyllis.' "

# CHAPTER XI

# The Family Come True

THE REVEREND Lou Sheldon had convinced many Hispanic, African-American, and Asian fundamentalist ministers that lesbians and gays wanted to take away from Latinos, blacks, and Asians their status as legitimate minorities, and that to protect themselves they must exert political pressure on the State Assembly to block the passage of AB-101, the lesbian and gay civil rights act. To counter Sheldon, leaders of the African-American community, including the Reverend Cecil Williams, who wished to show their support for lesbian and gay civil rights, stood with Cleve Jones on the steps of the State Building in San Francisco's Civic Center. ACT UP's tactic was, of course, different. They sent Mr. Sheldon a pile of manure.

It was Jesse's third birthday, and the party was to be held at Fairyland in Oakland, the oldest children's theme park in America, where no one more than forty-eight inches tall can fit on the rides. Everyone was to meet by the Big Shoe. Cheryl went on ahead to greet our guests, but Jesse would not get out of the car. He was afraid of Fairyland. He believed that he might go inside and never be able to get back. He might have to roam Neverland with the Lost Boys forever. And Tinker Bell was moody. And what about the crocodile who had eaten Hook's hand?

I opened the car trunk and carefully lifted the large glazed pastry in the shape of a crocodile. A Mexican baker in the Mission District of the city had baked it for me. The crocodile was quite impressive, complete with dangerously sharp-looking scales, open jaws exposing white frosting teeth, and a great big red jelly tongue.

Jesse quivered when I held it before him. "Is it alive?" he asked me.

"No, dear. It's pastry. Do you want to eat it?"

"Eat the croc?" he asked, and I knew I had truly heard the sound of wonderment.

"Mm-hmm," I said. "Eat the croc."

He was nervous, but he smiled as I broke him off a claw. He chewed on it, and he seemed to become more confident. As he swallowed the crocodile's claw, I asked him, "Do you want to go into Fairyland now? Mama Cher and all of the children are waiting for you."

"Give me a piece of the tongue," he commanded, and after he had swallowed it, he informed me that he was now ready for Fairyland.

While Jesse was conquering Fairyland, Jonathan attended his brother's graduation from Yale. President George Bush was the speaker, so Jonathan wore his PROMOTE QUEERNESS shirt. There were hundreds of American-flag ties, hatbands, and lapel pins in the commencement crowd. His middle brother asked him not to disrupt the President's speech, but Jonathan could not promise that. He happened to see a friend from ACT UP carrying a banner, and he waded across the crowd to join them. As George Bush began to speak, Jonathan stood on his chair and held the ACT UP banner high above his head. He chanted, "Act up! Fight back! Fight AIDS!" and he was punched in the jaw, but he didn't fall from the chair. The banner was still up, and that was all that mattered. Three rows in front of him was a middle-aged, fat alum who picked up his chair, folded it, and lifted it over his head to throw at Jonathan. The alum's wife was horrified. "Honey! Honey! Calm down, honey!" she begged. Jonathan knew it was easy to hit the suburbs, even Hollywood, but he wanted to hit the universities, especially the Ivy League. Yale was one of the most hostile crowds in which he had ever been. They immediately acted violently, Jonathan explained, because as social brahmins, they had never experienced a challenge to their status quo. The center of blue-blood culture, where the real power rested, now earned a special place on Jonathan's list of targets. He had taken to heart Harvey Milk's words, "No one is going to give you power. You have to take it."

When Jonathan came home, I watched from his back porch as he and Kurt picked strawberries in the garden with Jesse, and I wondered if there would ever be a day when we could just live our lives.

❖

The report from the Department of Social Services was in my hands. I was alone, as I wanted to be. I opened it slowly, and read.

The minor is not free for adoption and the State Department of Social Services recommends that this petition be denied.

The minor is equally well bonded to both women and considers both of them to be his mothers. The birth mother wishes to consent to the adoption but wishes to retain her parental rights. The State Department of Social Services does not believe that this adoption is in the best interest of the minor and recommends denial of the petition because the best interest of the minor is served by fostering and maintaining a secure and stable relationship between parents and children as promoted by legal marriage.

The petitioner and her lesbian partner have lived in a stable, monogamous, marriage-like relationship for five and one-half years. . . . He appears to be a bright, lively, well-adjusted little boy. . . . His teacher indicates in her reference letter that the child is well adjusted, and appears well cared for. . . .

A normal, affectionate, parental relationship is well established between petitioner and child. However, the State Department of Social Services does not believe that this adoption is in the best interest of the minor, and recommends denial of the petition because the best interest of the minor is served by fostering and maintaining a secure and stable relationship between parents and children as promoted by legal marriage.

In view of the foregoing facts, the State Department of Social Services recommends that the petition of the adopting parent be denied.

This is known as a positive denial, meaning the Department of Social Services will leave the final decision to the judge. It is the best possible result, yet it was humiliating. It confirmed the utter disregard in which the State held my relationship not only with Jesse, but with Cheryl. Pain is an amazing thing, even when it is expected; if it is deep enough, it is no longer pain, but an extraordinary and horrible adventure that will either destroy you or make you so powerful that nothing can hurt you ever again. I saw a picture on TV of a heterosexual family on vacation; it made me furious. The anger helped the pain. It helped me to stand up, go to my car, and drive to the Women's Building and the Queer Nation meeting, where I made the announcement: "I have just had my adoption officially denied. I don't want to make an action. I think it will be all right. But I do want to say, 'I'm here. I'm queer. I'm his mother, so get used to it.'" Annette put her hand on my arm, and I stayed in the room for a while with Pam, Jonathan and Kurt, Tanya, John and Mark, the partisan avantgarde of the thousand militant homosexuals of light.

I left the Queer Nation building only to find that my car window had been shattered. It was like a dream, or maybe that's what I had to turn it into. We had been warned to leave the meeting in pairs, that there had been some bashings, that people had been followed, chased, beaten. I had no idea if someone had watched me enter the Women's Building, or if the smashing had been simply random. It took a long time to remove the glass, sliver by sliver. They make the glass so that it does not break in shards, but when you try to pick it up, you find that it still cuts; it still draws blood.

❖

I received the notice of the adoption hearing, and I decided to work out some of my anxiety by planning a traditional lesbian family adoption party. If something happened, if the adoption was denied, I would turn the party into an action.

The adoption would be heard in Superior Court in City Hall;

I hand-delivered a letter to Mayor Agnos, telling him what was happening and requesting that he greet my family and friends in his office after court. If something went wrong, I would ask him to make a statement. I began to feel better. Taking action eliminated anxiety. Experiencing pain without self-pity and fear is empowering. A telephone message came from the mayor's office: He would absolutely be there on the twenty-ninth. He wouldn't have it any other way.

It was now the Saturday before the Monday court date, and I was contacted by Everett Denman, an activist who regularly monitors the televangelists and Sacramento-based fundamentalist political organizations. The fundamentalists were now attacking on an almost daily basis, with an intensity reminiscent of Anita Bryant and John Briggs. When had they, how had they gotten such control of political committees and commissions? A Dr. Cameron, consultant to Congressman William Dannemeyer, explained over the radio waves: "Homosexuals ought to be castrated and homosexual females ought to have a one-inch hole drilled through the cartilage of their nose." Many of our straight liberal friends, and a certain number of lesbians and gay men, told the activists not to pay attention to such extremists, who were just a bunch of crazies with no real power.

Everett Denman, however, had something he thought I should see: a particular videotape of Pat Robertson's *700 Club*, a fund raising show that masquerades as a religious broadcast. Swords clashed at the opening of the show, and the words SPIRITUAL WARFARE appeared, followed by those spokesmodels for the radical right, Pat Robertson and his sidekick, Sheila. They explained that all good Christians had to be at war with the great Satanic forces of evil that had unleashed themselves in the world. As proof of the presence of these evil spirits, they showed a videotape of the Lesbian and Gay Freedom Day Parade and of the GHOST demonstration against the Prayer Warriors who had come to San Francisco on Halloween to exorcise Satan from the gay community. Both tapes featured Gilbert Baker as Pink Jesus. They played Gilbert's movements in slow motion so that he would appear more snakelike.

They then held up a children's book that they claimed was

absolute proof of the militant homosexual agenda and its desire
to recruit children for wicked purposes as a result of possession
not by street-level, but by high-ranking demons. They opened up
the book for the viewing audience, and displayed a drawing of
two women holding hands with a little girl.

"They actually have this for children," said Pat Robertson,
former candidate for President of the United States.

"Disgusting," said Sheila.

They wanted everyone to be on the lookout for this book, to
be sure to get it off the library shelves if it ever appeared. It was,
of course, a copy of Jesse's book *Heather Has Two Mommies,*
by Lesléa Newman.

The demonization was reaching toward my child. Pat Robertson did not look at the words that were printed on that page, but
if he had, this is what he would have read: "Each family is
special. The most important thing about a family is that all the
people in it love each other."

The *700 Club* airs in forty-four countries, and claims that "six
million people made a decision for Christ this last year." My
anxiety was so terrible. I had the fear, perhaps absurd, perhaps
not, that the Family Court judge would watch the *700 Club* the
next night and, right before my adoption hearing, make a "decision" for Pat Robertson's version of Christ. I had once believed
Pat Robertson to be just a quack, and I would have continued to
believe that but for the work I had done with Queer Nation. I
now knew the power of media, especially television, and that the
radical right had been working TV for years, since the time of
Jerry Falwell and the Moral Majority. Yet none of us, straight or
gay, Democrat or moderate Republican, had any way of knowing that Pat Robertson would actually be elevated so high in our
society that, in 1992, he would be sitting beside Marilyn Quayle
in the GOP convention's vice presidential box, that the images
the Republicans would choose to embrace would include a beam-
ing Jerry Falwell and Pat Buchanan, that Vice President Dan
Quayle would specifically announce at his press conferences and
in interviews that families like mine were built on an immoral
foundation, that Lou Sheldon, that extraordinary point of hate,
would be an honored guest and an adviser to the 1992 Republi-

can presidential campaign. R. J. Rushdoony, a consultant for Lou Sheldon and his Traditional Values Coalition, had together with Sheldon successfully blocked California's lesbian and gay civil rights legislation. Mr. Rushdoony said of homosexuality: "Wherever a society refuses to exact the required death penalty, there God exacts the death penalty on that society. Every state and every society thus faces a choice: to sentence to death those who deserve to die or to die themselves." Pat Buchanan, standing at the podium on national television and representing the Republican party, would second this declaration of a religious war in America, and offer as proof the words of the "militant homosexual" at the Democratic convention, who stated that Bill Clinton was more supportive of lesbian and gay rights than any presidential candidate in history. The "militant homosexual" he was referring to was Supervisor Roberta Achtenberg. Clearly, Mr. Buchanan had not yet met Jonathan Katz.

Sunday morning, I was extremely agitated. I was driving everyone crazy, but I could not be reassured. Jesse was napping, and Cheryl decided to go outside and weed the boxes she had planted at the base of the trees in our front sidewalk. I watched her from the window. I knew I had been difficult to live with, that my anger was affecting our lives. And then I saw them, coming again, the three church ladies with their purses over their arms and their *Watchtowers* in their hands. What did I have to do to get rid of them? Cast Satan *into* them? I was so furious that my hands were trembling and I had trouble opening the window. I could see Cheryl become engaged in an animated discussion with them, and I wanted to save her from them. When I got the window open, I heard Cheryl say, in a sweet voice, "Oh, yes, I do believe in God. Isn't God wonderful? I'm a Unitarian Universalist. I teach Sunday School. God is love, isn't He? Pure love." The ladies were getting a bit uncomfortable, and I remained silent. Cheryl stood up. "Pure love," she repeated. The church ladies clutched their purses and *Watchtower* magazines as Cheryl took one step toward them, her gardening tool dangling from her hand at her side.

"You look thirsty," said Cheryl. "You look so thirsty. You could all use a glass of water. Let me give you some water."

"Oh no no," said the church ladies. "We wouldn't want to trouble you." They were very uncomfortable, and I realized they were frightened of Cheryl, who was now inviting them into the house, telling them that they looked terribly, terribly thirsty, and wouldn't they like to come in and talk about God's love? Cheryl's voice was smooth and comforting. The church ladies literally backed away from her and up the street, politely declining her generous offer of water, and they would never return for fear of the sweet tongue of the devil attempting to convert them to the way of the infidel. By opening her arms to them and welcoming them as her spiritual path taught, Cheryl had accomplished what I could not with all of my confrontational theatrics. Sometimes, "any means necessary" includes love. Cheryl went back to her weeding, just taking up where she had left off, as if nothing had happened, and I quietly closed the window.

That night, I joined her in the bedroom, where she was reading a hardcover book that did not look familiar.

"Come sit under the covers beside me," she said. The adoption hearing was the next morning, and I was so nervous that it was hard to sit still, but I would try.

"What are you reading?" I asked.

"This is a 1952 edition of Amy Vanderbilt's *Complete Book of Etiquette*," she said.

Maybe Cheryl had gone off the deep end.

"There's nothing in there for us," I snapped. My attitude was beginning to annoy even me, but I felt helpless to improve upon it.

"You're wrong," Cheryl said.

"Oh I am, am I?" I was getting all twisted and twirled about Amy Vanderbilt's *Complete Book of Etiquette* being in my bed.

Cheryl remained unruffled. "Look here now, Phyllis," she said, and I forced myself to read where she was pointing. There was a small section on adopting children, and how to properly prepare the announcements.

"How should we do ours?" she asked.

I began to cry, and Cheryl held me. I didn't think she understood what I was going through on an emotional level, but she was reaching out to me anyway.

\* \* \*

At nine o'clock the next morning, July 29, Cheryl, Jesse, and I appeared in Family Court in City Hall with Abby Abinanti. We brought Terry and my dear friend Michael LeBoff with us. I could see that they were both nervous, although Cheryl seemed absolutely calm. As we sat in the courtroom, Michael leaned over to me and said, "So you think it's going to be okay, right?" Terry heard him ask me the question, and she leaned toward me to hear my answer. Cheryl simply stared ahead, her eyes fixed on the judge's closed chamber door.

I assured Michael and Terry that everything would be fine, but I was not really certain. We were called into the judge's chambers, and I followed Abby, holding Jesse's hand, Cheryl and our friends behind me. The judge, seated behind her desk and wearing the black robes of power, first looked at me carefully, and then at Jesse.

"The adopting parent should be sworn in at this time," she said.

"Raise your right hand, please," said the court clerk, and I complied. Jesse looked up at me, raised his hand, too, then faced the clerk. The judge remained expressionless.

"Do you solemnly swear that the testimony you shall give, in the matter now pending before this Court, shall be the truth, the whole truth, and nothing but the truth, so help you, God?"

"Yes," I said.

We all stated our full names for the record. Abby and I sat before the judge, as Cheryl and our friends stood behind us. As I turned to take my seat, my eyes caught Cheryl's; I saw that she was fighting back tears, and I knew then that she understood.

Jesse insisted on sitting in my lap. He took my hand in both of his, and looked at the judge with his complete attention, his little back absolutely straight. He seemed to be trying to make himself more impressive. He was wearing his suspenders, and his red tie with the blue polka dots, of which he was especially proud.

The judge studied Jesse for a moment. He lifted his chin, and pulled my hand closer to his chest. The judge said, "I do not think it necessary that I ask this child any questions."

There was the sound of the court reporter recording all of the words, but then the clicking stopped. She could not record the silence, or the quickening pace of my heart.

"Let the record reflect," said the judge, "that I have reviewed the supplemental report of the State Department of Social Services. The Department of Social Services recommends against this adoption apparently because the child is being adopted into a family that consists of two lesbian parents.

"For the record, I will state that I am planning to approve the adoption, and I think that it is an appropriate adoption in the best interest of the child."

My breath had almost stopped. It was so simple, what the judge was saying, and yet it was the most powerful thing that anyone had ever said to me.

The judge asked me, "Do you in fact consent to adopt this child and to treat him in all respects as your own lawful child, and to have him enjoy all the rights of a natural child as your own, including the right of inheritance?"

"Yes."

"I will approve this adoption and will hereby order, adjudge, and direct that the petition is granted. That the minor is now the adopted child of the petitioner, and shall be regarded and treated in all respects as her lawful child. That she shall sustain towards the child and the child towards her the legal relationship of parent and child. Each respectively shall have all the rights and be subject to all the duties of natural parent and child."

As the words came from the judge's mouth, it was like a dream. He was legally my son. I was legally his mother.

"I will sign the declaration at this time," said the judge, and she scrawled her signature across the paper.

"Congratulations," she said.

I could only whisper, "Thank you. Very much," and I kissed the top of Jesse's head. Should something happen to our Cheryl, no one could take him from me. I would not have been able to withstand the pain of losing him. It was this fear that had created the shadow between us, but the shadow disappeared when I gave Jesse that one special kiss, which I had somehow been withholding from him.

Outside the courtroom, I asked Abby if she thought there

might one day come a time when there would no longer be automatic denials of lesbian couples seeking adoption. She smiled sadly. "Your question is difficult because it involves politics," she said. "Which way are we going? I'm not sure. We're in the middle of a stream here, and sometimes it's hard to tell which way it's rushing." Sometimes it is hard to talk to Abby because she always tells you the truth.

I held Cheryl's and Jesse's hands and we walked together, with our friends, to the office of Mayor Art Agnos on the floor below, where he greeted my family with great warmth. He had arranged for the city photographer to be present, and Jesse had his photograph taken sitting in the mayor's chair while the mayor knelt beside him. Jesse got to hold the mayor's baseball and touch the mayor's elaborate crystal wand. Yes, indeed. The mayor of San Francisco had a crystal wand on his desk, and beside that wand on a polished brass stand was the flag of the city, a phoenix rising from the ashes of its own destruction. The gold-and-black flag that had been designed by Gilbert Baker in the time of Mayor Dianne Feinstein. The phoenix hovers above a ribboned scroll bearing the Spanish words ORO EN PAZ; FIERRO EN GUERRA. "Gold in peace; iron in war."

We left the mayor's office, and Cheryl and Jesse and I stood at the top of the grand staircase, beneath the rotunda. Harvey Milk had said that we should always take the stairs and be visible, and today of all days, we would do just that. Jesse surveyed the hall, and I could see that he was feeling quite powerful. I had one great hope for Jesse that day. When he came of age, I wanted him to know when to fight and when to step back, which is the wisdom of the great warrior, and the way to peace.

"I Captain Pan," he said, as he took a closer look at the roaring golden lion's head in the iron banister.

"And I'm Mama Phyllis," I said.

"I know that," said Jesse.

"We always knew that," said Cheryl.

The next morning, I went to a small park on Larkin Street, above Ghirardelli Square and Fisherman's Wharf. Tourists rarely go there, unless they stumble upon it. The park overlooks the spectacular San Francisco Bay and the Golden Gate Bridge. I was looking for a special place upon which I, too, had once stumbled. It was shortly after J.'s death, during the time that Anita Bryant was raising money for "rehabilitation camps" for lesbians and gays under the auspices of Save Our Children, during the time of the John Briggs witchhunt for lesbian and gay teachers and any heterosexual teachers who believed we should be allowed to keep our jobs. I had walked for hours and miles, day after day, in a time when I could not have even dreamed that I would have the privilege of being a mother, and I can only hope that any lesbian or gay adolescent who is thinking of suicide can know this: Things can change, and that which seems utterly impossible can be made real.

The sky was darkening as a wall of fog moved in, and only the massive yet elegant pedestals of the Golden Gate were visible. I soon found what I was looking for and, as St. Francis said, that which was looking for me. I was afraid that someone might have torn it down, or that it would be covered with graffiti, but it was perfect, exactly as I had remembered it. In a small clearing, at the top of the hill, there was a stone upon which had been engraved a poem about San Francisco by the long-dead poet George Sterling:

> Tho' the dark be cold and blind,
> Yet her sea fog's touch is kind,
> And her mightier caress
> Is joy and the pain thereof;
> And great is thy tenderness,
> O cool, grey city of love!

❖

*My Dear Jesse,*

*Sometimes it's hard to talk about private things in a very public way, and I hope it's okay with you, when you get to be grown, that I wrote about you. You see, there are six million children in this country who have lesbian moms, and most of them aren't as lucky as our family. Many of those mothers can't say anything about it, or their children might be taken away from them. And a lot of those children feel ashamed of their moms because the only thing they hear is that being lesbian is bad. It's very hard to hear that the person you love the most is bad, even if it's not true.*

*I hope that when you get to be older, and you go through what every other boy goes through, and you have to get away from home and be on your own, you'll always remember one thing: We love you unconditionally, no matter what, forever.*

*You taught me something just a few months ago that I'll never forget. You had the chicken pox, along with all of your little friends, and you were covered with sores that made you itch terribly. You scratched them and scratched them, and Mama Cher and I were afraid you'd get scarred, so we put gloves on your hands, and gave you oatmeal baths, and tried to stop the itching for you, but nothing, nothing could help.*

*You were miserable from the itching, and when I held your hands away from your skin, you got so angry that you broke away from me and ran to your room. You came right back into the kitchen, though, and you had put on your Neverland Cap, the one Mama Cher made for you. I said, "Jesse. How are you?" and you said, "I'm not Jesse. I'm Peter Pan." You were defiant, and you pulled yourself up to your full three feet. So I said, "Well, Peter, how are your chicken pox?" And you informed me, in a patient but firm voice, "Peter Pan doesn't have the chicken pox." You got your paper sword and went about the very serious business of playing at Neverland in the living room, and as long as you were Peter Pan, you didn't itch. Not one bit.*

*As you grow up, and you find out that your family really*

*is a little different from most other families, I hope that you remember your gift of imagination, a gift that opens a door to another world and allows you to go beyond anything, anytime, and to create new places that are safe. Your gift is so powerful that you can even bring other people with you.*

*At the end of* Peter Pan, *as you well know, the Darling children want to go home, and they are sure that their mother will have left the window open for them so that they can fly right into the nursery. Peter is not so sure about that, though. You might remember, he thinks mothers are highly overrated. So I want you to tell Peter, should he ask you, that Mama Cher and I will always have the window open. Always.*

*Mama Phyllis*